THE
SECRET
MIRACLE

THE
SECRET
MIRACLE

THE NOVELIST'S HANDBOOK

EDITED *by*

Daniel Alarcón

A HOLT PAPERBACK
HENRY HOLT AND COMPANY
NEW YORK

Holt Paperbacks
Henry Holt and Company, LLC
Publishers since 1866
175 Fifth Avenue
New York, New York 10010
www.henryholt.com

Distributed in Canada by H. B. Fenn and Company Ltd.

Library of Congress Cataloging-in-Publication Data

The secret miracle : the novelist's handbook / edited by Daniel Alarcón.—1st Holt Paperbacks ed.
    p. cm.
  ISBN: 978-0-8050-8714-7 (pbk.)
  1. Fiction—Authorship—Handbooks, manuals, etc.   2. Fiction—Technique—Handbooks,
manuals, etc.   I. Alarcón, Daniel, 1977–
  PN3355.S388 2010
  808.3—dc22   2009028330

Abner Morales translated the answers of Mario Bellatin, Rodrigo Fresán,
Mario Vargas Llosa, José Manuel Prieto, Santiago Roncagliolo.

Henry Holt books are available for special promotions and
premiums. For details contact: Director, Special Markets.

First Holt Paperbacks Edition 2010

Printed in the United States of America
1   3   5   7   9   10   8   6   4   2

CONTENTS

THE
SECRET
MIRACLE

INTRODUCTION

BY DANIEL ALARCÓN

Apart from a few friends and many routines, the problematic pursuit of literature constituted the whole of his life; like every writer, he measured other men's virtues by what they had accomplished, yet asked that other men measure him by what he planned someday to do.

—*Jorge Luis Borges*, "The Secret Miracle"

In December of 2004, just before Christmas, I wrote the last sentence of my first (and for now, only) novel. I wasn't done, nor was it a first draft exactly, but composing this seven-word sentence certainly felt like some kind of milestone. At the time I was renting a room in a big, lonely house in the Eastlake neighborhood of Oakland, California. There was a yard of overgrown grass in the back that I never once set foot in. The landlady was my age, with sandy hair and a thin, mousy voice, polite to the point of being nearly invisible, and we shared the space like two people in the waiting room of a doctor's office. Her boyfriend lived in Los Angeles, and every few weeks she'd go see him and leave me to care for the house, which entailed nothing at all. The lights and the heat went off and on by electronic timer; there were no pets, no plants. Whether she was home or not made no difference to me: either way, I spent most of the day inside my room, venturing to the kitchen only to make coffee or lunch. I wrote all morning until I got too hungry to keep going. I had no distractions: baseball season was over, the disappointing presidential election had come and gone, and besides my sisters, I had essentially no friends in the Bay Area. For months, that hadn't mattered; I had my novel. And I knew I was close, knew I was approaching the end of *something*, but when it finally happened, I was caught completely by surprise.

I saved the document and closed the computer. I paced nervously around the house for an hour or so, then sat back down to reread the last paragraph, not sure what I would find. To my astonishment, it was still there—that last sentence—and the sensation I had was unlike anything I'd felt before, or have felt since. Not happiness or pride, not fear or abandonment, but some unholy combination of all four of these discrete emotions. I'd been thinking about this book for five years, been writing it for more than two, and suddenly I'd come to the end. My fingers tingled. My head ached. I had nothing to do.

The next day I put the document on a USB drive and biked over to a shop on Grand Avenue to have a few copies printed out. It was a beautiful day, clear and sunny, the sort of December morning that makes one appreciate California living. The rest of the nation shivered through winter, but I wore a T-shirt and sunglasses, and had finished a novel (or a version of something that would three years later be a novel). I told myself this over and over, feeling at once carefree and agitated. Only when it was done, when the copy shop attendant passed me the three copies, did I realize how much it weighed. I'd never seen the entire thing printed out, never held it in my hands, and in my haste, I'd brought nothing to carry it home in. I couldn't very well ride with this much paper under my arm, could I? I was too impatient to leave it at the shop and come back later, so we found a plastic bag, put the novel inside, and I pedaled home with three copies of the manuscript swinging happily from the handlebars. I was only a block from the shop, feeling quite content, when the novel got stuck in the spokes of the front wheel. The bike jerked to a halt, flipped dramatically, and sent me catapulting onto the asphalt.

I was not that hurt, and the street, at least, was warm. I lay on my back for a moment, catching my breath, as cars swerved around me, running over the manuscript pages strewn about the road. Someone came to ask if I was all right. "I'm fine," I said, and it was true, just skinned elbows and sore wrists, but the fall must have been spectacular. A small crowd had gathered to watch me. This kind stranger helped me gather my things and push the ruined bike to the relative safety of the sidewalk. My front wheel was hopelessly bent, the bike unrideable. One of the copies of the novel was damaged; the other two, thankfully, were fine.

. . .

This little episode was so noxiously, so self-evidently, meaningful—a man nearly killed by his novel—that I decided to take a trip. I gave up my room, set the book aside, and flew to Buenos Aires, where I spent a week and spoke to no one. Without my characters I felt very alone, but I was mourning a lot of things then, not just the end of a book. I drank a lot; I watched people; I tried to have fun. When I got bored, I went to Chile, and a few months later I found myself in a small town on the Pacific Coast called La Serena. It was the *Feria Internacional del Libro*, though it seemed mine was the only international presence in town, and I was only there by accident. Alejandra, a novelist friend of mine, had come up from Santiago to give a reading, and we were going to meet up after the festival with some people she knew and head to the beach. Or something like that. I can't remember exactly. I do remember, however, very clearly, milling around after her reading and noticing a rather small, hunched, and nervous-looking man hovering about the edge of the gathering. He was around fifty years old, with short, light brown hair, and a face lined with worry. His metal-frame glasses kept slipping down the bridge of his nose. Alejandra was signing books and talking to the writers who'd just been on the panel with her, and this man circled around them, looking for a way to join the conversation. Everyone was deliberately and quite obviously ignoring him. They knew him. Eventually, he gave up and turned to me. He asked if he could give me a book.

"Sure," I said.

A poetry reading had begun by then, and we stood listening. The novelists took their conversation out of earshot, and the man giving away his books watched with envy as they wandered away. Chileans— God bless them—live and breathe poetry, and a very attentive crowd had gathered to listen to the reading, but the man next to me was not impressed. He spoke in a shrill whisper. Free verse has ruined poetry, he told me, and now anybody could claim to be a poet. "Do you hear that?" he said, waving a dismissive hand at the stage. I tried to listen. The reading disgusted him. "Sonnets, young man! Sonnets! What is classic never goes out of style."

I nodded, and he took the opportunity to introduce himself. "Enrique_____, the most published writer in Latin America."

"How many books?"

"Three hundred sixty-three," Enrique said, beaming, and then recited a few notable figures from his vast bibliography: ninety-three books of essays, sixty-seven books about women, forty novels, one hundred or so books of sonnets.

Naturally I let him keep talking. He'd moved to Chile some thirty years before—that is, he left Spain just after Franco died and relocated to Pinochet's Chile. I did the math and took a step back. He owned a few buildings and lived off the rents, which allowed him to dedicate all his time to literature. He started writing in 1998, he told me, and spent a day or two on each book. "I think in meter," he said at one point, in a voice that can only be described as harrowing.

When I told him I was Peruvian, he said he'd written a few novels about my country, and those were the ones he'd like to give me. If it was okay with me. A few novels—this was the phrase he used. I found it astonishing. It's not even his country, I thought, and this man has written a few novels about it? What have I done?

"Of course," I said.

He came by my hotel the next morning with two books: one called *Resentment*, about a Peruvian who hates Spaniards because of the Conquest, and another called *July 28, Day of Peru*, a novel/sonnet in honor of the natural beauty of my country. Both were slim, printed with humongous type, and far be it from me to say what is and what is not a novel, but . . . Of course, it is all very obvious now: Enrique was crazy. In his lunacy, he exuded a vulnerability and sadness that perhaps all writers share to some degree. He ran his fingers lovingly over the cardstock covers of his books, and explained how he had come to write them, what he was trying to say with each. I sat in the hotel lobby, sipping coffee, listening to this tender recitation, and was moved. At every other moment, Enrique spoke brusquely, without adornment, but now there was great affection in his voice, as he discussed the process, the discovery, the joy with a certain cluelessness I recognized. We don't know what we're doing, and for this very reason, we find it impossible to stop. And when we talk about writing, we are sometimes reduced to this: sentiment instead of insight, because describing what actually happens and how is next to impossible.

Because I was running late, I let him give me a ride to a local radio station where my friend was being interviewed. We were leaving town that afternoon. He spoke without pause, relating how he'd been expelled from various writing workshops (jealousy, he said), and fought with the mayor and the editor of the paper over local political controversies not worth getting into. He'd written a book called *Letter to the Pope*, which he mailed to the Vatican, and had even received a note from a representative of John Paul II in return. A very nice letter, he said, which led to his follow-up *Response to a Letter from the Pope*, the "novel" he was most proud of. *I* should be on these panels at the book fair, Enrique said, after all, he had the most number of books at the local library! I was silent. I hadn't brought my manuscript with me. I'd done my best to put it out of my mind and not be a writer for just a little while. In spite of my best intentions, I thought about my characters every single day. "I'm going to the beach," I said. "I'm on vacation."

"How long?"

"Three days. Maybe four."

Enrique smiled. "By the time you come back, I will have finished another novel."

"Amazing," I said, nodding.

He shrugged, and looked tired all of a sudden. "If your friend Alejandra wants to leave me a book, she can," he said.

For a moment, I thought he might cry. His face clouded, his eyes closed, but then it passed and he was himself again. "If she doesn't, that's fine too. I've published many more books than she has."

. . .

It was the entire premise of writing turned upside down: the goal was to produce pages, meter, rhyme, and, finally, books in industrial quantities, all these words worth nothing unless they are bound and lining the shelves of one's own home. There is something narcissistic in the writing of a novel, to be sure, but I've never heard it expressed with such glaring honesty. My experience—I've abandoned more than five novels, and finished only one—couldn't have been more different.

I'm aware, of course, how ridiculous it is for someone who's written only one novel to be assigned the task of editing a book about how to write one. As I've been working on this project, I've been trying to write my own second novel, and it's been illuminating to work on both projects simultaneously. Perhaps this statement requires a little clarification: *illuminating* in the sense that as I go over the answers my colleagues have so generously offered me in response to our questions, I'm even more aware of how difficult it is to describe what it is that happens when one is actively communing with a given text. I don't suppose any of us really knows anything about how it happens, and so in this sense, maybe a first-time novelist is the best person for the job. Perhaps I'd be even more qualified for this role if I'd *never* written a novel, or even attempted to write one. Perhaps if I'd written three hundred and sixty novels, the mystery would be solved—but I doubt that. As the answers came in, I became increasingly aware of how unfair it was to ask my fellow writers to pull back the curtain, and was amazed again and again by the honesty, humor, and elegance with which they described what they found when they did. It's reassuring to be reminded that everyone works differently, that there is no single way to arrive at your destination, that, in fact, your destination is necessarily a very different place from anyone else's.

This book is not a how-to. No such book exists because it cannot be written. The caveats that would precede it would be longer than the book itself, rendering the entire project useless. This book, I hope, is not useless. I hope it inspires, consoles, frightens, prods, angers, and excites many of you who pick it up. I hope it leads you to the work of the fine novelists who have given so generously of their time and wisdom to make this book a reality, and if not to their work, then to that of the many writers they have recommended. We sought opinions and insight from more than fifty American and international writers, a wide array of veterans and first-time novelists, authors working in different languages and traditions, all in order to emphasize the universality of the novel as a genre. It is an almost infinitely malleable form, and its flexibility is the key to its survival and relevance: still, even today, there are those of us who attempt to make sense of the world—its terror, humor, and beauty—through the reading and writing of novels. Oftentimes writing can feel overwhelmingly lonely, a fool's errand, and it's gratifying to be reminded that at any given moment, there are thousands of others, working in hundreds of languages all over the world, engaged in much the same pursuit. They, like all of us, have good days, bad days, and days where it is more useful to sit quietly and read, to let the writing itself wait.

Novels are written in dialogue with other novels, and this conversation can be a shouting match or a whispered confessional or something in between. It can be joyful or torturous, and no single voice in this book will describe your experience or your relationship to your own writing. That's not the point. The goal of this book is simply to provide a glimpse into the way others approach the same task. Perhaps their combined knowledge and experience will have something to offer you. I sincerely hope so.

THE WRITERS

Meet Our Experts on the Art of the Novel

Every month at 826 Valencia, we gather a panel of published authors before an audience of aspiring writers. For three hours we grill the authors on brass tacks. How, exactly, do they do what they do? How does a vague idea become a completed manuscript? How do they get started? How do they finish? How do they do everything in between, and how do they cope once it's done?

It's a great forum with one major flaw: we can only fit fifty or so people in the building for each seminar. We wanted to bring the experience to everyone else, and that's what we've tried to do in The Secret Miracle. *We've gathered answers from several dozen of our favorite authors about the details of novel writing, from the most personal and esoteric to the most practical. All will be revealed: how to start and where to start; how to get to know your characters, and how to figure out who should tell the story; how to end and where to end; and why it all matters.*

CHRIS ABANI

Chris Abani's prose includes *Song for Night* (Akashic, 2007), *The Virgin of Flames* (Penguin, 2007), *Becoming Abigail* (Akashic, 2006), *GraceLand* (FSG, 2004), and *Masters of the Board* (Delta, 1985). His poetry collections are *Hands Washing Water* (Copper Canyon, 2006), *Dog Woman* (Red Hen, 2004), *Daphne's Lot* (Red Hen, 2003), and *Kalakuta Republic* (Saqi, 2001). He is a professor at the University of California, Riverside, and the recipient of the PEN USA Freedom-to-Write Award, the Prince Claus Award, a Lannan Literary Fellowship, a California Book Award, a Hurston/ Wright Legacy Award, a PEN Beyond the Margins Award, the PEN Hemingway Book Prize, and a Guggenheim Award.

CHRIS ADRIAN

Chris Adrian is the author of the novels *Gob's Grief* and *The Children's Hospital*, and most recently the short-story collection *A Better Angel*. His short fiction has appeared in the *Paris Review, Zoetrope, McSweeney's,* and the *New Yorker*. He recently completed a pediatric residency at the University of California, San Francisco, and is now a student at the Harvard Divinity School.

ALAA AL ASWANY

Alaa Al Aswany is the author of many novels, including *The Yacoubian Building*, which was a bestseller all over the Arab world, translated into nine languages, and made into a feature film. He writes a monthly opposition newspaper column in Egypt, and his literary criticism regularly appears in *El Araby El Nassery*. His most recent novel, *Chicago*, was published by HarperCollins in 2008. He lives in Cairo.

RABIH ALAMEDDINE

Rabih Alameddine is the author of several novels and short stories, including *Koolaids: The Art of War, The Perv and I*, and *The Divine: A Novel in First Chapters*. He is the recipient of a Guggenheim Fellowship, and divides his time between San Francisco and Beirut. His most recent novel, *The Hakawati*, was published in 2008.

PAUL AUSTER

Paul Auster is the author of fourteen novels, including *The New York Trilogy, Leviathan, Moon Palace*, and *Man in the Dark*. His many awards include the Prince of Asturias Award for Literature and the Prix Médicis Étranger. He lives in Brooklyn.

TASH AW

Tash Aw is the author of *The Harmony Silk Factory*, which won the Whitbread First Novel Award and the Commonwealth Writers Prize for Best First Novel. His work has been translated into twenty languages. His most recent novel, *Map of the Invisible World*, was published in 2009.

MARIO BELLATIN

Mario Bellatin is the author of *Flowers*, which won the Xavier Villaurrutia Prize in 2002. His work has been translated into German, French, and English. His other books include *Shiki Nagaoka: A Nose of Fiction*, *Pinocchio Tales*, *Hero Dogs*, *Lessons for a Dead Hare*, and *Beauty Salon*. He lives in Mexico City.

MICHAEL CHABON

Michael Chabon is the author of *The Mysteries of Pittsburgh*, *Wonder Boys*, and, most recently, *Maps and Legends*, a collection of essays. His bestselling novel *The Amazing Adventures of Kavalier & Clay* was awarded the 2001 Pulitzer Prize. He lives in Berkeley, California.

SUSAN CHOI

Susan Choi is the author of three novels, *The Foreign Student*, which won the 1999 Asian American Literary Award; *American Woman*, which was a finalist for the 2004 Pulitzer Prize; and *A Person of Interest*, which was a finalist for the 2009 PEN/Faulkner Award. She lives in Brooklyn, New York, with her husband and sons.

T COOPER

T Cooper is the author of the novels *Some of the Parts* and *Lipshitz Six, or Two Angry Blondes*, a *Los Angeles Times* bestseller also chosen as a Best Book of 2006 by the *Believer* and the *Austin Chronicle*. Cooper is co-editor of the anthology *A Fictional History of The United States with Huge Chunks Missing*, and has written for various publications, including the *New Yorker*, the *New York Times*, *Out*, and the *Believer*. Cooper lives in New York.

ANN CUMMINS

Ann Cummins is the author of a short-story collection, *Red Ant House*, and a novel, *Yellowcake*. Her work has appeared in the *New Yorker*, *McSweeney's*, *Quarterly West*, and the *Sonora Review*. She is the recipient of a Lannan Fellowship and teaches at Northern Arizona University.

EDWIDGE DANTICAT

Edwidge Danticat is the author of three novels, including *Breath, Eyes, Memory*, as well as a National Book Award–nominated collection of stories, *Krik? Krak!* Her second novel, *The Farming of the Bones*, won the 1999 American Book Award, and her most recent book, *Brother, I'm Dying*, a memoir, won the 2007 National Book Critics Circle Award for nonfiction.

RODDY DOYLE

Roddy Doyle is the author of many novels, including *The Commitments* and *Paddy Clarke Ha Ha Ha*, winner of the 1993 Booker Prize. His short fiction is regularly published in the *New Yorker*.

JENNIFER EGAN

Jennifer Egan is the author of *The Invisible Circus*, *Emerald City and Other Stories*, *Look at Me*, nominated for the National Book Award in 2001, and most recently the bestselling *The Keep*. Also a journalist, she writes frequently for the *New York Times Magazine*. She lives in Brooklyn with her husband and sons.

JOSH EMMONS

Josh Emmons is the author of two novels, *The Loss of Leon Meed* and, most recently, *Prescription for a Superior Existence*. He lives in Philadelphia with his wife, the poet Katie Ford.

ANNE ENRIGHT

Anne Enright is the author of four novels, including *The Gathering*, which won the 2007 Man Booker Prize. Her writing has appeared in many magazines, including the *New Yorker*, the *Paris Review*, *Granta*, and the *London Review of Books*. She won Davy Byrne's Irish Writing Award in 2004 and a Royal Society of Authors Encore Prize.

AURA ESTRADA

Aura Estrada (1977–2007) was born in Leon, Guanajuato, Mexico, and raised in Mexico City. She received her BA and MA from the UNAM and was studying for a PhD in Latin American literature at Columbia University and, simultaneously, for her MFA in creative writing at Hunter College. She published fiction and nonfiction in a number of Latin American and American journals and magazines, including *Etiqueta Negra*, *Letras Libres*, *Gatopardo*, *Wordswithoutborders*, *Book Forum*, and the *Boston Review*. Her husband, novelist Francisco Goldman, and friends have founded the Aura Estrada Prize (www.auraestradaprize.org) in her memory.

RODRIGO FRESÁN

Rodrigo Fresán is a celebrated novelist and journalist living in Barcelona. He is the author of many novels, including *Historia Argentina*, *The Velocity of Things*, *Esperanto*, and most recently, *Kensington Gardens*, published in the United States in 2006.

NELL FREUDENBERGER

Nell Freudenberger is the author of *Lucky Girls*, winner of the PEN/Malamud award. Her novel, *The Dissident*, was a *New York Times* Notable Book, and she was the recipient of a 2005 Whiting Writers' Award. In 2007 she was named one of *Granta*'s Best Young American Novelists. She lives in New York.

RIVKA GALCHEN

Rivka Galchen's first novel, *Atmospheric Disturbances*, received numerous accolades and has been translated into more than a dozen languages. Her short stories and essays have appeared in the *Believer*, the *New Yorker*, *Scientific American*, *Zoetrope*, and the *New York Times*.

CRISTINA GARCIA

Cristina Garcia is the author of four novels, including the bestselling *Dreaming in Cuban*, a finalist for the 1992 National Book Award. Her most recent novel, *A Handbook to Luck*, won the 2008 Northern California Book Award. She currently lives in Los Angeles, California.

GLEN DAVID GOLD

Glen David Gold is the author of the novels *Carter Beats the Devil* and *Sunnyside*. He has written comic books for Dark Horse and DC and his short stories, essays, memoir, and journalism have appeared in *Playboy*, *McSweeney's*, *Tin House*, and the *New York Times Magazine*. He lives in San Francisco.

FRANCISCO GOLDMAN

Francisco Goldman is the author of three novels, including *The Long Night of White Chickens*, which won the Sue Kaufman Prize for First Fiction in 1993. His second novel, *The Ordinary Seaman*, was a finalist for the 1997 PEN/Faulkner Award and the International IMPAC Dublin Literary Award. His most recent book of nonfiction, *The Art of Political Murder*, was published in 2007.

ALLEGRA GOODMAN

Allegra Goodman is the author of the novels *Intuition*, a *New York Times* bestseller, *Paradise Park*, and *Kaaterskill Falls*, a National Book Award finalist, two collections of short stories, *The Family Markowitz* and *Total Immersion*, and *The Other Side of the Island*, her first book for younger readers. Her fiction has appeared in the *New Yorker*, *Commentary*, *Ploughshares*, *Prize Stories: the O. Henry Awards*, and *Best American Short Stories*. She lives with her family in Cambridge, Massachusetts.

ANDREW SEAN GREER

Andrew Sean Greer is the author of three novels, including *The Confessions of Max Tivoli*, which was named a Best Book of 2004 by the *San*

Francisco Chronicle and the *Chicago Tribune*. His stories have appeared in *Esquire*, the *Paris Review*, and the *New Yorker*. He is the recipient of a California Book Award Gold Medal in Fiction and a New York Public Library Young Lions Award. He lives in San Francisco.

DANIEL HANDLER

Daniel Handler is the author of the novels *The Basic Eight*, *Watch Your Mouth*, and *Adverbs*, and far too many books as Lemony Snicket. He lives in San Francisco with his wife and child.

YAEL HEDAYA

Yael Hedaya is the author of *Housebroken*, a collection of novellas, as well as two novels: *Accidents* and *Die Sache mit dem Glück*. She lives in Tel Aviv.

ALEKSANDAR HEMON

Aleksandar Hemon's work has appeared in the *New Yorker*, *Esquire*, *Granta*, and the *Paris Review*. He is the author of *The Question of Bruno*, a short-story collection, and the novels *Nowhere Man* and *The Lazarus Project*, a 2008 National Book Award Finalist. He was awarded a MacArthur Foundation "Genius" Grant in 2004.

A. M. HOMES

A. M. Homes is the author of the novels *The End of Alice*, *Music for Torching*, and *Jack*, as well as two collections of stories. Her work has appeared in *Vanity Fair*, *McSweeney's*, and the *New Yorker*. She is the recipient of numerous awards, including a Guggenheim Fellowship and a National Endowment for the Arts Fellowship. Her bestselling memoir *The Mistress's Daughter* was published in 2007.

SHELLEY JACKSON

Shelley Jackson is the author of the story collection *The Melancholy of Anatomy*, the novel *Half Life*, and hypertexts including *Patchwork Girl*. The recipient of a Howard Foundation grant, a Pushcart Prize, and the

2006 James Tiptree Jr. Award, she has also written and illustrated several children's books, including *The Old Woman and the Wave*; *Sophia, The Alchemist's Dog*; and the forthcoming *Mimi's Dada Catifesto*. Her work has appeared in *Conjunctions*, *McSweeney's*, the *Paris Review*, and *Cabinet Magazine*. In 2004 she launched her project SKIN, a story published in tattoos on 2,095 volunteers. She lives in Brooklyn.

TAYARI JONES

Tayari Jones is the author of *Leaving Atlanta*, winner of the Hurston/Wright Legacy Award for Debut Fiction. Her 2005 novel, *The Untelling*, was awarded the Lillian C. Smith Award for New Voices. Jones teaches in the MFA program at Rutgers-Newark University.

STEPHEN KING

Stephen King is one of the United States' best-known writers. He is the author of more than forty novels, including *Carrie*, *The Shining*, *Hearts in Atlantis*, and *Dreamcatcher*. In 2003, he was honored with a National Book Foundation Lifetime Achievement Award. He lives in Bangor, Maine.

LAILA LALAMI

Laila Lalami is a novelist and essayist. Her debut collection of stories, *Hope and Other Dangerous Pursuits*, was published in 2005 and has since been translated into six languages. Her first novel, *Secret Son*, was published in 2009. The recipient of a British Council Fellowship and a Fulbright Fellowship, she lives in Los Angeles and is a Professor of Creative Writing at the University of California, Riverside.

JONATHAN LETHEM

Jonathan Lethem is the author of *Motherless Brooklyn*, named Novel of the Year by *Esquire* and winner of the 1999 National Book Critics Circle Award. He is also the author of *The Fortress of Solitude*, a *New York Times* bestseller, and most recently, *You Don't Love Me Yet*, a novel published in 2007. His writing has appeared in the *New Yorker*, *Rolling Stone*, *Harper's*, and *McSweeney's*. He lives in Brooklyn.

YIYUN LI

Yiyun Li's first book, *A Thousand Years of Good Prayers*, won the Frank O'Connor International Short Story Award, among other prizes, and the title story was made into a film by acclaimed director Wayne Wang. Li was selected as one of *Granta*'s 21 Best Young American Novelists in 2007, and her first novel, *The Vagrants*, was published in 2009. She lives in Oakland, California.

ADAM MANSBACH

Adam Mansbach's most recent novel, *The End of the Jews*, won the California Book Award Gold Medal in Fiction. His previous novel, *Angry Black White Boy*, was a *San Francisco Chronicle* Best Book of 2005, and is taught at more than sixty schools. A recipient of the Ford Foundation's Future Aesthetics Artist Regrant, Mansbach is the New Voices Professor of Fiction at Rutgers University.

DINAW MENGESTU

Dinaw Mengestu is the author of *The Beautiful Things That Heaven Bears*, which was selected as a 2007 *New York Times* Notable Book. He is the recipient of a 2006 fellowship in fiction from the New York Foundation for the Arts. He lives in Paris, France.

CLAIRE MESSUD

Claire Messud's novels include *The Last Life*, *When the World Was Steady*, and *The Emperor's Children*, a *New York Times* Best Book of 2006. She has been awarded a Guggenheim Fellowship, a Radcliffe fellowship, and the Strauss Living Award from the American Academy of Arts and Letters. She lives with her family in Cambridge, Massachusetts.

SUSAN MINOT

Susan Minot is the author of four novels, including *Monkeys*, winner of the Prix Fémina in 1988. She wrote the screenplay for Bernardo Bertolucci's *Stealing Beauty* and has been awarded the O. Henry Prize and the Pushcart Prize for her short fiction. Her most recent novel, *Rapture*, was published in 2002.

RICK MOODY

Rick Moody is the author of several novels, including *The Ice Storm*, which was made into a feature film, and *The Diviners*. His 2002 memoir, *The Black Veil,* won the PEN/Marta Albrand Award. His work appears widely, including in the *New Yorker, Esquire, Harper's*, and the *New York Times*. He lives in Brooklyn, New York.

HARUKI MURAKAMI

Haruki Murakami is the author of many novels, including *A Wild Sheep Chase, Norwegian Wood, The Wind-up Bird Chronicle, Kafka on the Shore*, and *After Dark*. He is one of Japan's most celebrated authors, and his work has been translated into more than thirty-five languages.

GEORGE PELECANOS

George Pelecanos is the author of numerous novels, including most recently, *The Way Home, The Turnaround*, and *The Night Gardener*. His 2003 novel, *Hell to Pay*, received a *Los Angeles Times* Book Award. *The Big Blowdown* won the International Crime Novel of the Year Award in France, Germany, and Japan. Pelecanos's nonfiction has appeared the *New York Times*, the *Washington Post, GQ*, and *Mojo*, and he received an Emmy nomination for his work on the HBO crime drama series *The Wire*.

JOSÉ MANUEL PRIETO

José Manuel Prieto is a novelist, essayist, and translator of Russian literature into Spanish. His novels include *Rex, Lividia (Nocturnal Butterflies of the Russian Empire)*, and *Encyclopedia of a Life in Russia,* and he is the recipient of numerous awards, including a Guggenheim Fellowship. He lives in New York City.

SANTIAGO RONCAGLIOLO

Santiago Roncagliolo's first novel, *Pudor,* was made into a feature film. His second, the political thriller *Red April,* received the prestigious Alfaguara Novel Prize, and was translated into English by Edith Grossman. His books have been translated into thirteen languages. He writes regularly for *El País,* one of Spain's most prominent newspapers.

AKHIL SHARMA

Akhil Sharma is the author of the award-winning novel *An Obedient Father.* His stories have appeared in magazines such as the *New Yorker* and the *Atlantic Monthly.* He currently lives with his wife in New York City.

ADANIA SHIBLI

Adania Shibli has twice been awarded the Young Writer's Award of Palestine by the A. M. Qattan Foundation. She is the author of the novels *Touching* and *We Are All Equally Far from Love.* Some of her short texts appeared in the United States in the *Iowa Review* and *World Literature Today.*

GARY SHTEYNGART

Gary Shteyngart is the author of two novels, *The Russian Debutante's Handbook* and *Absurdistan,* a *New York Times* Best Book of the Year in 2006. His work has appeared in the *New Yorker, Granta, Travel + Leisure,* and the *New York Times.*

CURTIS SITTENFELD

Curtis Sittenfeld is the author of three novels, including *Prep,* which was named as one of the ten best books of 2005 by the *New York Times.* She has written for the *New York Times* and the *Washington Post*, and her most recent novel, *American Wife*, was published in 2008.

MEHMET MURAT SOMER

Mehmet Murat Somer is one of Turkey's bestselling novelists. He is the author of the Hop-Çiki-Yaya series of gay noir detective novels, which include *The Prophet Murderers* and *The Kiss Murder.*

SAŠA STANIŠIĆ

Saša Stanišić is the author of *How the Soldier Repairs the Gramophone*, which was short-listed for the German Book Award and is being translated into thirty languages. Stanišić lives in Germany.

AMY TAN

Amy Tan's first novel, *The Joy Luck Club*, was a finalist for the 1989 National Book Award and the National Book Critics Circle Award and is a selection of the NEA's Big Read program. Her work has been translated into thirty-five languages. She has also written a memoir, essays, short stories, a screenplay, and a libretto.

COLM TÓIBÍN

Colm Tóibín is the author of novels such as *The South*, *Heather Blazing*, and *The Blackwater Lightship*, as well as a collection of stories. His novel *The Master*, a portrait of Henry James, won the International IMPAC Dublin Literary Award, was named the *Los Angeles Times* Novel of the Year, and was listed by the *New York Times* as one of the ten most notable books of 2004. He lives in Ireland.

MARIO VARGAS LLOSA

Mario Vargas Llosa is one of the most acclaimed writers in the Spanish language, and was awarded the Cervantes Prize in 1994. He is the author of dozens of books of fiction, journalism, and criticism, including novels such as *The Time of the Hero*, *The Green House*, *Aunt Julia and the Scriptwriter*, *The War of the End of the World*, and *The Feast of the Goat*.

ALEJANDRO ZAMBRA

Alejandro Zambra is the author of the novels *Bonsai* (2006) and *The Private Life of Trees* (2007). He lives in Santiago de Chile. His work has been translated into five languages.

CHAPTER 1

READING AND INFLUENCES

WHAT DO YOU LOOK FOR IN A NOVEL?

SUSAN MINOT: Transport. Enchantment. Guidance. Pleasure. Beauty. Novelty. Entertainment. Charm. Poetry. Truth. Solace. Wit. Wisdom.

MARIO VARGAS LLOSA: I look for the same thing that I try to achieve when writing a novel—a well-told story. I believe that is the most difficult thing, to tell a story in an absolutely persuasive manner. To make readers live that experience—not just as readers, but to really experience it. For me the novels that achieve that are the most moving and leave a lasting impression in my memory.

YIYUN LI: I look for a world—sometimes it is one as familiar as this one world we have, and sometimes it is a strange world that perhaps would only happen in a dream—but in either case when I read a novel I look to live in that world along with the characters.

PAUL AUSTER: Passion, power, integrity, beauty.

HARUKI MURAKAMI: If I want to read it again, it must surely be a good novel.

CHRIS ABANI: The most important thing for me is that a novelist has a philosophical engagement with the world, some deeper question about their place in all of this that emerges subtly and beautifully through the work they do, regardless of what the apparent subject is. So for instance, Toni Morrison wants to understand what love is and what it means to us and the ways in which we understand it, use it, and want to control it. For her, trauma, violence, and hate are symptomatic of our inability to face and accept all the facets of love. Language, exquisite prose is also essential: I cannot read a book for the story anymore, no matter how compelling. I also love books that challenge our ideas of convention, novels are meant to be just that, novel.

RICK MOODY: A certain kind of irreducible complexity, a mixture of very good and memorable prose, originality with respect to the form, and a density of thematic material. What I don't require and don't consider relevant: "likeable" characters, naturalism, epiphanic transformations, plotting, or a rationale for what is going on around us in the world.

ADANIA SHIBLI: I usually can only see the words, how they come to express what they express. I'm rarely interested in what they express; that is the being of the word rather than what it tells.

COLM TÓIBÍN: A novel looks for something in me. Meaning, there is no type of novel I like or look for, or no set of emotional contours or contexts I look for. But if what a novel exudes has not been felt properly or seriously or deeply enough by the writer, then it will show and I will become tremendously bored and irritated.

CRISTINA GARCIA: I look for poetry in a novel. And that means from the get-go it's singing to me in some particular, peculiar voice. And if that doesn't exist, it's hard for me to get interested.

STEPHEN KING: Entertainment and good language.

SANTIAGO RONCAGLIOLO: Emotions and ideas. I want a story that I can't put down, that makes me forget the real world but that, like Richard Ford said, brings me back better prepared to live it. I look for an experience that transports me to other lives, and returns me to mine after having looked at it from the outside.

JOSH EMMONS: I look for well-crafted language and authorial intelligence; with these in place every story can provide the aesthetic bliss Nabokov said was literature's greatest reward.

ALAA AL ASWANY: At this point I think of the novel as a life of the people, similar to our daily lives but more composed, more significant, more beautiful. What do I care about while reading a novel? The human experience, the human feelings, the human logic. This is the real challenge of the novelist.

RODDY DOYLE: Surprise and reassurance.

JENNIFER EGAN: The thing I most crave is to be sucked into a novel and feel that helpless sense that I can't stop reading, and that I'd do anything—give up anything, certainly a night's sleep—in order to *keep* reading. When I step back and look at what qualities in a novel inspire that sense of urgency (and I wish it happened more often) I'd say the top one is *surprise.* The surprise can arrive in many forms: a fresh, distinct voice; a story whose moves are counterintuitive or unexpected; the language stands out as being original, or innovative. What most excites me as a reader is the sense that I'm encountering material I haven't seen before.

JOSÉ MANUEL PRIETO: A different way of looking at the world, one that expands my way of understanding it—not through factual knowledge (data, dates, historical events) but with a new philosophy, a unique grammar of existence.

GLEN DAVID GOLD: Sheer entertainment.

ADAM MANSBACH: Truth and beauty. Soulfulness. Honesty. Emotional resonance. Insight into the human condition expressed in prose that is original and well-wrought—and funny, when possible. Beyond that, I don't know that I have specific criteria; certainly, there are topics that will make me pick up a book, because they dovetail with my own interests—the complexities of race in America, for instance—or because they offer clues about some problem I'm trying to solve in my own work. But I'm also learning not to trust my own interests too completely; to only read the books with obvious appeal is to miss out on a lot.

SAŠA STANIŠIĆ: I look for a novel to entertain and enlighten me.

RABIH ALAMEDDINE: After reading a great novel, I am not the same person I was before I read it. Now all that stuff we take for granted—great story, great structure, great language—that all makes for a really good novel. But a great novel is not the one that transforms the character but the one that transforms the reader. In a lot of workshops they tell you there has to be a movement in the narrator. For me, that's minor.

ALEKSANDAR HEMON: I look for what I don't expect. Great novels make you change your mind about what you know, what you expect. They teach you how to read them, which is to say that they force you to drop your expectations and aesthetic prejudices, they force you to read in a way you are not accustomed to. I want the reading of a novel to be a transformative experience.

MEHMET MURAT SOMER: For some time I've been discerning in my appreciation and my liking. As a reader I look at what I like, which is joy. It's very essential for me. And wit. I love to have a smile on my face, both while reading and for some time after, as residue in my memory.

As an author, I appreciate many books, even envy the way they were written, but do not like all of them. I don't feel comfortable with slaps to my face or fists in my stomach. Perhaps because I'm still in my never-ending rose-colored phase.

CLAIRE MESSUD: Ah—satisfaction and a challenge both. What exactly these entail it is impossible properly to elaborate; but suffice it to say that for me, no novel is satisfying without some challenge, whether narrative or structural or linguistic or intellectual or some combination of these; and yet, if a novel impresses me as all challenge—that's to say, without any tangible narrative satisfactions—then I'm unlikely to be won over.

TAYARI JONES: I am drawn to novels about families—I love the permanence of the relationships, the way they tend to box the characters in, forcing them to really stretch the relationship to the snapping point. I like sad and difficult stories. If something is blurbed as a feel-good story, I go running the other way. I want a story to give me hard truths. I want a novel that isn't afraid to follow a story to its true end, even if what is discovered there isn't good news.

T COOPER: Sometimes it's no more complicated than wanting to get out of my own head for a spell. But I suppose I also want the usual: to be surprised and moved, inspired to think about some small thing in some different way—and I guess I also secretly want a novel to inspire a little envy (I know it's the right book when I find myself ensnared in a desperate love/hate relationship with it).

DINAW MENGESTU: In general whenever I'm reading I'm looking for language first—for a strong, distinct, accurate, and even beautiful prose style. After that I think I tend to look for novels that feel like they have a real engagement with the world, for novels that look beyond certain conventions or settings.

EDWIDGE DANTICAT: A great story. Good plot. Beautiful language. Good pacing. I want a novel to grab me by the throat and not allow me to put it down.

GEORGE PELECANOS: An original voice.

NELL FREUDENBERGER: I look for characters in a novel. This is my bias, but beautiful sentences or a particularly compelling setting (and I'm a sucker for books that take place in countries, cities I've never visited) isn't enough for me. I like that shock of recognizing things about human beings that seem to be true, even if I've never been articulate enough to put them into words myself. I think of George Eliot as the master of this particular novelistic skill.

JONATHAN LETHEM: A sense of a created world with its own internal life, and a consistent possibility of surprise.

SUSAN CHOI: In reading I tend to follow hankerings, instead of reading what it seems I *should* read, and these hankerings are usually as irresistible and unexplainable as the craving to eat Chinese instead of pizza. Sometimes all I want is fussy drawing-room stuff, and sometimes all I want is politics-in-the-jungle stuff, and so I cast about, usually fairly blindly, for the book that I think will satisfy.

RODRIGO FRESÁN: I guess I look for the same thing I've always looked for—a guaranteed possibility of traveling to other planets without subjecting myself to brutal physical training.

RIVKA GALCHEN: Apparently the opening of Aristotle's *Metaphysics* is generally mistranslated as something like "Philosophy begins in Wonder," or "Philosophy begins in Curiosity," but apparently (I wouldn't know, but I'm told) the Greek actually means something more like "Philosophy begins with the Uncanny." That is, it begins with the moment when we are able to see what is familiar to us as, in fact, strange. And I guess that's kind of what I'm most attracted to in novels, regardless of how it's accomplished. (Maybe by all the characters being rabbits, or maybe through a Nabokovian focus on detail, or maybe through exaggerations of colloquial speech . . . there's endless ways, I suppose.) I love it when a novel constitutes a world that I both recognize and don't. Or when a novel makes vivid to me what normally would have no luster. Or vice versa. Or when a novel takes a situation or person that I feel like I know and reveals some sort of alien underbelly. I love, for example, the way that Kazuo Ishiguro opens his novel, *The Unconsoled*, where you're on the elevator with the bellhop for what just seems like way too long, the dialogue there goes on and on, and the suitcases start to seem immensely heavy, and as a reader you're like, all right, I recognize this universe— it's just like mine—but it's not mine, time moves weirdly there, maybe I recognize it from a nightmare or dream that I have forgotten. It's like the freakiness of seeing yourself in one of those reverse mirrors, those mirrors that show you to yourself not the way you're accustomed to seeing yourself, but instead in the way that everyone else sees you; you see yourself as you in fact appear, and it's totally unsettling! Or like in Kafka's *Amerika*, the brilliance (maybe accidental, but I suspect not) of the Statue of Liberty holding a sword and the Brooklyn Bridge connecting New York to Brooklyn—those kinds of wrongnesses that work just right.

A. M. HOMES: I like to be made to think, I like to laugh, and I am desperate to be dazzled.

MICHAEL CHABON: Flawless sentences, well-stocked with living words and phrases. A sense of living another's life. A good story but not too much of a good story. Intricate pattern that feels offhand.

ANN CUMMINS: I look for wily, psychologically messy characters with a natural inclination toward trouble. I like interesting, unpredictable sentences and paragraphs. I love dramatic fluidity where sentences, characters, events—all—combine to create a page-turner, but I want to turn pages as much to reflect on style and ideas as to discover how the plot will be resolved.

YAEL HEDAYA: Power, claustrophobia, a narrative that is a bit violent, grabs you by the neck and won't let you go. For me, it's more in the voice than in the plot.

HOW MANY BOOKS DO YOU READ IN A GIVEN MONTH? HOW MANY BOOKS DO YOU READ AT A TIME?

MICHAEL CHABON: Three in a month; seventeen at a time.

ANN CUMMINS: I might start a dozen or so in a month; I might finish one.

SHELLEY JACKSON: I probably finish ten to fifteen books a month. I'm not sure I can even count how many books I read at a time. Lots. The house is full of books with bookmarks stuck in them. I can see about ten from where I'm sitting.

AMY TAN: Depends on what I'm doing, meaning, what I happen to be writing. I might go for months without reading anything from beginning to end because most of what I'm reading is research. There are many months when I have a stack of manuscripts beside my desk, and these are always requests from people. I'm trying to get better every year at saying, "No, I can't read this for you," but I think I actually get worse every year.

ADANIA SHIBLI: Five to seven books, depending on how long they are. And I usually read five books, at least, at the same time, but in different hours of the day.

ANNE ENRIGHT: As I try to answer this, I realize how very eccentric I am getting about the question of reading. It is with reluctance that I admit to reading anything at all. My books are stored upstairs where visitors don't go: no one gets to peruse my shelves. I think it would be true to say that in childhood I read up to three books a day, in my early twenties I could read a book in one sitting—without moving, eating, or getting dressed—and that, as late as my thirties I could finish one book and start another in a full day of reading and nothing but. My recent statistics, however, are that I had two children and four books in seven years—meaning that I wrote four books in that time, not that I read four. In fact there was a year (2003? 2004? It's a bit of a blur) when I realized that I had written more books than I had read in the last while. It was, undoubtedly, a high-focus time for me, but I have met women since who abandoned reading when their children were small. Already tired, they said books just put them to sleep. But I also think I have never seen it in a book—the thing I needed to read, just then, and this feeling makes me agitated and restless: it makes me want to write the book where someone could find the thing I needed to read in the last seven or eight years. This restlessness could be the mark of a writer, but it might just be a mark of my age—it can be hard to find a man over forty who still reads fiction, for example, unless they are in the book business. These days I read almost exclusively for work. I am editing *The Granta Book of the Irish Short Story* and various short-story collections are piled in heaps around my bedroom. I also read new work by young writers, especially Irish ones, to see if I can give them an endorsement, because I like to keep that show on the road. I read nonfiction to feed my future books, and I also read, or at least look at, books that have a similar theme to the one I am writing at the moment. Or I may not read these so much as smell them, now and then. Some of these are totemic volumes that sit on the shelf closest to my desk, and some are more idle orderings that come in through the letter box and lie, half-read, all over the house.

I suspect that the Internet is really eating into my reading time. I think women come back to heroic reading when their kids are more grown, but I worry that, by being a writer, I have spoiled one of my great pleasures. At least I didn't open a restaurant (or a brothel).

CHRIS ABANI: Now with a busy travel schedule, I only read about three books a month; but I read them all at the same time.

RABIH ALAMEDDINE: Between three and four.

SAŠA STANIŠIĆ: I don't like to read that much. Maybe a book a month. I fall asleep often when I read. Might be some kind of allergic reaction.

CHRIS ADRIAN: I hardly ever get to read novels but end up reading goofy stuff for school or work that can be inspiring on the writing side in a weird way. It teaches you nothing about narrative or structure to read a depressing series of pediatric oncology case studies, but somehow being involved with these things sends me to my desk. I read a lot of different comic books in any given month, but perhaps these do not count so much.

RODRIGO FRESÁN: I guess about eight. And generally, I read about four books at the same time.

ANDREW SEAN GREER: I am very slow and deliberate, since I'm looking for techniques to take. So I end up reading a book a week, along with a longer book I always have in my office—*War and Peace, Middlemarch*, something.

JENNIFER EGAN: Only one at a time per genre, but ideally I'm reading fiction, nonfiction, and poetry all at once. However, with two little kids in the house, I'm often getting a lot less reading done than I'd like to. I don't really count the number of books I read—probably a good thing, because I'd only be depressed that I'm not reading more of them.

GLEN DAVID GOLD: It's all over the place. For years I've been reading Casanova's memoirs. In the words of my friend Bill, he's like the world's best traveling companion. I read a ton of nonfiction for my work, and fiction to relax (or to get highly competitive; it turns on a dime). But for the last three or four months I've been unable to read any fiction whatsoever. I seem to have reader's block. I'm not sure I know why.

SUSAN MINOT: Sometimes I'll finish three a month, or one every three months. I read about five or six or seven at a time.

ADAM MANSBACH: It varies greatly. Am I traveling? Writing? The father of a month-old baby? I tend to go on benders and read ten or twelve books in a month. Then I might only read a couple the month after that. Sometimes I'll be reading two or three at once, but unless they're widely divergent or there's a specific reason, like I'm teaching one of them, that might be an indication that none is fully holding my attention.

SANTIAGO RONCAGLIOLO: I read a book a week, more or less, but never more than one at the same time. If I don't like one, I abandon it and I begin another. There are lots of good books to be read. There's no need to obsess yourself with the bad ones. There are also good books that you read at the wrong time. In those cases, it's better to wait and try again later.

AKHIL SHARMA: Two or three. I try to read only one at a time. This forces me to finish books that I find boring (*The Magic Mountain*). This also forces me to concentrate on each book and helps me gain what I can from each book. One of the dangers of reading multiple books at the same time is that it can become like channel-flipping.

JOSÉ MANUEL PRIETO: That depends, if I'm on vacation, sometimes I read one or more books a day. If not I take longer, but I read similar books. I'm always reading a few at a time on different topics, and in particular, popular science and thought. Nowadays I find that more interesting than fiction, novels.

YIYUN LI: I read two books at a time, a novel and then a collection of short stories. I read four or five new books in a given month, but more of my reading time is spent on rereading.

MEHMET MURAT SOMER: It depends on the length of the books and where I am reading them. I can read more on trips. Airports, planes, beaches are perfect for reading. At home my attention is taken up by so many other things. . . . If I don't like what I am reading, I leave it after twenty pages. I usually read two books simultaneously, the second one in bed before sleeping unless somebody charming is present.

RODDY DOYLE: Between five and ten. I'm reading four at the moment.

SUSAN CHOI: Lately, with two kids under the age of four, it's more a matter of how many months it takes me to read a book. But I usually have a few going at once: one main preoccupation, one chunk of nonfiction I dip in and out of, and a few story collections that I'm working my way through.

TAYARI JONES: I probably read a book a month. Although, if I am on vacation, I can read four chunky thrillers in a week. How many at a time? Whether it's reading or writing, I am pretty monogamous.

ALAA AL ASWANY: It depends on the kind of books. Sometimes, for example, there are very heavy theoretical books that are very useful and important, that I keep reading while I am reading other books. I could give you an example: I kept visiting the very important book called *The Decline of the West* written by a German thinker named Oswald Spengler. He spent twenty years on this book. It's almost impossible to get through it at one time, but with poetry and novels, I usually read them all the way through. I begin a book and I finish it.

JOSH EMMONS: In a good month I read four books, which is fewer than I'd like but realistic considering how much other literary matter warrants attention: magazine articles, instruction manuals, poetry, album-liner notes, blogs, short stories, flyers, junk mail, etc. Ideally I have three or four books going at once, a mix of fiction read strictly for pleasure, nonfiction helpful for whatever I'm writing, fiction that friends or other people have given me, nonfiction to fill in gaps in my education, fiction the prose and momentum of which is inspiring, and nonfiction that promotes through its message or content better ways to think and live. Because we're all protean creatures whose inner worlds are defined by what we ingest mentally and spiritually, by reading widely we're able to write widely, which, when all goes well, will produce work that expands and confirms what we suspect is true of others and our surroundings. On a more practical level, reading randomly and systematically teaches us about subjects we'd normally not know about and so can inform and improve our work. By picking up a history of bauxite mining in Michigan's Upper Peninsula, for example, you'll be able to explain why your Finnish immigrant heroine loves saunas and fears cancer and considers ocean waves to be too violent.

YAEL HEDAYA: I cannot read more than one book at a time, and lately, I can't find the time to read at all, which is very sad for me, since reading was such a huge part of my life once.

ALEKSANDAR HEMON: I don't know—a lot. I don't count. I often read two or three books at a time.

CLAIRE MESSUD: I wish you'd asked me that question seven years ago, before my children were born. Up to that point, I read a great deal; and I made a point of finishing a book I had begun, even if I didn't care for it. In my life since, however, my reading time has been hideously curtailed. I'm still not sane unless I'm reading something; but it may take me weeks or sometimes even months to finish it. And I'm afraid I'm guilty of abandoning books along the way. That said, I'm rarely reading more than two books at a time; and I'm usually really reading only one.

COLM TÓIBÍN: Because I write long pieces for the *New York Review of Books* and the *London Review of Books* and always have two or three pieces on the go, I will read for those pieces every day. I read books by my friends. I don't read half enough at random anymore. There are some short stories or poems I will become obsessed by and will reread every day for a month or maybe more. I always have a project of my own that I am reading for, often uselessly.

A. M. HOMES: I am often reading for work, reading applications for things, reading for contests. Currently my reading for food for thought has been seriously limited—which isn't good—I'm starving for that kind of stimulation.

DINAW MENGESTU: My reading habits can vary widely depending on my own writing. Often when I'm writing well, I'm reading constantly—as many as three or four novels at a time, which comes to about twelve to fifteen books a month. There are of course spells, though, when it can take me weeks to get through a single book, or when I can't seem to find the proper novel to match my mood.

EDWIDGE DANTICAT: I always read one book at a time. I used to read about ten books a month before I had a small child at home. Now I average two or three.

GEORGE PELECANOS: Typically I read four or five books a month. There is my "A" book, usually a novel, which is the one that makes its way with me around the house. And then there is usually something (nonfiction, biography, or a film book) on my nightstand, for the reading I do before I go to sleep.

JONATHAN LETHEM: As a teenager I devoured a book a day, typically. I'd always dedicate myself to one at a time, easy to do when you're simply plowing through them from start to finish in a series of five or ten uninterrupted sessions, as I often did—and easy when you're reading pocket-sized paperbacks, which never need to be anywhere but on your person. I probably averaged three to four hundred books a year for a while there. Of course, I was often reading shorter novels, and plotty novels as opposed to novels dense-with-language. And my reading was sometimes dangerously cursory—rather than linger on sentences, I'd fillet books for their skeletal essence of story and character and concept.

Now I probably manage about five or ten books a month, a combination of novels, which I read much, much more gradually—and are often longer or denser than those I used to fillet—and nonfiction, which I tend to read as hungrily and sloppily as I once read fiction. I'm often in the middle of two or three books at once, and I don't always have them with me—so there might be a book in the office I'm reading slowly over weeks while something else by my bedside is going very quickly.

NELL FREUDENBERGER: I don't like to read more than one novel at a time, but I'll sometimes read nonfiction (especially if it has to do with what I'm writing) along with a novel. I'm always reading a novel, but I've never made a monthly tally.

HOW DO YOU BALANCE READING WIDELY, WITH READING THAT IS IMMEDIATELY USEFUL TO YOUR WORK?

CHRIS ABANI: Reading widely is what is immediately useful to my work.

SHELLEY JACKSON: I consider all reading useful to my work. Even cookbooks and yoga manuals give me ideas. So do spam mails and slips of the tongue. Language is language, and it's all up for grabs—the difference between a line in a novel and one spray-painted on the side of a truck is only in how you read it.

MICHAEL CHABON: I don't; I err consistently on the side of the latter.

RICK MOODY: There's no science to how I read, which is how I like it. One of the big challenges of the midcareer time of life involves carving out reading space for myself—that is, to the best of my ability, untouched by the industry and by expectations of friends and colleagues. My intention is to read exactly what I want to when I want to. It is, after all, the adventure of reading that got me writing in the first place.

STEPHEN KING: I never read for work, unless it's quick Google-gobbles (today it was some stuff about Martin Scorsese). I only read for pleasure.

ADAM MANSBACH: It differs for me with each project, as does how widely I'm willing to cast the net of "immediately useful." Usefulness, I'm learning, can come in unexpected ways; the utility of a Thomas Hardy novel to my own current novel about graffiti writers battling mysterious demons in the tunnels of New York City and consuming entheogenic rain forest drugs is not something I could have predicted had I not picked up *The Return of the Native*, grudgingly, on a friend's suggestion.

ANDREW SEAN GREER: I focus mostly on what is useful for my work—but by that I don't mean research and similar novels. Reading widely is the key to finding ways of telling a story that might solve a problem, so anything might work. I do put down wonderful novels if they're not helping me with my own. It's not their fault—it's my own.

HARUKI MURAKAMI: I read books for fun.

JOSÉ MANUEL PRIETO: One way or another, all books end up being useful in my work. When I'm researching, I read in specific ways, about a particular theme, but the truth is one never knows what type of reading will give an idea you can use in the book you are currently writing or a future one.

RODDY DOYLE: I read for pleasure in the early mornings and late evenings, and research—often a pleasure—during the working day.

SUSAN MINOT: I have no real reading plan. I graze. I will return to books that I know speak to something I'm working on, or that offered me something that I'm hungry for, otherwise I find new books by keeping a lookout and reading about books and browsing around. Sometimes I will NOT read books that I think might be too close to what I'm working on. (One must find one's own way. . . .)

TAYARI JONES: I never know what is going to be immediately useful. I read a book because I want to read it. Sometimes that is a really smart book and sometimes it is a middle-brow mystery. What always surprises me is that there is always something in there that benefits my work. For example, the mysteries remind me to keep the plot moving.

PAUL AUSTER: I do very little research for my novels; therefore, very little extra reading is required to write them. While working on a novel, I tend to stay away from reading fiction, concentrating on history, biography, science, politics. Since I spend my day in an imaginary world, it's good to find the real again when my work is done.

ALEKSANDAR HEMON: Everything I read is immediately useful to my work. Reading helps me stay inside literature all the time. It makes me think in a way that is conducive to writing. In fact it is the same thinking process. I read compulsively—preferably a book of my choice, but anything would do. I've read, with great interest, nutritional information on cereal boxes. I regularly read wedding announcements in the *New York Times*. Hell is being stuck at an airport without a book, surrounded by blaring TVs. Reading is a mode of engagement with the world without which writing is impossible.

CLAIRE MESSUD: Again, because of the abbreviated reading time aforementioned, much of my broader reading has been deferred. It's a great and rare treat to sit down with a book I am reading purely for pleasure—whether it's Dostoyevsky or Alice Munro—these days. Many of the books that I read I am reading for research, or to review. Even these, I read appallingly slowly. Recently, I had the great thrill of reading and rereading much of the oeuvre of Joseph Conrad, supposedly for a review of his biography; but in fact I took such a long time to read them all that I was too late to write the review; and hence had the retrospective pleasure of having read the novels for my own pleasure and general education. It felt great.

COLM TÓIBÍN: I don't read widely anymore, or not as much as I would like, and also I teach a literature class every year over one semester and this means I read two or three books a week for that, books that I have usually read many times before.

T COOPER: I don't differentiate much between reading that is good for my work and reading that is just plain good for me. Sometimes I get on jags where I read only magazines and periodicals (the *New Yorker* or *Harper's* or the *Atlantic*, or even just the *New York Times*, etc.), and that enriches me as much as a novel might during whatever phase I'm going through.

I remember a point when I was teaching high school writing and English, and it just clicked for me how important it was to tell students simply to read the newspaper every day. I think at that point I'd just finally realized how important it was for me to do the same (I was still a young, aspiring writer myself at the time). I know everybody's decrying the death of print journalism, but there's something about old-fashioned reporting that's unlike any other form of writing. . . . You just get the opportunity to hear from a chorus of voices you don't always get to hear from in your daily life, and I think this chorus truly has the potential to enrich one's fiction. It has mine, and countless other authors I know— some who have literally built stories out of headlines, and others in more indirect ways.

EDWIDGE DANTICAT: I now mostly read what is useful to my work. But sometimes I do read a book that simply sounds interesting for its own sake.

JENNIFER EGAN: It's difficult. As with most things in my life, I rely mostly on instinct. I'm not especially good at grand schemes. I find that reading is a lot like eating—there are times when I'm really in the mood for certain books, and times when I'm almost physically averse to reading them. I try to read things when I crave them, because that is most fair to the books and to myself. This strategy usually results in my reading a mix of books that relate directly to whatever I'm working on and books that have nothing to do with it.

GEORGE PELECANOS: I don't read as much crime fiction as I used to, and I don't like to read it at all when I'm writing a novel. My work involves getting out of the house, talking to people, and, most importantly, listening, because you have to get the voices right. Yes, everything you need to know in terms of factual research is probably available in the library or on the Internet. But there's no substitute for breathing the air and feeling the dirt.

RABIH ALAMEDDINE: I consider almost any good book to be immediately useful for my work. Almost all my books are inspired by other books. When people ask me "where do you get your ideas?," it's usually from other books. I use style, I use all kinds of things. Now for the last one I had to do something specific because I was looking for a story, so I got a lot of books looking for the story. So yes, that would be immediately useful for my work. But for the most part when I am writing I tend to limit myself to what I consider great writing. I'm writing so much that only a great book will get me going.

NELL FREUDENBERGER: I don't balance. I'm sure I should, but in terms of fiction I have no discipline: I just read whatever I want.

SANTIAGO RONCAGLIOLO: Reading a lot, and from a wide variety of sources, is immediately useful to my work. Ideas are everywhere. In fact, I read a lot of magazines and newspapers; I read in English, French, Spanish, Catalan, and Portuguese; I read essays, children's books, screenplays. I'm omnivorous.

GARY SHTEYNGART: It's a catch-22. If you commit yourself to writing novels that require a lot of research, you will lose out on the reason you became a writer in the first place—the love of good books. There's just not enough hours in the day, so the least you can do is disable your WiFi signal every Tuesday and Thursday and give yourself the gift of two good Chekhov stories slowly read.

IS THERE A NOVEL YOU GO BACK TO AGAIN AND AGAIN? IF SO, WHY? WHAT DOES IT TEACH YOU?

LAILA LALAMI: There isn't one novel I go back to, but there is a writer I always return to—J. M. Coetzee. He is a consummate craftsman and I often reread him for pleasure or for work. I like to see how he handles particular craft elements. For instance, I love to reread the opening to *Life & Times of Michael K* to look at how each sentence is put together, how it connects seamlessly with the one before or after it, how it works all at once to advance the story, create character, move time forward or back, etc. His sentences are marvelously beautiful and incredibly efficient. I also often reread *Waiting for the Barbarians* to study the way in which each character is fully examined and portrayed, with neither harshness nor indulgence, just a deep understanding of the human condition.

FRANCISCO GOLDMAN: The writer I reread most often is Saul Bellow. On drowsy mornings when I don't really feel like working, I reach for his prose like jumper cables. He is a constant for me, and so is Jorge Luis Borges, especially now, in my wife, Aura's editions of the collected works, nearly every page filled with her margin notes, so that really, it's like reading them both, in constant dialogue.

Lately, because of the book I'm writing, I've been returning regularly to a handful of books with first-person narratives, which are especially helpful to me right now, especially Gregor von Rezzori's *Memoirs of an Anti-Semite*, Colm Tóibín's *The Story of the Night*, Murakami's *Norwegian Wood*. For this book I've needed to cast off writing habits that maybe come too easily to me—a sort of digressive playfulness or jokiness that is inappropriate for this book, as it was for the last one, come to think of it. There is a beautiful unaffected austerity (that doesn't really apply to von Rezzori, of course), honesty, and gravity—lightly borne, if that's not too contradictory—in a lot of the prose that I like to read right now.

AMY TAN: I do—and I usually try not to read it from beginning to end. One of them is *Love in the Time of Cholera*. Another one is *Jane Eyre*. I love Charlotte Brontë's truthfulness.

HARUKI MURAKAMI: Some books I read again and again. What does it teach me? I want to write those kind of books myself, if I could.

ANNE ENRIGHT: I used to read *Ulysses* every five years to see how much I might understand, and what I might make of it, this time around. I look at *Lolita* now and then—I am interested how the novel has changed as society changed around it. I was both fascinated and bored by it when I read it first, at the age of twelve; I was crazy about it in college, and now . . . I think it just makes me cross. But I still like its failed structure—how the second half fritters itself away, and how this doesn't actually matter. It is a book that I am somehow creatively intimate with.

PAUL AUSTER: *Don Quixote.* I have been reading this masterpiece every seven to ten years for the past forty years, ever since I read it for the first time as a college student. Cervantes explored every possibility of narration in this immense book. It's a source of inextinguishable inspiration for me.

RODDY DOYLE: I reread Dickens regularly. To remind me of why I try to write.

SHELLEY JACKSON: Beckett's *The Unnamable*, for the ghastly humor with which it yanks the rug out from under its own feet; its pungent, contrary, stagger-on sentences; and its exemplary bravery.

JONATHAN LETHEM: There are many I go back to (and to skip ahead to the next question, yes, there are often different touchstones for different projects). *Alice in Wonderland, Through the Looking-Glass, White Noise, The Great Gatsby, The Long Goodbye, The Trial,* and *We Have Always Lived in the Castle* are a few examples—and certain stories by Thurber and Barthelme and others. I'm often seeking a specific trigger of visionary language or imagery that I can rely on to remind me of why I'm chasing the effects I'm chasing in my own writing. Of course, what they often end up teaching me when I return to them is how much I've changed, in seeing them differently—and how many different books can hide inside the same book, available to different versions of myself at different readings.

ALAA AL ASWANY: I reread all the Greek novels every three or four years or sometimes less. And every time I read *The Old Man and the Sea*, by Hemingway, I discover things I couldn't understand before because I was too young. The older you get, the more human experience you get, then the more you understand a novel.

ADANIA SHIBLI: There are few. There is *The Epistle of Forgiveness*, written by Abu al-Alaa' al-Ma'ari at the end of the tenth, early eleventh century. Al-Ma'ari is considered to have used in his writings the widest range of vocabulary in Arabic literature. This work is actually believed by many theorists to have influenced Dante and led him to writing *The Divine Comedy*. I also go back occasionally to the Arabic translation of the Bible by al-Yaziji and al-Bustani made in the late nineteenth and early twentieth century, which also presents a wide range of words, yet in modern Arabic. I also go back to reading *Ulysses* by James Joyce. These three books accompany me wherever I go. They in a way are like a "flask" of words that keep me going on and able to rediscover language and its magical abilities.

Sometimes I also get attached to a newspaper and would carry it for one or two months, to read from it. The simplicity of newspaper language is sometimes a break from language.

STEPHEN KING: I go back to the John D. MacDonald novels from the fifties, like *The End of the Night* and *One Monday We Killed Them All*. Great stories. The Travis McGee books are small beer compared to the stand-alones (the greatest is *The Last One Left*); the stand-alones are real American literature—rough, sure, but so's Thomas Wolfe. These books taught me how to write stories.

JOSÉ MANUEL PRIETO: Yes, *In Search of Lost Time*, by Marcel Proust. I don't tire of reading it, as much for what it says as for how it says it. For years it has been my nightstand book and the truth is I've never been able to find a substitute in that sense.

CRISTINA GARCIA: I go to Chekhov when I'm depressed about writing. And then I go to Juan Rulfo's *Pedro Páramo* when I want to be astonished and inspired by what's possible. That's the range, and then there's a lot of other people in between. Chekhov somehow always lifts my spirits in terms of the human condition, even with all the very melancholy people he writes about. There's just something incredibly redeeming about him and how he writes.

YIYUN LI: There are a few novels that I go back to regularly: *Two Lives, Fools of Fortune,* and *The Children of Dynmouth* by William Trevor, and *Disgrace* by J. M. Coetzee. There are many things to learn from *Disgrace,* and I can reread that novel a hundred times, but when I work on my novel I go to that novel to relearn pacing and rhythm. The Trevor novels offer everything I need for writing a novel—mood, narrative voice, wisdom—most importantly I think Trevor's work offers me a haven where I do not have to worry about interference from other people's narrative voices (and sometimes noises I pick up here and there).

SUSAN CHOI: There are certain novels that, for whatever reason, become inextricably bound up with certain projects of mine, and I read them so intensely for that period that I sort of demolish them. This happened to me with *The Great Gatsby* while I was writing *American Woman.* The uncoiling spring of that book's plot, the awful momentum that takes hold of the characters (and during the torpor of a heat wave!)— these seemed to me like the engines of those fateful cars the characters drive: intricate and powerful but ultimately dissectable, and so I took that book apart trying to figure out how he'd done it. Literally. At one point I had the book in pieces and the pages spread all over the floor. I went crazy. And what did I discover? That Fitzgerald's seemingly inevitable, flawless plot is in fact deeply flawed. The characters are obliged to do something utterly unbelievable, for the sake of the action, and yet it's almost impossible to notice this because the writing is wonderful. Moral:

great writing is more important than flawless plot. Write well and you can get away with anything.

MEHMET MURAT SOMER: Several. And the list is very eclectic. Patricia Highsmith's *The Talented Mr. Ripley* and *Those Who Walk Away* next to Honoré de Balzac's *Vautrin*, Turkish author Ayşe Kulin next to Japanese writer Junichiro Tanizaki. All for different reasons. I've learned different things from each and every one of them. I also realized that over time I forget novels. Not the one-sentence summary of course. But after some time, when I read it again, it's as fresh as the first time. Even early Harold Robbins or Armistead Maupin's *Tales of the City*, both of which I count as exemplary for their sense of pace.

CHRIS ABANI: Toni Morrison's *Beloved*. The language is to die for, the use of semiotics and image is unparalleled, the conflation of multiple characters into one while still maintaining individuality, the social, historical, racial, and gender engagements. It teaches what I still need to learn. Also, Salman Rushdie's *Shame*, Peter Orner's *Esther Stories*, Brad Kessler's *Birds in Fall*, Junot Díaz's *The Brief Wondrous Life of Oscar Wao*, Stewart O'Nan's *A Prayer for the Dying*. I learn everything I need to know about character, scene, language, and experimentation from these writers.

ADAM MANSBACH: If I had to pick one, it would be Baldwin's *Another Country* because there is an emotional precision to his inhabitation of each character. He's got a big cast, diverse in every way, and their inner lives and interpersonal relations are so sharp, from dialogue to gesture to inner monologue. He's making larger points, enormous points, about race and gender and sexuality and art, but he does it in subtle touches and intimate moments. He's able to leech the brutality out of tenderness, and vice versa. That book understands astoundingly well how closely those two things are linked.

A. M. HOMES: I go back to John Cheever; I think line by line he's brilliant. And he's working in both long and short forms and, well, I just think he's it—Cheever and Richard Yates.

RICK MOODY: There are books that I return to philosophically and consult episodically even if, on occasion, I don't reread them in their entirety. *Moby-Dick,* *The Recognitions, The Crying of Lot 49, The Rings of Saturn,* Beckett's trilogy, *To the Lighthouse,* the New Testament, Montaigne's essays, *A Lover's Discourse,* etc. The lessons are probably the same in each case. Don't compromise, don't back down, don't be faint of heart, don't curry favor.

SUSAN MINOT: William Faulkner's *The Sound and the Fury.* Proust's *In Search of Lost Time.* Anything by Virginia Woolf, Hemingway, Fitzgerald, Raymond Carver, J. D. Salinger, Nabokov. . . . They recapture for me that first inspiration I got from literature, which reminds me on an instinctive level why I write. And they demonstrate mastery.

MICHAEL CHABON: *Moby-Dick. Love in the Time of Cholera. The Long Goodbye.* I want to live in their worlds; in their language; in the lives and consciousnesses they portray.

SANTIAGO RONCAGLIOLO: No. I often get tired of even my favorite authors. It's like analyzing a magician's tricks: sooner or later they don't surprise you anymore. I'm a very promiscuous reader.

ALEKSANDAR HEMON: *Lolita* by Nabokov; *A Tomb for Boris Davidovich* by Danilo Kiš; *Austerlitz* by W. G. Sebald; *Madam Bovary* by Flaubert. *The Collected Works of Billy the Kid* by Michael Ondaatje. I also go back to Chekhov's stories. The list is long. These books rekindle my love for literature and reading, reenergize the magic. After I get depressed with the abundance and shallowness of the front-table books, I go back to the novels and stories I love to remind myself what it is all about.

I don't study them—for you can study crap and learn a lot. But, reading them, I redefine my aesthetic, I formulate what it is that I want from my books.

CLAIRE MESSUD: There are a number of novels I go back to again and again. *Portrait of a Lady* is one of them because Henry James is never more simultaneously lucid and rich in his exploration of character than in that book. I go back to Italo Svevo's *Zeno's Conscience*, because I love it, even as I recognize that any parsing of its structure reveals it to be an eccentric shambles—that's to say that in rereading it I am constantly reminded of how important a mess is to a great novel. Life is not tidy, and books should not be either. There are others too— I go back to *Anna Karenina*, again for Tolstoy's lucidity and complexity; and I go back to Proust, because I still haven't finished the darn thing.

YAEL HEDAYA: Until recently, I used to read Yaakov Shabtai's *Past Perfect* again and again, every time I began writing a new novel. It was my ignition book. Shabtai writes very long sentences, has a breathless narrative that I myself use. I love his work. When I was at a point in my career where I was deeply influenced, I was influenced by him.

COLM TÓIBÍN: I go back to *The Portrait of a Lady*, to *Pride and Prejudice*, to *The Great Gatsby*, to *The Sun Also Rises*, to *Amongst Women*, to name but five, not because they teach me anything—I hate teachers (except myself)—but because they fill me with pleasure.

T COOPER: There are so many. But I guess one that comes to mind is *Kiss of the Spider Woman* by Manuel Puig. Specifically, I go to this book to be reminded of all that can be done with dialogue. What's absolutely necessary, what's flabby or expository and should be excised, and just how much story can be conveyed without my "telling" the reader anything. The characters do it all through dialogue in this book.

EDWIDGE DANTICAT: Toni Morrison's *Sula*. It's so epic and economical and I can read the whole thing in one night. I learn a great deal from it about writing idiosyncratic and memorable characters, how to use time in a novel. Her language is so vivid and poetic.

GEORGE PELECANOS: *True Grit* by Charles Portis, for the storytelling and the incredible voice of Mattie Ross. It is an underrated novel and an American classic.

RODRIGO FRESÁN: Yes, Melville's *Moby-Dick*, Proust's *In Search of Lost Time*, and *Slaughterhouse-Five* by Kurt Vonnegut. Add to those John Cheever's stories and a bit of Denis Johnson. As far as what they've taught me, I prefer to not have a clear idea. I'm also not interested in finding out the exact influence they had, have right now, and will continue to have on me. In truth I prefer to think of all those titles as if they were an indissoluble and irreplaceable part of my DNA.

NELL FREUDENBERGER: I go back to stories more than novels, especially Grace Paley's and Alice Munro's. I think I'll reread novels more as I get older, but for now there always seems to be a lot I haven't read. I do go back to particular chapters in novels: for example, the one in *Anna Karenina* when Vronsky and Anna visit the Russian painter Mikhaylov, and we briefly see the two of them through his eyes. Tolstoy shifts the point of view briefly and abruptly so that we see his characters through an entirely different lens. Another chapter I go back to is the first in the second part of Peter Carey's *Illywhacker* in which Goon Tse Ying begins to teach the narrator how to become invisible. I like the way the whole novel (narrated by a notorious liar) integrates the fantastic into a realistic story, but I'm not sure I could learn from it—I think I go back to it because the narrator's voice is so powerful.

ANN CUMMINS: One of my favorite books is Kobo Abe's *The Woman in the Dunes*, though I've only read the English translation. It's just a slip of a book, more a novella than a novel. It starts off with a great dramatic hook—a man, an entomologist, goes missing while searching for bugs in dunes. The protagonist is a jaded, logical, lonely specimen, dissatisfied in his relationships with women, with his coworkers—in some ways, with the workings of his own mind. The dunes with their constantly shifting sands become annoying and then terrifying for this scientist. The villagers are communal, willing to sacrifice the individual for the good of the whole. While this theme of the tormented individual at odds with society plays out in many wonderful books, I love this one, which is akin to Camus' *The Stranger*, because it shows the incremental changes in perception one person experiences when thwarted. It's a layered book reflecting psychological and social schisms in Japan after Hiroshima, where the landscape is desolate. The community shovels sand, futile and metaphorically interesting work for a humbled, defeated society. So I love the book for all of the thought-provoking metaphoric layers, but I love it mostly because it's a page-turner, full of dramatic tension. The writing's economical. Every word drives the story. I wish I could write a book as elegant and riveting as this one.

ARE THESE TOUCHSTONE BOOKS DIFFERENT FOR EACH PROJECT?

CHRIS ADRIAN: So far they have been. For the last novel, I kept going back to *Moby-Dick* and the Bible. Part of this is because there is always someone who wrote about what you want to write about fifty or a hundred or a thousand years ago, and it is nice to get to know the ways in which you are destined to fall short of your goal, and deal with the misery of that, and move on. A bigger part is that there is a great deal to learn from the people who have already done what you want to do better than you will ever be able to do it. The novel I'm working on now is a retelling of *A Midsummer Night's Dream* set in the present in San

Francisco, so I keep going back to the play again and again, and the story itself is an odd sort of response to the play.

ANNE ENRIGHT: Yes, but they come around again, a few books on.

SUSAN MINOT: Not really. They don't have to do with subject, rather with literary excellence.

CHRIS ABANI: No. I read them all, all the time. I also forgot to mention that I love poetry and physics and math, so those too. I read those randomly.

STEPHEN KING: No touchstone books.

AKHIL SHARMA: I've only written one book and there was a certain style that was a touchstone for that (Hemingway, Tolstoy, Dostoyevsky). With this new book, my old style isn't working and so I need to learn a new style and this is causing me to think a little bit more about Chekhov and Joseph Roth.

ALEKSANDAR HEMON: No. It's all one big, continuous project. I do sometimes read books that are demanded by what I am working on. This is not research—it is more of a mood thing, and very similar to the method (if it were a method) of picking music I listen to when I write.

SHELLEY JACKSON: Yes, each project has its particular literary godparents, and I turn to them repeatedly—to catch a rhythm, sharpen my attention to a certain formal problem, or just remind me to be as true to my own peculiar vision as I can be.

CLAIRE MESSUD: I'm sure that if I returned to my earlier books I would be able to enumerate the books that had been so important in the shaping of those projects. For example, I remember that Peter Brown's biography of Augustine was hugely important to me when I was working on *The Last Life*. But there are other books—novels, mostly—like those aforementioned, which at least thus far have traveled with me through life and remained important always.

HARUKI MURAKAMI: No touchstone. I just love to read them. That is all.

JOSÉ MANUEL PRIETO: I think so. You more or less have in mind the book you are modeling, the one you want it to be similar to, without it ever being like it. But that book, that serves more or less as an admitted model, exists. For *Rex*, for example, it was partly *Pale Fire* by Nabokov, for its relation with commentary as narrative technique. But also a not very well-known work by Proust, *Pastiches et Mélanges*, as much for the writer as imitator as for the story it tells, about a diamond forger. For *Nocturnal Butterflies of the Russian Empire*, curiously, I didn't have any, but I did read an infinity of epistolary books, as anyone who has read it will note.

A. M. HOMES: YES.

MICHAEL CHABON: No, they are pretty much eternal.

RICK MOODY: There are always new lessons. The writer who feels that he or she is now fixed on certainties and is impervious to the surprise of the new is probably delusional. There are new discoveries along the way for me, as a reader, sure, but they are not yoked to specific writing projects. Discovery just happens.

COLM TÓIBÍN: For *The Master*, the novel I wrote about Henry James, there were about forty of them. For the other books I often don't know until afterward the extent to which I have been depending on another book for my book.

DINAW MENGESTU: There are a few novels that I find myself return-ing to over and over again. V. S. Naipaul's *A Bend in the River*, Marilynne Robinson's *Housekeeping*, and *Duino Elegies* by Rilke have all been consis-tent standards in my reading habit for the past several years now. Each is beautifully written, and each has a certain emotional weight or personal significance that reminds me why I love literature, and what it can do when it's done well.

SANTIAGO RONCAGLIOLO: Yes. In my novel *Prudishness*, John Cheever was decisive. In *Red April*, the book *From Hell* by Alan Moore, and the novels of Ian McEwan. In *The Fourth Sword*, Norman Mailer and Truman Capote. Now I'm into Philip Roth and Martin Amis. My interest in English-language literature is a constant. It's more direct, economical, and personal than Latin American literature, which tends to be more elitist and baroque.

MEHMET MURAT SOMER: Not for me. I don't have any touchstone books, films. . . . Perhaps only music, which affects my mood. I consider myself a monumental project, not my novels. If I am well-fed, intellectu-ally as well, I can craft them.

EDWIDGE DANTICAT: Yes. For my last book, which was a memoir, Jamaica Kincaid's *My Brother* and Joan Didion's *The Year of Magical Thinking* and Paul Auster's *The Invention of Solitude* were my touchstone books. I took turns reading those three books over and over as I was writing.

RODRIGO FRESÁN: No. They are simply places to return to and places I will never leave.

NELL FREUDENBERGER: No, I don't think so. I think foundational books—the books that made you want to be a writer—teach you things that you apply every time you write something.

ARE THERE CERTAIN AUTHORS YOU WON'T READ FOR FEAR OF UNDUE INFLUENCE?

RODRIGO FRESÁN: No. But I have to acknowledge that prolonged exposure to the very parasitic—for all the right reasons—Vladimir Nabokov as a certain risk. And on more than one occasion, certain key absences make a mark on the style as much or more so than certain current or assimilated present influences. I'll go further: maybe that is what style is in the end. Maybe, now that I think about it, a writer's style is nothing more than the ghost of his shortcomings rather than the reality of his virtues. I'll try to explain myself. You end up resigning yourself to what you can do, and throwing aside what you'll never be good at, and so others perceive as achievements what in reality are the dregs within reach, with luck, each time ennobled and purified. What a writer does and what he wanted to do are two different things, and, as time passes, what he does solidifies into the only thing he can do well, what he does like no one else. So, style then is like antimatter and, perhaps, in another dimension, on the other side of a black hole, there's another Rodrigo Fresán who loves to write nineteenth-century-style novels that the Rodrigo Fresán now reading and writing loves to read because—he's resigned himself to it—he knows he'll never be able to write them.

SUSAN MINOT: Like bad ones? As I said, sometimes the subject matter of a book might be too close to what I'm trying to write so I will stay away from it. But who knows? I don't read it so maybe it wouldn't have influenced me.

RICK MOODY: Yes.

PAUL AUSTER: No.

YIYUN LI: I don't think so, but I try to stay with the books I mentioned earlier when I am doing the most active writing.

SUSAN CHOI: I used to have that hang-up, and it stunted my reading and didn't help my writing. I got over it.

ALEJANDRO ZAMBRA: I don't believe in forbidden readings while writing. Neither readings nor experiences. But what I never do is read previous books of my own. I'm repetitive enough that I'm likely to go back over my own writing. I never reread what I've published because of the temptation to rewrite it, of reliving that writing period.

ADANIA SHIBLI: Yes, books or writing styles which are too conscious of making language smart, and/or smartly unpredictable. These are quite contagious, they would take over one's own language, or appropriate one's mind. I find this style especially in North American literature, such as Salinger and in magazines such as the *New Yorker*. In fact, each time (and these instances are quite rare) I read a piece in the *New Yorker* I feel I need a few days or so to detox.

JOSÉ MANUEL PRIETO: No, surely not. That's something that one fears when young, but not when you've consolidated a certain personal way of expressing things.

ANNE ENRIGHT: No. I love being influenced.

ADAM MANSBACH: As a teenager, I stayed away from Kerouac. Like me, he was a white dude from Massachusetts who was into jazz and drugs and black culture and fucking with authority figures, and I saw enough hipsters hanging out by the Harvard Square T stop with their ratty Beat Readers that I was like "no way am I reading this guy, because I'm either going to hate him or love him." Today, I have no such fears. I feel like my sensibility is well enough developed that I can read anything. Except Mitch Albom. He's just too goddamn good.

RODDY DOYLE: Hitler, Jeffrey Archer, all the cookery books.

JOSH EMMONS: No, but there are authors I read in the hope of being influenced. For majesty of thought and narrative control—for a consciousness that might be mistaken for God's in the best and least tyrannical sense—I read George Eliot, Leo Tolstoy, Marcel Proust, and Shakespeare. For thrilling, lapidary prose, Vladimir Nabokov and Don DeLillo and Edward Gibbon and Barbara Tuchman are unbeatable. For sympathy and insight into the complications of being human, I like Franz Kafka, Fyodor Dostoyevsky, Stendhal, Milan Kundera, and Saul Bellow. For whimsy and joy and delight—too little practiced these days!—I turn to Jane Austen and Lewis Carroll and Laurence Sterne and Salman Rushdie. For raw, unfiltered depictions of life's dark side, of subjects and people wrongly neglected and shunned, I find solace in Samuel Beckett, Hubert Selby, Jr., and Louis-Ferdinand Céline. For sheer comic ebullience, I read Martin Amis, Jonathan Ames, and Anthony Burgess.

TAYARI JONES: Nope. I welcome influence, actually. I understand myself and my writing to be products of what I have read, what I experience.

SHELLEY JACKSON: I usually welcome influence. None of us could write without it. But I did avoid reading novels about conjoined twins when I was writing one, not so much for fear of influence, but for fear of feeling constrained to avoid any *appearance* of influence—of hog-tying my imagination to avoid trespassing on someone else's territory.

A. M. HOMES: There's a point at which I think you feel too old, or too solid, to be overly influenced—I got there long ago.

GLEN DAVID GOLD: Funny. I can always tell when a student has been reading Bukowski, Hemingway, Faulkner, or Palahniuk. For me, the fatal guy is Henry James. I write a lot of action scenes and it's no good when my characters are suddenly gazing into the middle distance. And no, I'm not kidding.

ALEKSANDAR HEMON: No. That's absurd. I find that attitude both arrogant and insecure. Thinking that if I read Proust I'll end up unconsciously, without particular effort, imitating his sentences and philosophy is arrogant. To think that I could easily be brainwashed by a dead author is insecure. Besides, why not be influenced? It reminds me of a scene from Monty Python's *The Life of Brian*, when Brian is trying to talk his followers out of following him. He tells the devout mass not to listen to him because they are all individuals and they all repeat: "We are all individuals." Except for one guy who says: "I'm not."

SANTIAGO RONCAGLIOLO: To the contrary: I read all authors in the hope that they'll influence me. I want to learn from them.

TASH AW: Yes—writers who write with a very distinctive, exaggerated style. Nabokov and Burgess are two I stay away from when I write—I seem to assimilate their writing style without meaning to, and then I get paranoid that I've crossed the boundary into mimicry, which would be terrible.

COLM TÓIBÍN: It would be like saying: Do you refrain from sex when you are writing a novel? No, I don't.

T COOPER: For my last novel, *Lipshitz Six, or Two Angry Blondes*, at least, I was a little leery of reading Philip Roth. I've read a lot of Roth, but it was actually after my book came out that I finally got through *Portnoy's Complaint*. I was so relieved that I hadn't seen it before, because as it turned out, the first-person narrator of the contemporary, latter section of the novel skews Portnoy a bit.

And as it was, just when I was all proud of myself for coming up with what I thought was going to be the only "Jewish novel" that wove Charles Lindbergh's Nazi-sympathizing tendencies into a Jewish immigrant story, out comes Roth's *The Plot Against America*, which I read in galley form right around the time I finished a draft of my novel. I was momentarily (not to mention dramatically) devastated, but in the end, Roth's use of Lindbergh was completely different from my own—I just had to get over not being the first to stick a proverbial flag into the terrain. Oh, and also not being Philip Roth.

EDWIDGE DANTICAT: I won't read unpublished manuscripts that deal with the same subject matter for fear that something of the other person's might seep into my book.

JONATHAN LETHEM: No, never. I don't fear undue influence, I crave it. I like to be drunk on different writers as I go through my work, and my days—their tempo, their vocabulary, their irony or hesitation or punctuation. I rely on my own sentences to remain stubbornly my own despite absorbing these trace influences like drug effects—how could it be otherwise?

There are, however, a small number of books I'm reluctant to read because the force of my imagined version of them is so fascinating to me that I don't want to discharge it by learning what they're really like.

ANN CUMMINS: When I was starting out as a writer I was very susceptible to other voices, though I found them more inspirational than dangerous. Jamaica Kincaid's voice was in my head for some of my short stories, as was Leslie Marmon Silko's, and, in another mood, Raymond Carver's. But there were several years early on when I found reading difficult—humbling. I admired everything I read and couldn't fathom ever making my writing cohere the way other writers did.

NELL FREUDENBERGER: I would count myself lucky to be influenced by any of the writers I really admire.

MICHAEL CHABON: No, I can handle it.

WHAT DO YOU LEARN FROM OTHER ART FORMS ?

SHELLEY JACKSON: A lot! Even a device that's old hat in its own domain—say, musical counterpoint, or the site-specific art installation—becomes interesting when I try to imagine how I would do it with words. (Considerably more interesting than another conventional novel, however well written.)

PAUL AUSTER: Visual art and music have always been as important to me as literature. It's difficult to explicate exactly how a painting or piece of music can influence a work of writing, but I nevertheless feel that I have been influenced by the things I've seen and heard.

STEPHEN KING: It's not about learning, except by accident. Art makes me joyful.

JENNIFER EGAN: Other art forms are hugely important to me as I work. For each of my books, there is usually a constellation of visual art and music that seems to link up with that work in some deep way. For example, my last novel, *The Keep*, was partly inspired by a video piece by Bill Viola that I saw at the Whitney years and years ago: a video of what appear to be apparitions moving around a swimming pool. The book I'm writing right now is a fairly direct response to Proust, and really drenched in a sense of time passing. At the moment I'm playing a lot of music by Laura Veirs because it seems to touch the wistful, slightly melancholic place I'm trying to write from. And the album *Come from Heaven* by Alpha was a real touchstone for me as I worked on *Look at Me,* for reasons that are hard to explain. When I'm really stuck in my work, I often find that going to a symphony or an art museum is helpful. Engaging my nonverbal senses can dislodge verbal material that I'm having trouble shaking loose. I always bring a notebook with me, needless to say.

JOSÉ MANUEL PRIETO: Like Hemingway says in *A Moveable Feast*, you can learn a lot about writing from looking at a Cezanne. In my particular case, music has taught me a lot about how to organize my texts, particularly Mozart's Symphony no. 41 (41 not 40!), the "Jupiter." In it I've found the "musical mass" perfectly distributed, dramatically organized. If you listen to it with attention, what I'm saying will be understood.

MARIO VARGAS LLOSA: When you write a novel—and this might apply for any creative activity—all your accumulated experience becomes part of it. I believe you not only write with your intelligence, your culture, but also with your sensibility, your passions, your instincts.

In the creative process, the unconscious aspect plays an important role—and sometimes a decisive role—in what you do. If all experiences are raw material for the writer, then of course the other arts have a say in the formation of sensibility. Music, painting, film, photography . . . and of course personal experiences, friendship, love. They're always a manner of enrichment that becomes part of what you do, though you may not have a clear awareness of it. In creative endeavors you work with your whole personality.

CHRIS ABANI: Visual artists teach me how to think in terms of scale and dimension and their words on their own work teach me how to think through mine. Music teaches me structure and symphony and the importance of learning your own melody. Architecture teaches me plot and scene and setting and place, from car design I learn efficiency and streamlining, and from film I learn atmosphere, dialogue, and image.

ADAM MANSBACH: Everything. I think one of the best ways to understand an art form is often through other art forms: writing through music, photography through journalism, hip-hop through jazz, the basic concept of narrative through forms that lack it or push its boundaries, like modern dance. Sometimes I've transferred these things to fiction in very formalistic ways, like structuring a scene or an entire novel to reflect the conventions of jazz composition and performance—call and response, verse and chorus, soloist and ensemble, the tone colors of different instruments, characters as representative of those instruments, speaking or acting "percussively" or "modally" or whatever, the role of time and improvisation, the relative impact of internal and external forces on that improvisation, and so on. A lot of people, myself included, have discussed my work in the context of hip-hop, and certainly the aesthetic and intellectual pillars of that culture inform my novels: the studious, democratic, ecstatic collage-building that runs through all hip-hop's art forms, from beat-construction to the kinetics of break dancing, to give just one example. And on a more general level, some of my most inspiring moments come through watching dance, or music, or looking at art, and many of my most enlightening conversations have been with artists in different disciplines. Particularly with some of the musicians I've worked with over the years as an MC, or met when I was a roadie for the great drummer Elvin Jones.

AKHIL SHARMA: I listen to music and it moves me and so I think, I need to be brave and not give up. I watch a movie and I think I can leap from scene to scene or fragment narrative.

TAYARI JONES: I often hear music and I think, "That is what I want my novel to feel like." I don't know if it is the same as learning from music, but music often serves as a sort of spirit guide for my projects.

HARUKI MURAKAMI: Music has taught me many things about writing novels.

YIYUN LI: I feel I am learning a lot from classical music (Tchaikovsky, Mahler, and some Dvořák are what I go to regularly), and I feel that I am learning a lot from these composers about movement, how one sentence moves into the next sentence and how one chapter moves into the next chapter.

GLEN DAVID GOLD: Holy smokes! Humility. That's one of the best lessons, I think, up there with confidence. Narrative, detail, emotion, the way information is unveiled, but most of all humility.

RODDY DOYLE: I love the silences in good dialogue in a film or a play. Film editing fascinates me—I'm sure it's rubbed off on my work—I hope it has. Rhythm is the most important part of my writing; take away the rhythm, and there's nothing left. I don't just listen to music while I'm working; I try to climb into it.

RICK MOODY: I suspect it's essential for writers to engage with nonliterary art forms. Fiction that is uninformed by other media feels, to me, well, kind of dead on the page. By other media, I suppose I mean, in general, other media exclusive of film. Film as a medium exerts an undue influence on the novel. It's as if we have this cool elder sibling and we'll do anything he says, even if it's not good for us.

Myself, I am very, very, very, very, very interested in music, and the lion's share of my nonliterary intellectual consideration is given over to listening to music. Not just popular music, but serious music, including jazz, "classical," whatever that means, Old Time, music from other countries, and so forth. I also, however, love and admire contemporary visual art, especially painting and photography. I always find my work improved by any encounter with visual art.

ALEKSANDAR HEMON: If you think of art as a means of engagement with the world, then all art forms are continuous. You learn whatever it is that can be learned from (and in) art.

ANNE ENRIGHT: Being an Irish woman writer, I grew up in considerable amounts of silence, about many things. There were very few voices out there that sounded like my own. The harbingers of social change are visual artists, who don't have to excuse or complete their work—by which I mean that they are never prescriptive. I found great freedom and resonance in the work of Irish visual artists, particularly Dorothy Cross, but also Kathy Prendergast and Alice Maher.

YAEL HEDAYA: That there is such a thing as magic. Listening to music, for instance, be it Bach or Pink Floyd, gives me the opportunity to forget I'm an adult. Even though today I enjoy music differently—my ability to recognize the complexity, for instance, has developed as I get older—when I listen to something really great, I'm a child all over again. I understand nothing but I'm lured into something so huge, so magical, I'm elated.

Lately, I'm learning a lot from TV. I think HBO has changed the way people view TV. Series like *The Sopranos* and *Six Feet Under* have upgraded TV to a higher form of art. Really. I get the same high watching an episode of *The Sopranos* that I do reading Joyce or Nabokov or Faulkner.

RABIH ALAMEDDINE: I was in New York recently, and we saw all the galleries in Chelsea. Most of the art was cynical, ironic, sort of referred back to itself. There was one show where the painter was basically doing imitations of abstract expressionism. At best it was mildly interesting. Then all of a sudden we get into a show of W. Eugene Smith. He was a *Life* photographer in the '40s and '50s. He had one series of a Spanish village in 1950 during Franco's era and it was just stunning—stunning, stunning. This is a photojournalist who understood composition, understood dark and light, understood that the content meant something. The Franco soldiers, the old women. Smith showed death and dying and hurt and I realized what was missing in all the other work we'd seen was not just life, but the intention of doing something that mattered. Something that actually matters to the reader, to the artist. I've got no problems with irony as long as my intention is a little bit deeper than just commenting on something. I hate commenting on something.

ADANIA SHIBLI: I learn a lot from painting; how something can exist so well without words, without which I cannot even imagine my life. That is, painting teaches me that language is not as essential as I consider it; especially expressionist German painting and even silent cinema.

CLAIRE MESSUD: I think that structurally I learn a great deal from music, even though my musical education is rather, uh, patchy. But certainly my experience of narrative form is akin to my experience of music, and I often feel that certain narrative decisions are dictated almost by the musical chord they create.

The visual is important to me also—one of my great struggles as a novelist is to try to convey the simultaneity of experience, so well conveyed by the visual, through the inevitably linear medium of language. I'm not sure, though, that I've so far come to any particularly satisfactory understanding of how that might be done. And the visual is simply fundamentally important to me, in a way that music is fundamentally important to my husband: my apprehension of the world is intensely visual; so that I am always learning from visual artists' expression of their visions.

SANTIAGO RONCAGLIOLO: I've always been interested by the impact an image can make in film, and by the rhythm of music—two art forms that I've cultivated. My theater background taught me that in order to create a plausible reality, you have to be very deceptive. I'm also very interested in journalism, although it isn't an art form. Reality has a special narrative power.

NELL FREUDENBERGER: I like looking at paintings, and my last book had to do with visual artists in particular. But it's the story of how the work was made that I ended up writing about, rather than the work itself. I don't think I'm smart enough about other art forms to learn from them directly.

EDWIDGE DANTICAT: From music, you can learn pacing and rhythm. From poetry, you can learn to value the weight and power of one word. You can even learn from architecture about structure. Arundahti Roy, I believe, was an architect and she said she plotted *The God of Small Things* architecturally.

GEORGE PELECANOS: Everything. I was a movie freak as a kid and got my sense of story structure from watching films. Thematically, and in terms of the issues I like to explore, there is more Peckinpah, Don Siegel, Sergio Leone, Robert Aldrich, and John Ford in my books than there is Fitzgerald, Faulkner, or even Raymond Chandler. Which is not to say that books have not been a strong force. Writers like Steinbeck, Edward Anderson, Horace McCoy, John Fante, and A. I. Bezzerides, and authentic crime-fiction stylists like David Goodis and Charles Willeford, have had a tremendous influence on me and inspired me to reach. And then there's music. Rock and soul have been very influential in terms of energy. When I am writing I listen to soundtracks and instrumentals. They free my imagination and help me pace my scenes. If you walk by my office on a writing day, you might hear Ennio Morricone, Jerry Goldsmith, Lalo Schifrin, Jerry Fielding, John Barry, or *Get Up with It*-era Miles coming from my stereo. Movies, music, novels, and paintings all push their way into my books.

JONATHAN LETHEM: A great number of art forms have the advantage of being, compared to novels, light on their feet—full of immediacy and impulse and, in the case of performance arts like music or theater, the intimate sense of being created directly in front of their audience. I tend to believe that the novel, however characteristically ponderous, rather than just relying on its compensating advantages (it has many: capaciousness, immensity, thoughtfulness, etc.), should look to import as many of these light-on-their-feet qualities as it possibly can. There may never be a novel as irresistibly plastic and complete as a pop single or a Calder mobile, but it certainly can be interesting to reach for.

MICHAEL CHABON: I can generally find a way to feed my own obsessions by studying the results of others'.

CRISTINA GARCIA: Art teaches me that language is often superfluous. And somehow, even though it is, we still have to manage the impossible, to catch the uncatchable in a way, to translate silences.

RODRIGO FRESÁN: A lot. I feel formed—or deformed—as well by the paintings of Edward Hopper and the diction of James Stewart and Peter O'Toole as well as, especially for its atomized quality, "A Day in the Life" by the Beatles, and *2001: A Space Odyssey* by Stanley Kubrick, probably the most writerly director in the history of cinema.

A. M. HOMES: SOOOO much. I feed on art, on painting and photography and sculpture. In every city I go to on book tour, the first thing I do is visit the art museums. For me Art is the stuff of life.

HAS BEING A NOVELIST CHANGED THE WAY YOU READ NOVELS? HAS IT CHANGED THE WAY YOU APPRECIATE OR INTERACT WITH ART GENERALLY?

MICHAEL CHABON: Yes, fatally. Can't read ones that suck, that in particular are poorly or even just serviceably written, the way, once upon a time, I could. I read much more carefully and with an eye toward theft; always thinking, "I'd like to try something like that."

SAŠA STANIŠIĆ: Yes, maybe I'm more envious of all the great authors out there than I was before I myself wrote.

CHRIS ABANI: No. I have been doing this for a long time. I published my first novel at sixteen, so I grew up being a novelist, and I have always read like one, like a good magician trying to figure out the tricks of your competitors while still being in awe of them. I would say that most of my students read as readers and that changes over the course of study.

STEPHEN KING: Rarely. As to your second question, our survey says no.

ALAA AL ASWANY: Yes, of course. When you become cultured, when you become mature, then you have different visions of life. This will influence not just your reading, but your writing as well. I think this happened to me, and now I can appreciate many different kinds of literature. In the beginning, when I was really young, I was too enthusiastic for the kind of literature I loved, and I was not very enthusiastic about the other schools of writing. Now I think I have a much broader vision of art, and life as well. Your taste for the art runs parallel to your vision of life.

PAUL AUSTER: Yes. I am so demanding of myself as a writer, I tend to be just as demanding of the writers I read. I'm probably too tough, but it's an incurable reflex by now.

NELL FREUDENBERGER: Like almost all fiction writers, I was a reader before I was a writer, and I'm a writer because I'm a reader. I don't think I read any differently now than I did before I'd written anything of my own.

ALEJANDRO ZAMBRA: I hope not. Maybe I'm more sensitive to the junctures, affectations. I have less tolerance for tricks, especially when not confessed outright, for I like tricks, but I believe they have to be in full view. Nonetheless, faced with a good novel, my attitude is of total innocence. I let myself get taken wherever I may be taken. I get bored with too much literature, but when the story draws me in the last thing I want to do is guess what comes next. Also, I prefer a novel with fore-seeable, natural developments. The mystery is in the phrase, the atmo-sphere, not in the story. Even in detective novels, though I don't read many detective novels, because one already knows the assassin is always the author.

ANDREW SEAN GREER: I find that some of the joy is gone when I read for technique, but it's very easy for me to turn that off for certain books and enjoy them for themselves.

ADANIA SHIBLI: Yes. Sometimes I say to myself, for instance, this is how I never wish to write. If I weren't a writer, I would not say such an arrogant remark, but simply feel the book is not so good.

RODDY DOYLE: I've been writing novels for more than twenty years, so I think I've forgotten how I read back in the last century. I think now I probably admire the work that goes into making them, more than the art. With art generally, I'm constantly wondering how it was done, how decisions were made, etc. I tend to see artists as craftspeople.

SUSAN MINOT: Sadly, yes. I am not an innocent. Happily, yes. I see more of the expertise. And I am less patient with work that doesn't speak to me. Undeniably. But then I started writing when I was thir-teen, so who knows how I was interacting with art before that.

AKHIL SHARMA: I question my responses to a novel much more than I think I would have if I were just a reader. If I am moved by a novel, I ask, is this quiet, plotless narrative working because I am feeling full of self-pity and this protagonist has become a vessel of my self-pity?

ALEKSANDAR HEMON: I am not a novelist. I am a writer. And if being a writer is a vocation, rather than a profession, then I have been a writer my whole life. In other words, I don't remember ever reading differently.

COLM TÓIBÍN: It's a funny question, as though "being a novelist" meant anything much. I suppose I would prefer to say that I write novels sometimes, and have done five, nearly six, so far. But I don't feel like a novelist. It's not a profession, like being a doctor or a barber, but maybe they don't feel like doctors or barbers except when they are on call. Tomasz Stańko, the Polish jazz player, was asked if he got better as he got older and he replied: "Yes, my sensibility is more rich." I would love to believe the same and this means that a bad novel makes me bored much easier than before, and something good excites me still, but I would like to think that was age and a richer sensibility rather than being a novelist.

I write a column about painting for *Esquire* magazine, the UK edition, every month, and that helps me enormously with my fiction, I don't know why. It's something to do with looking closely and then trying to describe carefully. I can get more inspiration in a gallery than I can from a big wide river. I listen to music a lot, but never when working, mainly art songs and chamber music and Irish ballads. I am interested in the sonata form and try to follow it carefully, especially in Schubert and late Beethoven.

RODRIGO FRESÁN: I suppose so. I think as life progresses, the reader (which is the same as saying "the writer," since a writer is nothing more than a reader with superpowers) goes through different evolutionary stages. When reading and writing—as years and books go by—we are first absorbed by the image of the hero; afterward we are intrigued by plot; even later we are interested in the writer; and, finally, if we are really audacious, we arrive at the glory of concern for style, which is nothing else but the digressing from action.

T COOPER: I think that I don't get lost in novels as much now that I'm a published novelist. I'm so much more aware of looking at mechanics now, and I often end up just getting preoccupied with, "Gee, how'd they do that?" considerably more than when I wasn't actively thinking of myself as a novelist—or before I was published. While this may sound like a potential bummer, I'd say that my engagement with novels now, as a published author, is more active, like, instead of just being along for the ride, I'm more up there shoveling coal in and constantly in conversation with the text.

DINAW MENGESTU: I think I've always read books with a deep curiosity for how they work, both structurally and at a sentence level. The more I write, the better a reader I become, or at least I hope so.

MEHMET MURAT SOMER: I cannot discriminate. Or I cannot blame it on my novels. I've been writing management and personal development course notes, film scripts, music reviews all the time. But I discriminate strongly between what I appreciate and what I like, as well as between art and craft. And of course, "I did it my way." (Please read with its melody.)

EDWIDGE DANTICAT: Yes. I find myself reading a lot to learn. And when I really enjoy a novel, I read it again to see how the writer did the things he or she did. I think I have a sharper eye. I observe everything more closely.

GEORGE PELECANOS: I've been doing this for twenty years, so I no longer find novels mysterious. I know now that there is a man behind the curtain. Since there are only so many stories, it's how artfully one writes the story that interests me. Still, I read voraciously for pleasure, and that will never change. I also visit galleries more frequently than I used to. The Edward Hopper exhibit, recently displayed in Washington, D.C., was stunning. I don't think I would have appreciated it quite so much when I was younger. It was as much about how he chose to live his life, devoted to his work and not wasting a moment, as it was about the beauty of the paintings themselves. I am both frustrated and in awe of the art I cannot make myself. I will always stand in front of the stage and watch the band in wonder.

ANN CUMMINS: For many years, I lost the joy of reading because I was honing my critical eye and ear. I became much more attuned to craft, always reading for how a writer accomplished a certain effect, and lost touch with the reader in myself who loves to be told a good story. I think every writer must go through that uncomfortable stage of learning the mechanics of craft. I still lack the ability to become enrapt by a book, losing track of myself and of time, but by stages, I'm rediscovering the joy of reading. The critical eye never closes for me, but I'm learning to make it look on with disinterest while the reader in me reads.

RICK MOODY: It has made me impatient with work that doesn't challenge me in some way. I don't read in order to feel humanism vindicated or rationalized and work that has this as its primary goal tends to provoke in me the feeling that *I know what's going to happen*. This feeling bugs me.

A. M. HOMES: Yes, unfortunately. We become writers because we love to read, but all this reading and thinking carefully and critically ruins the general practice of reading for pleasure. I read with a mental red pencil in hand, and honestly I'd say most contemporary fiction could use a bit of a final edit before it goes to press.

WHAT DO YOU READ BEFORE/DURING THE WRITING OF A NOVEL? IS THERE A LOGIC TO YOUR READING?

ALEKSANDAR HEMON: There is a logic, but I can't define it. I like reading impulsively. I collect books, I have a lot of them, but most of them I have not read yet. I'll read them when they call me from the shelf. That does not change when I am writing, because, in a sense, I never stop writing.

TAYARI JONES: When I was a teenager, I used to consult the radio as an oracle on matters of love. I would randomly turn to a station and try to figure out what message the universe was sending me in the lyrics of whatever song I heard. When I am really writing, I pick books randomly and try to figure out what I am supposed to learn from them. I know on some level that this is ridiculous, but I can't make myself stop.

AKHIL SHARMA: It took me nine years to write my first novel and so I read as I would normally do. I do try hard to learn, though, from other writers.

RICK MOODY: I do like to read nonfiction that is related to the themes at hand. When I was writing my novel *Purple America*, e.g., I read a lot about neurological illnesses and the history of the American nuclear power industry. In those days, research was more book-oriented than it is now, because there wasn't yet Wikipedia, or, at least, I didn't know about Wikipedia yet. In the digital present, some of this research can be done more quickly. And yet Wikipedia doesn't stop me from reading voraciously on Mars, chimpanzees, stem cell research, and so forth. It is good to allow an appetite for facts to follow its bliss, as they say. As for fiction, despite my feeling that I am allowed to read anything anytime for any reason, it is true that there are certain writers I will avoid while writing a novel, because I don't want that sound in my ears. Faulkner, for example. Or the James Joyce of *Ulysses*.

A. M. HOMES: Logic that is internal but to the outside observer it would look crazy.

COLM TÓIBÍN: I read whatever I have to.

T COOPER: It depends on what the specifics of the novel are. I do enjoy the research period before delving into writing a first draft of a novel, even if the research is not officially or obviously related to the subject matter I'm working with for the book. The oddest things inspire me, sometimes films and videos I find on YouTube or on the Discovery or History channels, a lot of photographs, newspaper articles, and of course I spend a lot of time with nonfiction books that speak directly to the period or people or culture I'm working with in my novel. In the midst of the process, there doesn't seem to be a logic to my reading and note-taking, but pulling back and looking at it after the fact—and seeing what ends up finding its way into the book—it becomes clear that I've gravitated toward a particular selection of reading and research material for a reason. Like a lot of this stuff, it's instinctive, and I try to listen if something's calling to me.

HARUKI MURAKAMI: I don't care much about what to read when I am writing.

CHRIS ABANI: I read randomly everything from physics to ethics to cultural studies, I watch a lot of bad, trashy TV and lots of good TV and above all else, I consume books of poetry voraciously. And no, there is no logic to it; it makes sense but in a more organic way.

RODRIGO FRESÁN: For a time up to this point, I discovered that while writing fiction it helps me to read nonfiction. But I'm not 100 percent faithful to this. Working in journalism, I also have to read new novels and story collections. So then, in all honesty, I try to have the quality of the authors mark the "logic" of my readings.

RODDY DOYLE: I'm always reading and, also, when I've finished writing one book I go straight into a new one. So, if I didn't read while I work on a novel, I wouldn't have read a new book since sometime in the early '80s.

DINAW MENGESTU: If there is a logic, I've yet to find it. My reading patterns, particularly when I'm writing, are dictated entirely by what feels right for me to read at that particular instant.

NELL FREUDENBERGER: If I find a new writer I like, I often read everything else I can find by him or her. Otherwise I don't think there's any logic, and I guess I'm always writing something, so there's no particular thing I read during those times.

CHAPTER 2

GETTING STARTED

WHAT WAS THE TRIGGER FOR YOUR LAST NOVEL?

JENNIFER EGAN: I visited a castle in Belgium and had a particular feeling that I always get when I know I'm going to write about a place— a sense of excitement, almost of heightened perception, as if I'm suddenly aware of a larger narrative around me.

SUSAN MINOT: I set out to write a very short three-page short story about a lover's tryst. It got longer.

CLAIRE MESSUD: My last novel, *The Emperor's Children*, had several triggers, or catalysts—among them, a desire to write about friendship, and about a particular stage of relatively young adulthood; a desire to write about ambition; a desire to write about New York (which seemed to coincide well with a desire to write about ambition); a desire to write about life in the United States for the first time; and a desire too to write about the complications of privilege. That's a lot of triggers; but in retrospect I can't put them in chronological order.

RODRIGO FRESÁN: I couldn't exactly say. Maybe the need to write a love story and, meanwhile, destroy a couple of planets on the way there

(I'm in the middle of that). Although, in the case of *Kensington Gardens*, it was clearer and more precise: by chance tuning the television to a documentary about the life of James Matthew Barrie. And there we go, there we went.

COLM TÓIBÍN: I built a house in Cush in the southeast of Ireland where some of my novels had been set, where my parents fell in love, where I was conceived. (Yes, I know that this is mad.) I go there once a week and try and read and write and think and stay up late. One night I began to look at the first chapter of my new novel and I saw that in the first page there was a story that contained in itself a whole little novel which soon became a big novel. I saw it all that night.

RICK MOODY: The idea that television and contemporary spirituality are somehow allied, more so than we suppose.

ANDREW SEAN GREER: A family story that had much to be explained.

YIYUN LI: My last novel is my only novel yet in existence. I had always been fascinated by a case in China in the late 1970s, where a woman was executed for political reasons, and her execution sparked a mass protest, which led to the execution of another woman. I wrote an essay about the case ("What Has That to Do with Me," which I published with the *Gettysburg Review*), but the more I thought about the case, the more I felt an essay was not enough, so I began to write a novel about it.

MICHAEL CHABON: A Yiddish-English pocket phrasebook for travelers, published in 1958, called *Say It in Yiddish*.

DINAW MENGESTU: I wouldn't say there was any one trigger in particular. The opening of my first novel came to me while I was walking down the street, but I can see now that its origins are buried in a dozen different things—from stories my parents told me of Ethiopia, to research I had done while I was in college. As I began to write, I found that I had inadvertently done a lot of the historical groundwork for writing about Ethiopia, which is to say that I knew the information so well by the time I began to write fiction that it had become a natural part of my imagination.

ADAM MANSBACH: It was a story a friend told me about somebody's grandparents getting divorced. That was it: you now know everything I do about that situation. But it got me thinking about a number of things: the notion of profound changes coming late in life, about the conflict and the pain leading up to such an unusual event, about my own grandparents' difficult marriage, about how a family might react to such upheaval, about the practical and emotional implications for everyone involved.

ADANIA SHIBLI: It is a painful thing, which I feel too shy to share with anyone.

SUSAN CHOI: In the late '90s, my father and I were both interested in the Unabomber case—he particularly because he's a university mathematician—and then when the Unabomber was arrested it turned out my father had been classmates with him in graduate school. Years later, this clicked with me: I started imagining a novel about an aging math professor who turns out to know the serial bomber who's just murdered his colleague. Sometimes years after I read about or experience something it very abruptly erupts as an idea for a book. Something unconscious has been going on, but I have no idea what.

JONATHAN LETHEM: I don't think so much in terms of a "trigger"—by the time I've begun a novel, I've typically been thinking about it for years, accumulating impressions and concepts that seem in some elusive but necessary way to me to be inextricably related. In a way, a novel is for me a grouping of different problems or conundrums or unfinished thoughts that seem to promise to shed light on one another. The number of points of contact—or triggers, if you like—with my own experience and interests are so extensive that I've usually not even finished noticing and identifying them until long after I've finished. The process of understanding all the reasons why I've written something is not necessarily simpler—or smaller—than the process of writing it.

HARUKI MURAKAMI: Just a scene.

GEORGE PELECANOS: There was an incident near my home when I was a kid. Three white boys drove into an all black neighborhood, threw firecrackers and shouted racial epithets, and tried to drive away. Unbeknownst to them, the road dead-ended, and they were trapped. One was shot and killed, one was brutally beaten, and one ran into the woods and escaped. My question was, What happened to all of those boys? Where would they be today? It was enough to ignite the novel that became *The Turnaround*.

NELL FREUDENBERGER: There were three: a very glamorous house I'd visited as a child; a photograph by the artist Rong Rong of a performance by Zhang Huan ("12 Square Meters"); and the memory of a Chinese art teacher who visited my high school in 1991 and taught us to paint lobsters.

RODDY DOYLE: After writing a couple of novels set in the past, I was keen to write something set in present-day Dublin. I saw a woman on the street, trying to use her mobile phone, starting to lose her temper. As I passed, she smiled, a bit embarrassed, and said that it was new. That got me thinking.

CHRIS ABANI: In the case of *The Virgin of Flames*, the photo that was used on the cover, but usually all my books begin with a title.

DANIEL HANDLER: I got the idea for *Adverbs* on the subway in New York with my wife. I suddenly had the thought that I could be in love with this elderly woman near me, and I gazed at her with exaggerated lovingness while my wife cracked up. It got me thinking that love is more about a way of doing something than about the participants themselves.

CHRIS ADRIAN: I was a medical student doing a pediatrics rotation in Virginia and was on call for the first time. About halfway through the first night I developed the distinct feeling that I had been there forever and that I was never going to go home. So I started thinking about what would happen if none of us who were there all night could ever go home again, and somehow, over a while, that transmogrified into an idea about a hospital floating around after the end of the world.

SANTIAGO RONCAGLIOLO: I'd been trying to write for a long time about my experiences working in human rights after the counterinsurgency war that left seventy thousand dead in Peru. I was unnerved by the feeling that it was a war without good guys: both sides had been extraordinarily deadly. I began to play around with the idea of a murder-thriller series because I basically wanted to talk about a society of serial killers. One day I ran across *From Hell*, the graphic novel by Alan Moore that tells the story of Jack the Ripper. Then I knew what I wanted.

TAYARI JONES: For *The Untelling*, I was triggered by going to look at condos with a rude real estate agent. I started with that, but by the time the book was done, it was a novel about motherhood and urban renewal. I thought for sure that it would be a novel that used real estate as some big metaphor, but it just didn't happen.

ALEKSANDAR HEMON: The trigger was a book a friend of mine gave me because he thought I might be interested. It was called *An Accidental Anarchist* and it was about a young Jewish immigrant who was shot by the Chicago chief of police in 1908. It is a slight historical book, written with passion and intelligence. As I was reading it, I realized I wanted to write a book based on it.

STEPHEN KING: It was time, that's all I know. I had the idea thirty years ago and tried to write it then. Gave it up. I wasn't ready. It was too big. Now I think I might be ready. Also, I read two Ken Follett novels, *The Pillars of the Earth* and *World Without End*. I loved the way those books move narratively over a long distance. It excited me to see books in which the characters, although good, were secondary to events.

JOSÉ MANUEL PRIETO: The novel I'm writing is titled *Vox humana*, which is the name of a stop on an organ, the musical instrument. It's something I've known for a long time, due to my interest in classical music, and at some point I thought of the idea of someone obsessed with the possibility of imitating the human voice, all of its shades, its infinite expressive possibilities. Something impossible, as is recognized toward the end of the novel.

AKHIL SHARMA: I wrote a short story. It was well regarded and I wondered if I could open it up into a novel that would matter for me.

RABIH ALAMEDDINE: I've been a collector of stories—all kinds of fabulous stories—since I was a young, young boy, even the age of four or five. So what triggered it finally was an understanding that we are the stories that we tell about ourselves. Here was a family sitting down to talk, each with different stories about the father. I began to understand what I wanted to deal with: who is the family, what is the family, what is the culture, who are we within the context of storytelling.

T COOPER: The novel was triggered by a much mythologized story that was passed down through the generations of my family: when my grandmother immigrated to the United States from Russia around 1900, her young brother was lost at Ellis Island, and never heard from again. It was a story that always baffled me as a young child, and I always thought it would make more sense as I grew older. It made only *less* sense, however, as time marched on and the generations disappeared. So that loss of a child and the speculation about what might've happened to him pretty much anchors the novel, though it spins off wildly from the moment in the prologue on Ellis Island when the child disappears. I thought that kernel of a story that had been passed down (and inevitably changed) through the generations would serve as a good starting place to ask some questions about the notion of "truth," and whether any information we get about history and people and family can ever be verified as completely "true" and faithful accounts.

EDWIDGE DANTICAT: A conversation with a friend.

YAEL HEDAYA: My children. Being the mother of three, my life is very noisy. Especially my inner life. I had always hoped that I'd have better communication with them than I did with my own parents, that the lines would be open and we'd always "hear" each other. But I'm discovering this is impossible, there's so much static, interference, it's like talking on a cell phone. Sometimes you're out of range. You can't hear them. Or they you. My new book is about people lost in parenting. It's about the dynamics one has with small children, and with one's own childhood. It's about how rewarding and traumatic it is to be a parent. And it's also an opportunity for me to get back at the psychological establishment. Especially child psychologists.

SHELLEY JACKSON: I had been doing a series of drawings of a two-headed woman, her arms and legs crossed—a self at odds with itself, though with a strange air of triumph. I wanted to write about what it was like to be that person, or people. Around then I read that Nabokov wanted to write about the sex lives of conjoined twins but that his wife forbade it, and it struck me that the coming-apart-or-melting-together I had been treating as an extended metaphor was a physical reality for conjoined twins. Which made it richer, complicated enough to sustain a longish novel.

ALAA AL ASWANY: My latest novel is called *Chicago*. I am a dentist as well as a novelist because you can't make your living from literature in our world even if you are very famous. I studied at the University of Illinois in Chicago, and spent some years over there. I love Chicago, I think I know the city very well, and I was lucky to be there. It is a very rich place as well, in the sense that you have almost everything that is essential about American culture in Chicago. And from my very first day there, I had in mind the idea that I must keep my eyes open, and must keep myself open to the experience, because one day I might, I could, write a novel about Chicago. That's exactly what happened.

GLEN DAVID GOLD: You know that's one of those questions that's never answered the same way twice. Don't you think? Don't you have ideas all the time for novels that don't actually turn into novels? Only . . . one or two of them actually do? This time, I can follow five or six different tributaries that seemed to collide. I think the biggest one is that the pub date for novel no. 1 was September 11, 2001. It tended to make me wonder what the point of fiction and storytelling was. I was also fascinated by a couple of photographs of Charlie Chaplin and some mysterious, fragmented history of the U.S. involvement in the Russian revolution.

ALEJANDRO ZAMBRA: For *The Private Lives of Trees* it was a poem, a friend's poem, Andrés Anwandter. It goes like this: "Like the private life of trees/or that of the shipwrecked . . ." When I read, years ago, this poem (I wasn't a friend of the author then) I thought I would like to write a book titled *The Private Lives of Trees*. The idea stayed with me for a long time, a few years, until life put me in a situation where the meaning of that verse became, for me, exact: a man telling a girl what happens in a park when everyone leaves, when the trees are alone. The private lives of trees.

GARY SHTEYNGART: Heartbreak usually gets one going, heartbreak for a love that didn't work out, for a homeland that has lost its way, for a generation that didn't quite make it. Give your protagonist that heartbreak along with the cruel hope that he or she can improve upon their lives. And then there will be a novel.

ANNE ENRIGHT: Sitting down and writing it.

FRANCISCO GOLDMAN: I was trying to get *The Divine Husband* off the ground. The novel needed to open in a convent. I had never written a so-called historical novel before, and so perhaps I was overly obsessive in my research about convents. When I look back at that time, it seems I read every book on nuns' convents, every nun's hagiography, ever written. I practically felt as if I was going around in an invisible unwashed woolen novice's habit, with a barbed wire belt tied around my waist, and even imagined that I found it strangely delicious and wonderful—okay, I was really losing it. My head was crammed with nun and convent knowledge, but how to turn that into narrative? How to give it life? Every day that summer in Mexico City I tried to start my novel, and failed.

One night I went to a party at Mario Bellatin's house. He had a bartender there, making frozen daiquiris, but they ran out of ice. I was in front of the bartender's table, empty cup in hand, hoping for a refill. He had a novel solution—he began scraping woolly ice from inside the freezer into the blender pitcher. If I remember correctly, he also found, embedded deep inside the freezer, a frozen tray of Pleistocene Mexican tap water. It was enough for another pitcher of daiquiris. I drank mine down, and I swear, within minutes, felt something like a mule kick deep inside my stomach. I'm going to be sick, I thought. I went home, and was sick, and got into bed, and sometime that night I woke up feeling rotisseried with burning fever and sweat and quite literally hallucinating. I saw a

19th-century Guatemala City street, and some women with shawls over their heads, convent servants, walking along, looking for indigent Indian men to bring back to their convent so that their prioress could use them in her personal mortification ritual. I got out of bed, wrote the scene down, and went back to bed. Later, another scene came to me, and I got out of bed again. I was like that for about 48 hours. And it was with those two hallucinated scenes that novel finally got under way.

DO YOU DO ANY RESEARCH BEFORE YOU BEGIN WRITING? IF SO, DO YOU FIND IT HELPFUL, OR DOES IT CONSTRAIN YOUR IMAGINATION?

LAILA LALAMI: Because I write about my home country while living mostly outside of it, I always like to make sure that descriptions of the physical setting are correct. I might remember that a particular building is on Zerktouni Boulevard, when in fact it is on Green March Avenue. So I always make sure to consult current and old maps, for example. If the story has any kind of historical reference, I read up on it as much as I can—newspaper articles, essays, memoirs, novels, and so on. I've also done interviews with relevant people. But the problem with research is that it doesn't end; there is always more to discover. So when I sit down to do the writing, I set all my research aside. I try to focus on my task as a writer, which is to say to create characters and tell their story.

COLM TÓIBÍN: I needed to research how paintings were made for *The South*. I asked a painter to show me. I needed to know all about Irish law for my second novel but that was easy because I had already, when I was a journalist, written a history of the Irish Supreme Court. For the next novel I needed to know about the oil industry in Argentina. I found an expert on the matter and called her. The next was *The Blackwater Lightship*. For that, I looked into my heart. (That was the hardest research.) The next was *The Master* and for that I did huge amounts of reading. For the novel I just finished, I needed to know about Brooklyn in the '50s. I read some books on it. I also needed to know about baseball. I went to a game. (It is very slow and strange, like watching paint dry in the company of maniacs.) You need research only for details so it should not constrain your imagination.

STEPHEN KING: No.

GLEN DAVID GOLD: Yes, tons of research, and I love it more than I love writing. At a certain point you have to stop researching.

AMY TAN: I do too much research. I'm afraid of being inaccurate. I fall in love with the research.

ADANIA SHIBLI: Yes, I do research during and sometimes even after I have finished the first draft. It has often been "field research," or research that does not involve reading but visiting places and exhibitions. For instance in writing my second novel, which revolves around love and hatred, I regularly visited courtrooms and was present in discussions between couples and their lawyers asking for divorce, etc. Although I never wrote about this, for me it was a way to be inside love and its absence.

For the present novel I visited a lot of shows and museums and places. I even got arrested once during one of these visits to museums. It was a war museum in Tel Aviv, and the Israeli police and security arrested me thinking I was a spy. In these visits I could find faces for my characters, movements of their bodies, their clothes, and sometimes the soil they could have walked on.

JENNIFER EGAN: Depends on the book. For the one inspired by the castle, *The Keep*, I read a lot of gothic fiction all the way along but did very little research initially. That worked fine for the gothic parts of the novel, but much of it also takes place in a contemporary high-security prison. I read a lot about prisons, but that wasn't enough: I needed to actually spend some time in a prison to capture the textures and feel of the place. But I was already well into *The Keep* by the time I did that research.

GEORGE PELECANOS: I do all my research before I begin to write. Sometimes, as in the case of a sprawling historical novel like *Hard Revolution*, this involves months of library time, street time, and oral history work. When I'm satisfied that I've got what I need, I start writing, and try not to leave the house too often. Otherwise the book does not get written.

ANNE ENRIGHT: My rule is that you must do the bulk of the research after you have written your novel, and not before.

ALEKSANDAR HEMON: I do research, if research is required. But then I forget about it. That is, I let myself absorb the stories that I had collected in my research and don't care much about the facts.

SHELLEY JACKSON: I do research, not before, but during the writing process. Early on too much research cows my imagination with its superior level of detail, but toward the end that detail helps my vague ideas take a more intricate, precise, and particular form.

ADAM MANSBACH: I do a tremendous amount of research informally before I begin writing, but I never really think of it as research because I'm conditioned to think of research as a deliberate act. But the truth is that, for instance, *Angry Black White Boy* is brimming with shit about New York and hip-hop and race that would take somebody else years to research; I happened to have accumulated that knowledge before I began writing, through life experience. The same is true of *Shackling Water*; I was a roadie for a jazz band, so my research was extensive, but I never thought of it that way. With *The End of the Jews*, I had a lifetime of conversations with my grandparents that went into those characters.

And with the new book, I've got a storehouse of graffiti lore that is coming into play, although I did do some a priori research about ayahuasca and plant sentience before I wrote those sections.

HARUKI MURAKAMI: No research.

JOSH EMMONS: I do research on a need-to-know basis. If my story's action comes to a place I'm not familiar with, or if my character has a job I know too little about, I'll read just enough to make the setting or profession believable, and invent the rest. Too much research can delay writing too long—given the resources available to us now, it's easier to get lost in background reading than it was for *Middlemarch*'s Edward Casaubon, whose "Key to All Mythologies" is for that reason never written—and it can confine you to the version of truth that has long impaired creative nonfiction. When one of my characters turned out to be a practicing Wiccan, for example, I read a book and a half about modern paganism so that her language and activities would be legitimate.

MEHMET MURAT SOMER: Depends on the material. For example, when I was writing an eight-episode television miniseries script about Hürrem Sultan, the wife of Suleiman the Magnificent, I read history for almost a year. While writing my bestseller *Catwalk*, I needed details about the fashion world, trends, the diets of models, even brands of makeup. That was another kind of research or reading material that was very helpful for me. At least to get the inside view, even if I don't use all the material I've gathered.

MICHAEL CHABON: Always. It's helpful up to a point after which it is constraining, right up to the point that it becomes helpful again.

SUSAN CHOI: I've done a fair amount of research for all three of my books, before commencing the writing, but with each successive book I've done less. The first time, I felt I needed to know everything before I started writing, and this was obviously impossible. The second time I tried to do just enough research to jump-start the plot; then I went back and plugged in small holes, like the actual names of the guns that the characters carried; up to the next-to-last draft the book said things like "Pauline shouldered her Big Gun TK." With the most recent book I followed the same basic rule—just enough research to get the plot going, then plug the holes later—but the amount of research I needed to get going was much less and the holes I left to plug were much larger. Regarding huge portions of the story where I would have, in previous efforts, prepared with extensive research, instead I just winged it. I made all the FBI procedural stuff up. So that once I was finished I didn't have holes to fill but chasms. Large portions required total rewriting. Yet this book was still completed more quickly, and more to my satisfaction, than either of its predecessors, which goes to show that research should be conducted as sparingly as possible. Too much and it's a crutch, a distraction.

CHRIS ADRIAN: I did a great deal for my first novel, which took place during the Civil War. I didn't even really know the dates of the Civil War before I started, so there was a lot to learn. It was profitable for all sorts of reasons, though not necessarily because it allowed me to get the facts straight . . . it was more that I was able to properly make shit up once I got the facts straight. Also, the research often led to surprising narrative turns as I learned more about people who had actually existed, and the possibility of their committing some imagined act turned the story in different directions. The chief danger of research for me was that I consistently got lost in the reading (which was all very interesting), and the research felt like work in a way that defused my usual guilt over not writing, so it ultimately could be pretty nonproductive.

EDWIDGE DANTICAT: Yes. I did about two years worth of research before writing the first draft of my last novel, *The Farming of the Bones*. I found the research really helpful in terms of finding plotlines that I had not thought of before I began doing the research.

NELL FREUDENBERGER: I think it might constrain you if you did it beforehand. In my case I have to figure out who the people in the story are before I can do any research. Once I've determined that, for example, I'm writing about an art student from Beijing, I know that I have particular questions to answer before I can continue, and the research often leads me in new directions in terms of plot. In terms of character, I have to figure it out in the writing rather than in the research. I also think that you write naturally about what you're interested in, and so you're often doing research for novels long before you start writing them—studying a language, interviewing people, traveling, etc.

CLAIRE MESSUD: With other books—such as my novel *The Last Life*, or my novella *A Simple Tale*—I've had to do considerable amounts of research before I started writing. In neither case did my imagination feel constrained; but it is true that there's always the problem of when to *stop* researching. You can procrastinate indefinitely by researching.

ALAA AL ASWANY: For *The Yacoubian Building*, I had to go to very small, very poor, and sometimes risky parts of Cairo in order to capture the actual fear in these places, so that when I wrote about these places, hopefully, they felt true.

CURTIS SITTENFELD: I heard an excellent piece of advice about doing research at a reading by Mona Simpson. I'm paraphrasing, but she basically said you should write up to the point when you know exactly what information you need—you shouldn't bury yourself in general research beforehand. So you write a scene, and you have two characters having an argument about ice hockey, but you yourself know nothing about ice hockey. You put X's or TK's or other placeholders in for their dialogue, but you write the rest of the scene. Then you go and find someone who does know something about ice hockey and ask them what your characters should be saying. This is a small-scale example, but you can do it for bigger questions too. And while of course I rely on books and articles for research, it turns out 95 percent of people, whether friends or strangers, love to be asked about subjects they know more about than you do, especially for purposes of your novel. I'm not sure why people love this, but thank God they do. When I finished a novel about a sixty-year-old woman who'd grown up in Wisconsin, I asked four sixty-year-old women (all non-writers) who'd grown up in Wisconsin to read it and vet it for mistakes or stuff that just sounded fishy. Part of my novel is also set in the White House, and I had a woman who'd worked in the White House read it. I'm sure I still made mistakes, but I hope they aren't as obvious or frequent as they might have been.

RODRIGO FRESÁN: I do all research while writing the novel. I don't like to sit to write with everything under control. I like to feel—at least a little—like a reader of my own novel, without sacrificing the pleasure of surprise, of surprising myself.

ANDREW SEAN GREER: I do lots of research and then try to forget it all. I find that images are most helpful when I'm stuck, as I can always find some way for a character to try on a glove, go to the seashore, etc.

SUSAN MINOT: If I do research it happens along with the writing. Research is fun; it takes you somewhere else. Why I don't do more research, I don't know. I guess I feel that the most unique thing I might have to say is going to come from the place I know best: my experience. As Fitzgerald said, when asked why he wrote about what he did, It was my material! What else did I have?

ANN CUMMINS: I did extensive research for my novel, *Yellowcake*, but not before I began writing it. My research took the form of problem solving once characters and plot began to form. Some of the research was great fun. One of my characters ties fishing flies for a living and lives in a houseboat in Marathon, Florida. I knew nothing about fishing, houseboat living, and I've never been to Marathon. I did a lot of research via the

Web and interviewing fishermen for that character, and I surrounded myself with beautiful hand-tied fishhooks. All fun.

RABIH ALAMEDDINE: Rarely. And not because I believe in the question here: "Does it limit my imagination?" I'm one of those that believes nothing can limit my imagination. I don't know if there's any external influence that can do that. I rarely do research because I always believe that when I write fiction, the idea for me is to make fiction believable, not to make it accurate, which is a different thing. So you will find probably lots of mistakes in my books, but the beauty of it—I hope—is that it's believable. Just as I hope that it's unexpected. My dream is to write a story in which I make the reader believe the sky is red. To make believable something that's completely unbelievable.

CRISTINA GARCIA: I always do research. And then, I always do too much research, and this is the process: I get swamped by the research. And I reject the research. And then somehow in that process what's necessary filters into the work.

YIYUN LI: I did not do a huge amount of research about the two women I mentioned earlier, one reason being that that part of history was mostly unavailable now. The other reason was that I did not want the research to constrain me in any way, as in the end the novel would be more about the community instead of about the two women. I did, though, ask my husband to draw a very detailed map of his hometown circa the late 1970s, as I wanted to set up the novel in a provincial town in China, and thought his hometown's name fit my course. Muddy River was the town's name but in an effort to beautify it, the town's name was changed to White Mountain in the 1990s, so I felt I had the right to own that discarded name for my novel.

RODDY DOYLE: I prefer to do the research as I write. But I did no formal research for the last book. It's about a year in the life of a woman, summer '04 to summer '05. So, stories I heard on the radio—she heard. The Pope's death—she watched the news. The White Stripes played in Dublin—she saw them.

CHRIS ABANI: I am reading all the time so that most of what I write about or use is already stored in some part of my head, but I do research now and then. It never constrains my imagination. In fact the very opposite is true, it releases my imagination. You can never have too much information, but you have to be careful about giving too much information.

YAEL HEDAYA: No, I'm too lazy to do any research. In my second novel, *Accidents*, both protagonists, the man and woman, are writers. Readers found this interesting, and I would get questions about what my intention was, why I chose to make them both writers, was I trying to say something about male writers and female writers, etc. After making up semiintelligent answers, I finally caved in and admitted I made both protagonists writers since I was too lazy to research other professions and a writer's life is something I know about.

TAYARI JONES: Yes, I did all this research on real estate in Phoenix, Arizona. The book didn't even end up being set in Phoenix. I guess the message is that you can research all you want, but the novel is going to be what it wants to be.

RICK MOODY: One mistake I have tried to correct in the last six or seven years is the mistake in which my love of research somehow preempts or forestalls the writing itself. I made that mistake while composing *Purple America* and *The Black Veil*, but I am hoping to avoid it in the future. These days, there is no preliminary research, and I'm not allowed to avoid writing because I don't yet know everything about telomerase or the length of a strand of DNA. It will be diverting to look into these topics, but it's going to happen in my free time.

A. M. HOMES: I'm always doing research. I do work from the imagination but I need to be sure it's correct, so for *This Book Will Save Your Life*, I spent a lot of time living in Los Angeles and reading about everything from tar pits to plant life.

HOW LONG DOES IT TAKE YOU TO FINISH A DRAFT?

SAŠA STANIŠIĆ: I don't really do drafts.

JONATHAN LETHEM: I used to do three very specific drafts, back when I worked on a typewriter. My first three novels were written this way. The first, and certainly most important, usually took less than two years. The next two drafts were done quickly—five or six months, pushing through, honing the language. Now that I work on a computer, my process has gradually evolved away from this notion of "drafts"—I tend to write a novel incrementally, perfecting most of the language as I go along, and arriving at a very satisfying finishing point two or three years after I begin (very much depending on the length of the book, of course). This consists of a kind of combined first and second draft. All that's left is a brief and systematic polishing draft (apart from rewrites that come out of the editing process).

JENNIFER EGAN: I usually write pretty quickly, by hand, so I can churn out a draft in a few months. Then I spend years trying to make it be an interesting and worthwhile book.

AMY TAN: Years it seems. For different reasons. It took me three years to write three stories for *The Joy Luck Club* and then four months to finish the rest of them. It took me a year and a half to write a draft for the next book. It takes me longer and longer. It took me very long to write *Saving*

Fish from Drowning because I got ill and I couldn't even write a sentence for a while. For different reasons I get delayed or paralyzed at some point because of the idea that someone's going to read this and it's going to get published and I wonder: Is this truly the book I want to write? Is this truly a book I want to get published and let go into the world?

ALEJANDRO ZAMBRA: In relation to the novels I've published, I wrote them by letting the search grow, without forcing myself to reach port. When I "saw" the books, after erring for a long time, the process was quick more or less. But my novels are very short. Maybe I've never finished a manuscript. Perhaps I prefer to publish the advances of a book, which, if I were honest, I would let grow like weeds.

COLM TÓIBÍN: I work in longhand and it varies. The first draft of my fourth novel was written in seven months. My first novel took four years.

MICHAEL CHABON: Call it a year.

ALEKSANDAR HEMON: I don't think about writing a book in that way. I don't know where one draft ends and another one begins. I don't break up the process into quantifiable units, or even phases. In some ways, every part of the process happens simultaneously.

JOSÉ MANUEL PRIETO: That depends on the book. Usually, a year, year and a half.

SHELLEY JACKSON: It took me fifteen years to write the first draft of my novel! I sincerely hope that is not typical. Later drafts took me a couple of months.

SANTIAGO RONCAGLIOLO: I tend to hit a couple of dead ends before getting to the end of a project. For each one, I write between eighty and one hundred pages before sinking. But it's during those fits and starts that my ideas begin to take shape, circling and settling into each other. When I sit down to write a definitive novel I've usually been thinking about it for five years and I've made two or three false starts, but it takes me about six months to write it. Then I spend a year letting it settle and making corrections.

ADANIA SHIBLI: To finish the first draft I may need one year, the following drafts take each about half a year, and I usually do seven drafts.

JOSH EMMONS: In my early twenties, I finished a draft in eight weeks. It was not good, which six months of subsequent work didn't change. The first drafts of my last two books took a year each and were followed by two years of revision. Anything short of ten years is a reasonable period to spend on a first draft. Beyond that, when you reach latter-day Ralph Ellison and James Joyce time frames, you may want to reconsider your pace.

DANIEL HANDLER: Usually about one year, uninterrupted, though such a year has never existed.

AKHIL SHARMA: Many years. When I finish a draft the book or story is very close to being as good as it is likely to be.

EDWIDGE DANTICAT: A year, more or less.

ANDREW SEAN GREER: A year and a half. Then another year to rewrite.

CLAIRE MESSUD: Ages and ages.

YIYUN LI: It took about four months to write the first hundred pages of the novel, and then I gave birth to my second son, so I waited for a year to get back and finished the rest of the first draft in twenty-one days in a writers' retreat. But revision took much longer than that.

RODRIGO FRESÁN: I don't write thinking about a first draft. I edit all the time while writing. Because the first finished version is the only one (and maybe it is the tenth or twentieth draft).

RICK MOODY: Somewhere between eighteen months and three years.

GEORGE PELECANOS: Historically it's been roughly five months. Keep in mind that, when I'm writing a book, I write seven days a week, two sessions a day. Mornings are for writing and evenings are for rewriting. So it's a relatively short but intense period of time.

SUSAN MINOT: Of a novel: Usually it's been about two and a half to three years.

TAYARI JONES: Two years if I am lucky.

NELL FREUDENBERGER: I've only written one novel. It took three years to write, and maybe two years to get to the last sentence for the first time. I didn't really think in terms of drafts with the novel, but with stories (especially when I have an editor) it works that way. I've only written seven stories that I wanted to publish, but each of those happened pretty quickly, sometimes inside a month. Then I obviously spent many more months working on them.

PAUL AUSTER: It all depends. The short novel I have just completed, I wrote in approximately four months. Other novels have taken me ten years.

RODDY DOYLE: The last book, a year. The one before, five years. The one I'm currently on, two years and counting. The shortest, six months.

STEPHEN KING: Depends on how long the book is. The new one is 810 pages long, and not quite half done. The 810 pages have taken six months.

CHRIS ABANI: Two weeks to three months. It depends. But the novel cooks in my subconscious for over a year or two before I actually begin writing. So at the draft stage I am translating what's been brewing in me for a while.

SUSAN CHOI: My standing record is about two years. I'm not a fast writer.

MEHMET MURAT SOMER: Between one and two months.

T COOPER: This varies for me. My first book took a couple of years to get a decent draft. My second, maybe four years or so. My third book I'm still in the research period (it's been about a year), and I'm hoping I can get a workable draft, once I sit down to write, in about a year's time. I've found that I do my best work at writers' colonies, so when I've been fortunate enough to be awarded residencies, I get a lot more work done than when I'm trying to fit it in between the requisite stuff of life at home.

CRISTINA GARCIA: There's a lot of back and forth even within a draft—some sections are rewritten a lot, and others not so much. But I would say it takes me at least a year if not longer, a year to a year and a half to just get down the rough, messy terrain of the novel, to be able to print it out and lug it around, feel its heft, feel like I have something. And that's delusion part one. The subsequent delusions are all these messy drafts to follow. It's all very, very layered, like peeling paint on a wall.

ANNE ENRIGHT: I don't do a "draft." The book is not a stable object for me, it shifts and is rewritten everywhere, all the time. You might say that my first draft happens with the submitted manuscript, which is, in my case, usually very close to the published work.

RABIH ALAMEDDINE: I started the first story in *The Hakawati*, my most recent novel, in 1999. It took five years not knowing what I was doing. In 2004 I had 330 pages of the possible 1,300-page novel. It's a different experience and I don't recommend it to anybody. For me, I'm lost most of the time, totally terrified. I didn't know how words form sentences. I would look at the page and think "Oh my God, not a single sentence works here." Then somewhere along the line I began to see a structure. When I begin to see a structure, I feel more comfortable. But still I don't know if it works.

A. M. HOMES: MANY YEARS!

HOW MUCH DO YOU KNOW ABOUT THE PLOT OF A NOVEL BEFORE YOU BEGIN?

SAŠA STANIŠIĆ: For my only novel I knew a lot beforehand but then soon noticed that my knowledge was tricky and not really reliable.

SHELLEY JACKSON: Not a thing. I would have very little interest in writing a book if I knew what I was going to say ahead of time.

PAUL AUSTER: A general sense of the shape of a story, a feeling for the beginning, middle, and end, but once I begin working, things always change and the book I thought I was going to write when I started often turns out to be a different book.

RICK MOODY: Ideally, I know the beginning and something about the end. But even these are not requirements. Discovery is the fun part.

ALEKSANDAR HEMON: I don't think about a plot. There are limits to my narrative situation—otherwise the writing would go on indefinitely—but the sequence of events grows out of the space defined by those limits. The plot, as it were, is the last thing that becomes part of the book or the story I am writing.

GEORGE PELECANOS: Very little. I have a situation, and a vague idea of where I want to end up. I'm much more focused on finding the characters. Once you do that, the book begins to write itself.

ANDREW SEAN GREER: Almost all of it—though there is always something wonderful for me to discover. A surprise that I then am able to spring on the reader as well.

ANNE ENRIGHT: I don't do plot.

ADANIA SHIBLI: Hardly anything. I only know the beginning and the end, and I let the writing walk from the starting point to the ending point.

SUSAN CHOI: It's been different every time. With my first book I had a situation and scattered vignettes, and I had to string them all together. With the second, I knew *exactly* where the characters were going to wind up at the end—the very room in which they would be arrested, the very emotional condition they'd be in, the thing they'd be doing—but I didn't have any idea how they would get there. With the third book, I knew all those things I just listed—the room, the emotional state, the character's actions—about the very first scene, and after that I had nothing. Novels in progress seem to me sometimes like landscapes seen through fog. You're always going to make out something different, have a different handhold at the start, and then you grope your way along.

COLM TÓIBÍN: Everything.

HARUKI MURAKAMI: Almost nothing.

JENNIFER EGAN: Very little. All I need is a time and a place, a sense of atmosphere. That seems to give rise to the people, oddly enough. The most critical thing is to find a voice early on; if I don't have that, I really can't move forward. And since my books are all quite different from each other, they have very different voices. But time and place are what give rise to the voice, for me.

MEHMET MURAT SOMER: I start writing my thrillers with every major point of the plot clearly decided. I work more with logic and arithmetic than inspiration and "que será, será."

ALAA AL ASWANY: The experience of writing a novel is very close to the experience of falling in love. You have no rules, but you want to be lucky to have a wonderful story. I work very hard on the characters. When I begin the writing, it's like taking a friend by the hand and going for a promenade. I have a general idea about the plot, but I write and wait for the other moment: when I no longer have any control over my characters. My characters become independent and they decide for themselves, and every morning, I see what my characters are doing and I simply describe what I see.

T COOPER: It's usually blocked in my head or roughly outlined on paper or file cards before I begin. But I don't hold myself to anything just because it's where I thought the book might go. If something feels right and it's a totally different direction, I'm always going to follow that because I'm a firm believer that if it feels right or I'm being pushed down a certain road, it's definitely worth investigating and playing out until it either works or it doesn't. But either way, I have to find out, and it's never lost work in the interim.

DANIEL HANDLER: Pretty much, usually; it's hard for me to think about a story's beginning without picturing its end.

TAYARI JONES: I begin the book under the impression that I know lots about the plot. I foolishly imagine these great scenes at the end. But when the book is done, it often has gone in a different direction.

RABIH ALAMEDDINE: I would say I know more about characters than I know about the plot. I'm one of those that sits down and makes things up as I go along.

DINAW MENGESTU: My first novel took me roughly three years to complete, but of course I wasn't able to work on it for long stretches of time. I never knew where the novel was going, which made the long gaps in between writing both difficult and exciting since it also gave me time to just think about my characters without making them do anything. Every time I sat down to write, though, I never knew what would come out next, even if I thought I had a vague idea in my head.

CLAIRE MESSUD: I usually have a fairly simple outline. In the case of *The Last Life*, I had ten things in order on a piece of paper. In the case of *The Emperor's Children*, it was somewhat more elaborate than that, but not much. Which is to say that I know the bones of the plot; but not necessarily the details. In fact, not the details at all—if I did, I wouldn't need to write it all down.

YIYUN LI: I knew the novel would start with one execution and end with another, and I knew the novel had three parts and each part would have at its center a public event. Other than that I did not know a huge amount about my characters' fates before I began.

RODDY DOYLE: Not much. I plan as I write.

AMY TAN: You mean the story? Plots are more mechanical: you've decided it's going to go this way or that. The story line, though, this has to be somewhat clear, including a vague knowledge of what an ending might encompass. But I don't know when the story's going to move until I'm physically and emotionally moved—and how could I have that plotted out? How could you plan to fall in love? You can set it up and be ready . . . but you can't force it. Or then you end up with the wrong person. Forcing it only lands you with the wrong person.

RODRIGO FRESÁN: Just enough so that the characters may be sufficiently interesting to me to spend a few years with. I don't need to know who their grandparents were or their passport number.

STEPHEN KING: Almost nothing.

JONATHAN LETHEM: Usually much less than I imagine I do. Somehow I always tell myself I've visualized the shape of the whole thing, which is perfect nonsense. I find I'm having to invent something every day to get me to the next day, and that process of improvisation completely exposes the illusion of foreknowledge. Yet there's something—a sensation, I suppose—that passes, importantly, for knowing.

YAEL HEDAYA: Nothing. I'm in pitch darkness.

MICHAEL CHABON: Some. The one-sentence summary. Or so, at the time, I believe.

SUSAN MINOT: I know the whole arc of the story and probably 60 to 70 percent of the elements that must be there. But there's lots of room for new material in the nailing down of the details. And those details are what make up the story, after all.

TASH AW: I think I know a lot, but in fact I know very little. I try and map out as much of it as possible—beginning, middle, and end, as it were. But what invariably happens in the writing of the novel is that the plot and characters don't go where I want them to go—what I had planned turns out not to be right, or feels forced, and I am obliged to change tack. By the end of the novel the plot doesn't resemble my original plan. But I think it's important for me to have something to start out with, to feel as if I know vaguely where I'm going, at least at the beginning, when the novel feels so vast and daunting and blank. Having a plan reassures me, even if I know I'm going to depart from it.

JOSÉ MANUEL PRIETO: What I know about the plot keeps changing, even though I have it more or less outlined. Only the accidents change, but I have a pretty clear idea of where the novel is heading, the wide margins of the plot. Still, that supposed cliché—that characters influence the plot—I've found to be true.

ANN CUMMINS: My work, both novels and short stories, grows from the inside out. It starts with a character I have a feeling for; complications grow around that character, and I slowly eke out a plot. Really, plot comes last for me. I need to know what's driving my characters before I can even think about what happens to them.

WHAT'S THE DIFFERENCE BETWEEN WRITING A NOVEL AND WRITING A SHORT STORY? DO YOU APPROACH THESE FORMS DIFFERENTLY?

ANDREW SEAN GREER: They are utterly different for me. The fear with a short story is that it won't be perfect. The fear in a novel is that it was a terrible idea to begin with. But the payoffs are commensurate with the fears—for me, there's nothing like the experience of writing a novel. A story does not seem to transform me in the same way—or send me into such deep despair.

A. M. HOMES: In a story each line needs to be in place before the next line can come—the architecture is much more specific and refined.

JENNIFER EGAN: I approach them the same way. Stories are scarier to me because I find they're like magic tricks, or games of solitaire—many times they simply don't work, and it's hard to know whether they'll work ahead of time. I've lost lots of time to failed short stories. A novel feels safer because once I get deep enough I usually have some confidence that it will work—that whatever force has pushed me that deeply into the material will also push me successfully through and out of it. I feel more of a margin for error while working on a novel—with stories there seems to be almost none.

YIYUN LI: I love stories, and so far I love the process of novel writing, but I think you have a different relationship with the characters from a story versus a novel. I could imagine the characters from my short stories live on in their own lives, and I could imagine running into them now and then in life, or in a story, but with a novel I feel that I've spent so much time with them, that in the end they do not have much left to themselves. Characters in a novel are more exploited and less spared.

RODDY DOYLE: I write short stories much more slowly—I examine every word. I never let myself write too much, as I tend to do when I'm writing longer fiction, knowing I'll go back later and cut. I cut as I go when writing short fiction—I don't move on until I'm happy that I have finished the previous paragraph, that I'd be happy to read it if published. I tend to be more relaxed as I write the novel—I give myself more elbow room. Moments in short stories are more significant, so they need more attention.

SUSAN CHOI: I haven't the faintest idea how to write a short story. It's as mystifying to me as is the writing of plays. I can't do it.

ALEJANDRO ZAMBRA: For me the difference is given in what is considered a book. As short as my novel *Bonsai* may be, while writing it, I thought of it as a book. It was, for me, an autonomous entity. I never thought of adding it to another story, for example. That's the reason I prefer to talk about books and not novels. Novels are periods of life. Stories or short poems are solitary mornings or afternoons. A book represents a period in life: not the time that motivated the writing, but what occurred while you wrote it. The life that passed through you while you stayed inside writing a book.

TAYARI JONES: When I write a short story, I often know what is going to happen. The end is always close enough that I can see it. With a novel, I am writing to find out what is going to happen. I am more confident when writing a story because I do believe I am going to be able to complete it. With a novel, there is always a chance it will die on the vine.

CLAIRE MESSUD: To my mind, a novel and a short story are as different as a novel and a poem. One way in which I approach these forms differently is that I don't approach the short story. Maybe someday I will be visited by the ability to write a decent one; but it hasn't happened so far. I think my breath, as it were, is novelistic. It's just my way of seeing the world. Some very fortunate people have the ability to write in many different literary forms; I wish I were one of them.

ADAM MANSBACH: Knockout versus decision, as the saying goes. Short stories are a pleasure for me because they get written in a couple of weeks, and you get to experience the joy of a finished product, a set of discrete challenges that gets resolved and lets you move on with your life. I don't know why I don't do more of them—oh, wait, I remember now, it's because nobody publishes them anymore.

AKHIL SHARMA: A novel, because it is longer, needs to be more interesting and needs more interesting characters, plot, issues.

MEHMET MURAT SOMER: I am not good with anything short or small. I don't want to sound like a size queen, but for me the size matters. I tried writing short stories several times with unsatisfactory results. Better stick to what I feel comfortable and easy with: the novel. I cannot write economically, nor can I talk in brief.

ANN CUMMINS: For me, they're very similar. Usually they start with a kernel that becomes a full-bodied character as I develop the character backgrounds, phobias, desires. . . . The process for both short-story and novel writing is a long exercise in trial and error. I look for characters and events that will cohere into a story. There's one difference, though. With my novel, *Yellowcake*, I learned that I had to rein my characters in more than I would in a short story. *Yellowcake* is multicharactered, and once I discovered the plot that united them, I wanted them to serve the plot and not to pontificate on their own. Since my short stories usually center around one pivotal character, I don't rein that character in, though I do try to use economy, given the shortness of the form, in evoking them. Generally, I see short stories as miniature novels.

NELL FREUDENBERGER: This is stating the obvious, but the difference is the length. You can see the end of a story much faster than the end of a novel, and often there are fewer characters to get to know. One or two points of view can carry you through a story, and so you reach that moment when you know you're going to finish it—that it's going to work—much faster. With a novel, I'm constantly writing pages in hopes of finding a new point of view, and then getting rid of them.

COLM TÓIBÍN: Your main job is to finish everything you start. It is easier, because quicker, to do this with a story. Just write it down and stop thinking. But with both, you have to wait until the opening comes to you as rhythm not as opening. It comes as a sound and then as a sentence and then you can start. I can never start because I have an idea.

RICK MOODY: A novel takes a lot longer to write, obviously. It also tolerates a larger cast of characters and more digression, which is maybe why I think I'm a better novelist than a short-story writer. Stories often go from event A to event B to event C, but these are not the stories that I care about. I would like to herd all of these sorts of stories into an internment camp.

EDWIDGE DANTICAT: Someone said a short story is like a date and a novel is a marriage. I tend to agree. It's easier to wrap an entire short story around your head than it is a novel. A novel has inevitable surprises, more time and opportunity to roam and digress from the central idea. A short story forces you to focus more closely. It's tighter, more economical. I won't start a novel until I have a big chunk of free time ahead. I can write a short story with distractions in my life.

DANIEL HANDLER: I'm hopeless at the short story. All of mine generally become novels.

ALEKSANDAR HEMON: Most obviously, a novel is bigger than a short story. I start with the story I want to tell—some of them can be told in seven thousand words, some in twenty-five thousand, some in eighty thousand. I usually know how big the space I am entering is—that is, I know whether it would be a novel or a story in terms of the length—but I don't see any difference in the method of writing or the so-called techniques.

DINAW MENGESTU: I haven't learned how to write a short story yet. I'm still trying.

T COOPER: I would say that I do less research and preorganization when I'm writing shorter fiction. When I've been inspired to write short stories, there's usually a character, or a situation, or some small moment I'm starting with, and the story just feels more condensed and focused right out of the gate. With novels, that "story" or moment is more involved and takes longer to reveal itself to me—not to mention to the reader (well, hopefully, if they're going to be along for a much longer ride with me).

SHELLEY JACKSON: I have a particular taste for stories in which the nature of the reality in which they take place remains uncertain to the very end—in which nothing can be taken for granted, and the sentences seem to be inventing their way across a sort of plasma of infinite possibility, into which they melt back as you pass. Beckett has shown that it's possible to write a novel like this, but I've only managed it in the short form. In my novel, I grudgingly decided that I had to allow at least a few things to become givens in order to strap together the pieces of my weirdo plot. Well, and to establish a norm against which strange occurrences could actually register as strange, instead of disappearing into the general haze.

SANTIAGO RONCAGLIOLO: I generally use a certain tone of intimacy in my short stories. I try to tell a story that someone could tell you in private conversation, over a drink, all in one sitting. I usually take bits and pieces from my personal life and leave a lot of loose ends in order to create a certain atmosphere of mystery. Novels, on the other hand, imply creating a universe in which every detail serves a structural function. Every character that appears must develop his or her personal story, and it all has to fit together.

STEPHEN KING: Novels are longer and have more shit in them.

JOSÉ MANUEL PRIETO: Yes, short stories can be written more or less in a moment's inspiration. A novel requires major work. They're two different types of work, of conceptualizing prose. The novel is more through accumulating details. And it requires a fine carpentry job, whose written order is not always what appears in the book. For example, in *Nocturnal Butterflies of the Russian Empire* I left the first chapter until the end, which I find particularly advisable, because it evades accumulating excessive information about the history, characters, from the beginning that later in the text is resolved in a much more natural manner.

CRISTINA GARCIA: I seem incapable of writing a short story. They never just suggest themselves in a contained way. I've tried a few times, but the only times they've worked is when I've backed into them. They're outtakes from novels that somehow never belonged, and then something chemical happens and I can salvage them.

SUSAN MINOT: One is much much longer. For both forms, I always seem to write in a kind of mosaic. Pieces here and there, beginning, end, middle, writing it as if I were making a giant mosaic. For a short story it may begin with more of a linear structure but pretty soon those mosaic fragments enter in.

MICHAEL CHABON: Novels take a lot longer. When I write stories it's always in the hope and expectation of getting them over with quickly.

CURTIS SITTENFELD: I think the possibilities for a novel should feel too numerous to squeeze into a story; you should feel as if there's just *so* much to say on the topic. Also, before I start, I want to be totally fascinated by the characters and situations because I'm going to live with them for a long time.

CHRIS ABANI: I really don't write short stories. It's a form I struggle with so I can't answer that.

HOW POLISHED DO YOU TRY TO MAKE THE PROSE IN A FIRST DRAFT?

HARUKI MURAKAMI: I am just curious about what is going on. So I don't care much about the prose in a first draft.

ANNE ENRIGHT: I work the sentences and the rhythms all the time. I can't move on from a bad sentence; it gets more and more painful, like leaving a child behind you on the road.

RICK MOODY: Less polished than when I was younger. I think rewriting is the soul of the craft, and I trust the rewriting phase. From patience comes all good things in writing. Novels that hurtle, that sound as though they were rushed, especially in the last fifty pages, are disappointing. There are a lot of them around. People probably need to worry less about early drafts and more about the responsibilities of revision.

T COOPER: I don't worry too much about prose in a first draft, though I constantly have to remind myself not to worry. Wait, what if I die and the first thing that is found on my laptop is this crappy draft of a crappy book that I'm working on, supposedly in private, where had I not died, all of this embarrassing dialogue and purpley prose could've otherwise been erased with a mere click?

AKHIL SHARMA: Very polished. For me, discovering the internal psychological logic of the book requires discovering the internal logic of the sentences.

ALEKSANDAR HEMON: It doesn't work that way for me. The word "polish" describes a treatment for antiques, or at least shoes—it is about appearances. I edit as I write and write as I edit until all the parts, all the sentences and paragraphs and chapters, collaborate in holding up the structure of the narrative.

ANDREW SEAN GREER: Very. The pleasure every day lies in the sentences, and I find I will use much of what I've written later by cutting and pasting. It also is crucial for me to find the language for the novel, and that all takes place in the words.

ADANIA SHIBLI: I do not try that at all. I prefer for the first draft to be as crude and intuitive and uncontrolled as possible. The later six drafts will only be concerned with polishing the crudeness of the first draft.

JOSÉ MANUEL PRIETO: I write longhand. Then, when typing it up, I continue polishing what was already written. Then I polish it more. But I find that one should write continuously, not word by word; the capacity for prose to flow is noticeable when a text is finally read. But the job of polishing is interminable; as has been well noted, books aren't finished, they're abandoned. . . .

CHRIS ABANI: I don't think about it. I just try to get the shape out as fast as possible and then the work begins with the second through to the sixteenth or so draft.

SUSAN MINOT: Pretty well polished. Though I do line edit afterward. But the polish is the difference between good writing and average writing.

TAYARI JONES: My first drafts are a hot mess.

MEHMET MURAT SOMER: I prefer it stays as it was written. I am not good with polishing, brushing up. Of course I do, as soon as it is written, not after a longish rest, and I try to keep the retouches to a minimum. No glitter in singular sentences or prose, but an overall glamour is my motto.

RODDY DOYLE: I tend to write too much in the first draft, but I try to make it as clear and as "good" as possible without letting the quality of each sentence become an excuse for not carrying on. Editing already-written sentences is often easier than inventing new ones, so I try not to be too fussy. But a certain fussiness is important. The novel isn't just plot. I try for a balance between the number of words I write in a day and the quality of the sentences and paragraphs that contain the words.

EDWIDGE DANTICAT: Not polished at all. I just try to get it all down.

SHELLEY JACKSON: I polish sentences—if my words don't interest me then the story doesn't either—but cut very few of them. Every idea I like, every phrase, every image stays, because I don't know until I'm done what will turn out to matter most. The result is extravagant and indigestible, bristling with beautiful dead ends. Later I will cut many of them, freeing the shape of the book I want to write from the fragments of other books that sprouted from it.

ADAM MANSBACH: Pretty polished, but not so much that it slows me down. I do a lot of editing as I go; I'll often begin a day by rereading and polish the previous day's work, or the previous week's. Because my writing is often interrupted by travel these days, I have to engage in the laborious process of getting back in, and for me that usually means rereading huge portions of what I've got. And rereading means editing.

STEPHEN KING: I want it to be perfect. It never is, but that's what I want.

JOSH EMMONS: I spend the first hour of every writing day looking over past work and tinkering with the prose—the perusal is in order to get back into the story, and the tinkering is because better phrases then present themselves—so after a while the prose gets polished almost in spite of itself. I recommend against perfecting every sentence as you go along, because you may get discouraged by how long that takes.

CLAIRE MESSUD: Doesn't everyone always try to write as well as they can, at any given moment? I can't imagine not caring, whatever draft I'm dealing with. It's a matter of aesthetics, as much as anything—infelicities, it seems to me, should be deliberate, not a matter of inattention; because they mean something too.

RABIH ALAMEDDINE: I'm one of those that doesn't really have a first draft. I usually edit and polish the prose as I'm going. Usually I write late at night, and when I wake up in the morning I go over it and start polishing. I've been known to send things away before they're ready, because I also believe that things should be sent out. Get it out of the way! If I could go back to my early works I would definitely rewrite them completely. So at some point it has to go out; it's as simple as that.

COLM TÓIBÍN: I try and make sure when I am working that I will never have to go through this again. So I write as though I will never get another chance. It is so disappointing to find that you cannot get things right just because you decide you should.

ANN CUMMINS: Too polished. I'm trying to unlearn my tendency to polish each sentence of every draft. I've thrown away drafts with pristine sentences. For me, maniacal revising and polishing is a type of treading water. While biding time, waiting for the next idea to gel, I revise and reread.

MICHAEL CHABON: As polished as polished can be. Just in case it turns out I nailed it and I'm done.

DINAW MENGESTU: I think, like most writers, I take apart my sentences over and over. A bad or unpolished sentence or phrase can ruin an entire paragraph for me so I try as much as possible to work over each sentence without destroying any of its initial integrity.

GEORGE PELECANOS: Since I rewrite as I go along, my first draft is, in essence, the manuscript that gets sent up to New York. Again, I spend hours every night rewriting and polishing what I've done in the morning, so putting an accurate count to the number of drafts is tricky.

NELL FREUDENBERGER: I don't really think in terms of drafts. I certainly do a lot of revision, but I don't think it's a discrete process, separate from the writing. I usually start writing in the morning by going over what I've written the day before, and I don't continue until I'm satisfied with it. I don't think you can build a novel on a shaky foundation of messy sentences.

PAUL AUSTER: I struggle every day to write sentences and paragraphs that are as good as I can possibly make them, which means constant revision in the first draft. Subsequent drafts are more a question of fine-tuning than rewriting from scratch.

A. M. HOMES: As polished as I can.

SANTIAGO RONCAGLIOLO: That's hard to say. Many sections remain fuzzy as I advance, but I know that their meaning will make itself known—including to me—down the road. When I write, I'm constantly going back to refine a scene or a paragraph once I have a broader perspective on its potential and its consequences within the greater whole. I do that throughout the process. Sometimes entire chapters that I'd thought were finished are subjected to reform.

SUSAN CHOI: My tendency is to neurotically polish and polish to a high sheen even when I'm not sure I'll use the scene I'm working on, and so I'm always trying to counter that impulse. I'm always trying to learn to write messy.

CURTIS SITTENFELD: I hammer out a first draft of each chapter as fast as I can—which is often not very fast—then I clean it up before moving on to the next chapter. (My chapters tend to be long—easily sixty pages.) A teacher I had in grad school, Chris Offutt, once suggested starting every day by looking only at the last sentence you wrote yesterday and then moving forward, and I think this is brilliant advice and try to follow it. Even if I change direction midway—let's say I make the brother character into a sister—I don't go back and change it from the beginning; I just write forward as if I had. To me, it's so much easier to improve upon written pages that exist, even if they're messy, than to try to fix a hypothetical piece of writing I haven't finished. I strongly feel that trying, in a first draft, to make every sentence shine and be perfect before moving on to the next one is a recipe for never finishing a novel (or possibly even a paragraph!).

WHAT IS MOST DISTRACTING FOR YOU? HOW DO YOU DEAL WITH IT?

CLAIRE MESSUD: The honest answer to this seems to me highly gendered. The most distracting thing for me is life itself. I honestly feel that I am less able to ignore the demands of the people I love than are most men I know, and particularly male writers. I can't say I deal with it very well. But I'm working on it—a lifetime's project. As Rebecca West said, a house uncleaned is better than a life unlived. But when it comes to the health and well-being of close family members, it's rather harder to harden one's heart. I would hate to think that I had sacrificed my work in order to be a decent human being; but sometimes that's what the dilemma feels like.

GEORGE PELECANOS: I've weaned myself off the Internet. It's like kicking cigarettes or drugs. Once you do it, you realize that it was a tremendous waste of time. Kids, dogs, and general noise have never been a problem for me. I've never written a book in a quiet place.

PAUL AUSTER: Noise. I shut the window.

GLEN DAVID GOLD: The Internet—eBay, specifically, although at this very moment (the evening of the 2008 Indiana primary), hitting "refresh" on dailykos.com has eaten into my work time. I deal with it by taking my damned computer off the Internet for a few hours at a time.

SHELLEY JACKSON: I'm perpetually assaulted with brilliant ideas that would entail rewriting the entire book. Sometimes I pursue them, but if I didn't eventually buckle down to one approach I'd never finish anything. So I write them down as notes for future use. And then don't use them.

JENNIFER EGAN: The phone used to be a distraction; now of course it's the Internet. I find that there is some part of me that is always looking for a way to pull myself *out* of a state of deep concentration; it's diabolical. The Internet is a naughty accomplice to that desire. In all these years I still haven't figured out why I want to break my own concentration, but I don't think I'm alone in the habit. A writer friend of mine, Lisa Fugard, once told me that she had a sign next to the door of her office that said, "Why are you leaving?" Many times she found herself walking through that door with no idea of why. Then she made herself sit down again and continue working. I try to have a mental sign that asks why I'm leaving when I find myself suddenly typing something into Google for no particular reason, as if I had nothing else to do.

ADAM MANSBACH: As of six weeks ago, it's having a kid to take care of. I think the solution is going to be, as GZA said, making it "half short and twice strong"—working more efficiently now that I have less time. Preparing more, so that when I do get to sit down, I'm ready to go. Writing while I'm on the road doing lectures too. And turning down gigs and assignments I don't really want or need.

ANDREW SEAN GREER: The Internet. I have removed a Web browser from my computer.

RODDY DOYLE: Football news on the BBC Web site. I give in and read it. Then I get back to work.

HARUKI MURAKAMI: Baseball games.

ALEKSANDAR HEMON: The most distracting thing in being a writer is being a writer. In some ways, I am a writer only when I write. Outside of that, I live up to my professional obligations, do what a professional writer is supposed to do—respond to e-mail, give interviews, negotiate hack jobs, talk to publishers, teach. A lot of it is a complete waste of time as it does not advance my writing in any way, or at least not more than living an unauthorly life and talking to people. And if I had that time, I would not write more. I would read more.

STEPHEN KING: Interruptions. I try to get rid of the interruptors as quickly as possible. And kindly, but sometimes I blow up.

MEHMET MURAT SOMER: Invitations to play canasta are the biggest distraction for me. Then comes cruising. My way of dealing is not resisting the urges. I accept the invitations.

COLM TÓIBÍN: I go online. That takes ages. I go to America. That takes longer. I go to meetings. I am a member of the Arts Council in Ireland and I enjoy looking at everyone talking. I teach because it gets me out of the house. I go to parties. But never enough. I go and see my aunt. I love her. I go to London. And come home like a drowned rat. I have no intention of dealing with distractions. I intend to look for more. Anyone with any ideas can get me via my publisher.

ANNE ENRIGHT: Nothing distracts me from the desk, at least when the children are out of the house. When I am there I probably spend too much time online, but I don't have a major problem. I think a lot of distraction is anxiety. If I am too anxious to work on the piece at hand then I work on something else. I distract myself from a novel by writing short stories.

SUSAN MINOT: Life! The desire to be off IN life, running around and interacting with people and places, going to movies, seeing things, doing something practical. I deal with it behaviorally. I tell myself: this is your work. Do it.

RICK MOODY: Everything is distracting to me. If I am trying to write, I suddenly need to know *everything* about the Alan Parsons Project, even though I never liked the Alan Parsons Project and don't like them now. But suddenly I need a complete discography, writing credits, and so forth. I try to deal with this need by severely curtailing my online time.

JOSÉ MANUEL PRIETO: Noise. I try to work in environments where there's little noise, and at dawn, when everyone sleeps.

AKHIL SHARMA: My own depression at not being able to get the book to work. I handle this by trying to be grateful for the many good things in my life (my wife, living in New York, my friends), by respecting the fact that this struggle is part of the literary life, and by appreciating that I get to do something that is meaningful to me.

DANIEL HANDLER: The phone. Occasionally I must throw it across the room.

DINAW MENGESTU: The Internet has the power to suck out whole days from me. My newest solution is a bit extreme: I live in a foreign country, in a very old building without a phone line or Internet access. If I want to see my e-mail, I generally have to leave the house, or wait until the evening when a neighbor turns on his wireless connection.

CHRIS ABANI: Focusing on the project at hand, as my mind is always coming up with new things to do. I still haven't worked out a way to deal with it. Watch lots of TV?

A. M. HOMES: Answering questions—trying to articulate a process that comes largely from instinct—I deal with it by typing as fast as I can.

MICHAEL CHABON: The Internet. No doubt. Worse than children. I deal with it by turning it off; can't do that with the kids.

YIYUN LI: A lot of excuses not to be at my desk and work: my children and all sorts of needs from them, everyday errands, teaching, and many other things. I think in general to live in daily life proves to be a huge distraction from living solely in the world one creates. How do I deal with it—I don't think I deal with it well. Or I would have finished another book or two by now.

NELL FREUDENBERGER: It's hard to choose just one thing! I think the only way to deal with distraction is to be disciplined about a writing schedule.

YAEL HEDAYA: LIFE! I'm in an eternal state of distraction.

RODRIGO FRESÁN: Almost everything. Not that I find it difficult to write: it's difficult to *sit down* and write. The issue is with successfully climbing the stairs and reaching the chair. Having a one-and-a-half-year-old son has further complicated the process. I'm not complaining. On the contrary. But that's where things stand.

CURTIS SITTENFELD: E-mail and the Internet are my main distractions, which probably means my own lack of willpower is my main distraction. The days when I check e-mail once or twice are always better than the days when I check it twenty times. And I can't count the number of times I've thought, "Oh, I'll just glance online for a second before getting started," and then I look up and three hours have passed, I'm reading some news item about a B-list celebrity's mother's plastic surgery, and it's time for lunch. I have fantasies about having two desks with two computers, one with Internet connection and one without, but it hasn't happened yet. I also try to avoid meeting people for lunch. Somehow lunch out takes me hours to gear up for (what my friend Jim once called "getting ready to get ready") and to wind down from. I think I've spent entire days meeting people for lunch.

T COOPER: Life is distracting. Trying to be a good, present person to friends, loved ones, strangers, my partner, my little dog, my body, and myself, all while needing to hole myself up selfishly for hours on end to get any quality work done. These two pursuits are often at odds, so it's a constant challenge.

EDWIDGE DANTICAT: Having to do events sometimes while I'm working, things where I have to talk about writing. I try to reduce the amount of these things I do when I'm in the thick of it, really in the middle of a book.

SANTIAGO RONCAGLIOLO: Work. I could earn a living in literature, but I do a lot of things because I enjoy doing them: translations, travel, a radio program, children's books. I used to get anxious because those things took time away from writing novels, but I've learned to take advantage of them. I use them specifically so as not to write too quickly. I'm taking my time with the novel I'm writing now because I consider each section over an extended period of time, and because working relieves the pressure after periods of focus.

WHAT ONE PIECE OF ADVICE DO YOU WISH SOMEONE HAD GIVEN YOU BEFORE YOU BEGAN WRITING YOUR FIRST NOVEL?

RABIH ALAMEDDINE: Don't do it.

SUSAN MINOT: Advice is pertinent only when it rings true, which means you somehow know it already. Maybe: "It always takes longer than you think it will and usually goes past the point when you are interested in it, but that doesn't mean you can stop. Keep going."

ANDREW SEAN GREER: Don't listen to anybody; you are the only one who knows what you're doing.

AMY TAN: Don't take on major projects that are distracting. Don't be persuaded by other people. Don't be a good girl. Don't be a good girl and do blurbs for books. Don't be a good girl and do what other people pressure you to do.

AKHIL SHARMA: Writing a novel is very hard and the fact that you will find it very hard doesn't mean that you are stupid.

JONATHAN LETHEM: To let the necessities of character and language generate what is ordinarily called a "plot," rather than thinking I somehow had to master that chimera on its own terms.

JOSH EMMONS: Writing a novel is not hard in all the ways you think it will be, but in others it's much harder.

RODRIGO FRESÁN: Write it as if it was your last novel.

A. M. HOMES: Ask yourself what you want the reader to come away with.

RICK MOODY: Take your time.

JENNIFER EGAN: It's one of those pieces of advice that I probably wouldn't have been able to use even if it had been given to me, but it would have been this: *Don't worry about what other people are doing.* That worry is like a sickness; it accomplishes nothing but to make you feel inadequate. And the thing you don't—can't—realize when you're really young is that everything is going to shift over time anyway; the rivalries and jealousies you have right now will seem funny one day, if you remember them at all. The hardest thing is to write well consistently, and to get better—and if you manage that, you will have won whatever there is to win. I think that's pretty good advice, but it may be advice that you can only understand after a certain number of years.

ALEKSANDAR HEMON: I don't think I would have listened to any advice. I think making "mistakes" is an essential part of the creative process and therefore of becoming and being a writer. In writing, you can make nine wrong steps and the tenth one is perfect. I cannot imagine ever writing without making mistakes, without writing awful sentences to convey stupid situations, without trying out things only to find out they cannot possibly work. Arriving at the right thing through the thick forest of confusion and sloppiness and humiliation is precisely the most exciting thing in writing—and it is much like life. I possess no skills as a writer, because there is nothing to possess. I figure it out as I go along and the only thing I've learned over time is not to get nervous or desperate or worry that I can't do it. I keep writing through the nine, or ninety-nine, wrong steps and then when I hit the right stride I recognize it because I am an experienced, good reader.

EDWIDGE DANTICAT: Go easy on yourself. It's never going to come out the way you imagine it. The mind is infinite, but there are only so many words in any language.

SHELLEY JACKSON: I sat on an unfinished first draft for years because I suspected, correctly, that I didn't know how to finish it. When I finally went back to it, I still didn't know how, but I went ahead and did it anyway. I wish someone had told me in the beginning that I would never know how to write a novel, only how to carry on despite near-total confusion and doubt, and how, once I finished a draft, to figure out what I'd done and make it better.

MEHMET MURAT SOMER: "What are you waiting for? Go at once! Now!" I've been writing and keeping them for myself for a long time. I am kind of a late bloomer.

JOSÉ MANUEL PRIETO: I don't believe there's advice that works for the whole world. What worked for me was the advice given by a professor of mine, a woman who was not a writer but a great reader: to keep a diary. I was eighteen years old back then, and I think it was very useful, because it helped me put down ideas, to think while writing.

COLM TÓIBÍN: John McGahern was a great help to me. He had a gap between novels of ten years when I knew him first. He moved slowly and deliberately and was a real perfectionist. He once said to me slyly: "I hope I do not have another idea until after Christmas." It was still the spring. I wish he had said more wise things like that.

CURTIS SITTENFELD: The writing is the best part. A lot about writing a novel isn't incredibly fun, but nothing that comes later, not money or acclaim, will match the level of engagement you feel creating your story. It sounds cheesy, but it's true.

DINAW MENGESTU: Be patient—more patient than you've ever been with anything else in your life, and just when you think you've been patient long enough, wait even longer. A novel can take years to write, and years to publish. If you're not patient with yourself, the silence and frustration that comes with waiting to see a work completed or published can begin to seem unbearable.

CHRIS ABANI: Focus on the big picture and finishing the book. Sweat the rest later.

SUSAN CHOI: Write the first draft straight through as quickly as possible, without showing parts of it to anyone. Resist the longing for reassurance or validation or whatever it is that makes you want to run to the first willing reader with the precious partial draft in your mitts, just to hear them say, Hey, this is great! I can't wait to read more! Until you have the whole shape of your novel blocked out, that reader really can't help your novel; he or she can only help your ego.

DANIEL HANDLER: Just about everybody has written a first novel that they throw away before writing their actual first novel.

GEORGE PELECANOS: I have not been particularly diligent about planning my career, though I've been blessed with having a literary agent who has advised me well. I'm going to go against the grain here and say that young writers should not become obsessed with the business aspect of publishing. First, live a full life so that you will have something to write about. Then bear down and focus on the work. The rest will follow.

MICHAEL CHABON: "Don't be such a smarty pants."

CLAIRE MESSUD: I don't know that any advice is useful in such a circumstance. Everyone has got to make the mistakes they've got to make; so advice is only ever so useful. The advice I give my own students is that if they cannot write, then they should not write—you should only choose a life of writing if you can't possibly avoid it. I wasn't given such advice; but it wouldn't have stopped me.

GLEN DAVID GOLD: "Glen, you're mistaking clever for genius."

YAEL HEDAYA: Take your time. Don't rush to publish. Mature. Ripen. REVISE.

NELL FREUDENBERGER: Slow down and make sure you're happy with every part of it, at least before it's published. Don't feel pressure to finish by a particular date, even if you love your editor and your agent and desperately want to make them happy.

RODDY DOYLE: Don't bother, and go straight to the second one. My first novel has, rightly, never been published; the second one was *The Commitments.*

YIYUN LI: Not to spend too much time on polishing the prose!

SANTIAGO RONCAGLIOLO: Try to write a novel that encompasses many emotions: that makes the reader laugh, cry, become afraid. Then it'll resemble life. And don't stop narrating: you can describe, reflect, or argue, without ever stopping narrating. Stories must remain in constant movement.

STEPHEN KING: Don't expect instant acceptance.

TAYARI JONES: Actually, I wrote my first novel without advice and it was a lovely experience. I wish on my second novel someone had said, "It's not your first run and it's not your last try." That way, I would have been less worried.

HARUKI MURAKAMI: I should have used a nom de plume. That is the only thing I regret now.

WHAT SHOULD A FIRST CHAPTER ACCOMPLISH?

SAŠA STANIŠIĆ: Leave the reader speechless and erotically longing for the second.

A. M. HOMES: First chapter should set the tone, lay the groundwork, and most importantly should convince the reader of why they should suspend the living of their own life to enter the world you are putting before them.

JONATHAN LETHEM: Ideally, practically everything. I think the best first chapters—I may only have attained this once or twice—should contain the DNA of the entire book in miniature, making themselves a kind of microcosmic engine or index the writer can rely on and consult throughout the work, and which should seem to produce the rest of the book as a kind of inevitable exfoliation of its essential motifs and rhythms. How's that?

MICHAEL CHABON: It should render the reader helpless to do anything but read on.

RODDY DOYLE: I don't really understand this one.

JOSH EMMONS: It should establish the novel's voice and several of its key concerns. Whether it addresses the full range of heuristic questions—the who, what, when, where, and why—is up to the narrator.

COLM TÓIBÍN: A novel's job is to hit the reader's nervous system. The job of a first chapter is to get this going. Nothing else.

PAUL AUSTER: A number of my books do not have chapters. But if we think about the beginning of the book, the opening pages, then I feel it is imperative that the writer get down to business quickly and draw the reader in to such a degree that he or she will not want to stop. I once ran into the crime writer Mickey Spillane at a book fair in Sweden. In his gruff, barroom manner, he said something that has stayed with me ever since: "Nobody reads a book to get to the middle."

SUSAN CHOI: The reader should find it impossible to put the book down. Actually, that's what the first page should accomplish.

RODRIGO FRESÁN: A first chapter must have a web you want to fall into.

ADAM MANSBACH: The same thing the novel as a whole should: draw you in and not let you go. Make the reader feel comfortable as a passenger in the car you're driving. It's like chess openings: there are a lot of possibilities, from aggressively bringing out your queen to patiently advancing your pawns, from pulling a slick, unexpected attack to entrenching your troops for the long haul. Any of them can win you the game, as long as you know what you're doing. But you shouldn't write a check with your first chapter that your novel can't cash: if you can't sustain the energy or the wit or the pace of your opening, you're in trouble. I think character is paramount; it's more important that you make me care about the people in your first chapter than about the plot, or the themes, or the setting.

MEHMET MURAT SOMER: What are we aiming for? Which audience? I myself prefer rose-colored pop. You know, it's a kind of middle-age crisis. Not just the first chapter, the first page should be catchy, witty, and possess an obvious or hidden joy.

CLAIRE MESSUD: Any rule about what a first chapter should accomplish would be undermined by one or another remarkable but unexpected first chapter. In fiction, as in life, you can get away with what you can get away with. If you're good enough, you can get away with murder. If you're not—and most of us are not—you can't.

ANDREW SEAN GREER: It should make the deal with the reader in terms of tone, imagery, scope, and theme. If it's a magical story, for instance, there should be a little flash-powder on the horizon.

ALEKSANDAR HEMON: Nothing in particular. I don't think it is more important than any other chapter. The worst thing you can do, though, is think that you're going to catch yourself some readers with the first chapter.

STEPHEN KING: Engage the reader. Make him or her impatient to continue.

DANIEL HANDLER: It should have at least one delicious thing and the promise of many delicious things to come, usually in that order. I always think a first chapter says, "Okay, this happens, and the book is going to be about these things, and I'm telling it like this, are you ready?"

AKHIL SHARMA: Be interesting. Establish the issues and stakes.

TAYARI JONES: The first chapter is an introduction. It should give the reader a sense of what's around the bend. This is why I always come back and work on the first chapter once the novel is done. How can I introduce the story before I know what it is?

NELL FREUDENBERGER: It should make the reader sympathize with the person telling the story enough to want to keep listening to it.

GEORGE PELECANOS: From the author's standpoint, reading it should inspire you to continue writing and push on. You should look at it and say, I've got something here. I'm not talking about that the-first-paragraph-of-the-novel-should-hook-the-reader bullshit. I'm saying, the voice should be strong and it should be compelling.

EDWIDGE DANTICAT: It should grab the reader by the throat and make the book impossible to put down.

JOSÉ MANUEL PRIETO: Set down the keys of how the book will be read. This is important as long as there's a unique narrative mechanism for each book. For example, in my *Encyclopedia of a Life in Russia* there are no proper chapters, but I do introduce an article or voice that explains how to read the book: not chronologically, etc. Nevertheless, as I mentioned above, I find it useful leaving the writing of the first chapter for later, because there's a tendency to say so many things, to inform the reader of details, that might otherwise appear naturally within the very development of the novel. When the novel is written, one sees that it is not necessary to overburden the first chapter. One needs only to place the story in its proper air.

SUSAN MINOT: It should bewitch the reader enough so she wants to read on. I do admire a first chapter that somehow touches upon in a hidden way all the things the book will be about—but that's an extra bonus, not required.

YAEL HEDAYA: It should be like a punch in the stomach. The readers should be knocked off the couch, rolling around on the floor holding their bellies, and then getting up and begging for more.

RABIH ALAMEDDINE: You've asked the right person. I wrote a novel, *I, the Divine*, all in first chapters, so I've thought about this a lot. The main difference between mine and Calvino's *If on a Winter's Night a Traveler*, is, of course, that Calvino's is a lot better—but also, that my first chapters are all written by the same character. She is trying to write a novel, start a memoir, and can't go past the first chapter. A first chapter has to grip me at some point, but it doesn't have to explain anything. I think a lot of people get in trouble because they feel they have to explain things in the first chapter, and set the scene for the second. I get bored with that. The very first line has to give you an idea of what the novel is about, and the first chapter has to go beyond that.

YIYUN LI: Building up a world, a mood, a situation, anything that will keep a reader interested.

GLEN DAVID GOLD: Oy. *Should. Should* is a negative word for me. And, remember, one good novel, four bad ones, and one in the pipeline that could either give me a .330 or .200 batting average. So take my advice with a grain of salt, but: your first chapter should make your reader want to read chapter two. This is done by being welcoming and engaging and getting the hell out of the way of the story. The first chapter should pose a question or two, at least.

CHRIS ABANI: Mesmerize a reader. Really the first sentence should do that. The chapter should steal their soul and make them a slave to the book until they are done reading it.

RICK MOODY: It's likely that it introduces the theme and perhaps one of the principal characters, but I don't honestly believe that it *should* do anything at all. It should do whatever it wants to do and that initial prolegomena of narratorial pleasure is enough for me.

CHAPTER 3

STRUCTURE AND PLOT

DO YOU OUTLINE? IF SO, HOW CLOSELY DO YOU FOLLOW IT?

ANNE ENRIGHT: I might have a doodle—an arc, a straight line or two, maybe a couple of asterisks for significant moments. I have a strong sense of the emotional shape of a book, and I hold on to that. I used to plan endlessly, but it never made much difference. Everything happens in the actual writing, for me. Now I just live in a book for three years or so. The computer is always on. I make decisions. I revise decisions. The book falls apart. The book comes together in a different way. The new book falls apart. I hold my nerve. The book I start writing—the easy, confident, public book—always turns fraudulent, for me, and I realize that I have to write the real book that lies beneath. This process isn't easy, but I have found, over the years, that a lot of my work involves abandoning plans and structures, not making them. I don't construct books, I sometimes think, so much as grow them, like mushrooms, in the dark.

MICHAEL CHABON: Yes, but not at first. And never with a whole lot of detail. And usually about three-fifths of the way in I start to go off the plan and never entirely get back to it. Often I end up hating the person who wrote the damn outline.

JENNIFER EGAN: I outline *after* I have a first draft, to clarify what I've got, exactly, and how it needs to change. My outlines are unbelievably long and comprehensive. My first revision outline for *Look at Me* was more than eighty pages long, single-spaced, in ten-point type.

COLM TÓIBÍN: I outline only in my head. Writing for me is hard. It is a sort of whispering. Taking notes about a novel sounds like a way of wrecking its sanctity before you start.

DANIEL HANDLER: I outline lots and lots and then ignore most of it.

AMY TAN: I used to say no and I think that's a lie. I outlined in certain ways—not the outline that your third-grade teacher taught you to do. Sometimes I write down in a flash form what I think is the overall story structure. They're cryptic notes to myself. Or I'll sit down and write a summary—three to ten pages of what I think it's about. Or I'll write down the movement of a particular chapter. It's good to have that because I can then move to the next part and say, Oh, I needed to include this or that.

ANDREW SEAN GREER: I write a very careful outline and then abandon it halfway through. It is always a difficult moment for me, but of course I know that it is crucial to follow the way the story has grown, even if it means leaving the road and bushwacking my way to the end.

JONATHAN LETHEM: Never at all. The sense of carrying the story around in my head, and the pressure of its need to be expressed, is an essential motivation for the long journey of a novel's writing. I'd never be tempted to discharge that tension into any kind of elaborate or systematic outline. All I do is jot random notes when essential items of language or other detail occur to me, so I don't lose them. But I avoid even putting those into any kind of sensible order that would resemble a plan or outline.

EDWIDGE DANTICAT: I don't outline, but I do have a general plan in my mind of where I'd like the book to go.

HARUKI MURAKAMI: No outline. It would be a bore if you knew the punchline before it is told.

CHRIS ADRIAN: I generally know where things are headed, and sometimes figure things out in detail before really starting to get most of the composition done. For *The Children's Hospital*, I had this goofy four-foot-long outline on a piece of poster board that had every chapter outlined. That was a little ridiculous.

T COOPER: I do outline, but not so far ahead that I've necessarily got the whole book mapped out before I start. I generally block out scenes or chunks of action as I write, so I try not to end a day of writing without knowing vaguely where to pick up when I get started again the next day. For both of my published novels, I've actually even outlined *after* I've written a draft, or halfway through a draft; what I do is I get a large roll of butcher paper and roll it out on the floor, or on a wall if I have the space, and I summarize scenes chronologically, leaving room to add ideas or dialogue or other scenes or questions that need answering in between. Sometimes I have little drawings, or photographs. Actually, a drawing I used to represent a scene from my second novel actually ended up being used in the final published book: it was a little caricature I sketched of a Jew sucking the blood of a Christian child—and it ended up serving as a pretty significant plot point for the book (sparking the pogrom that eventually inspired the titular family to leave Kishinev, Russia, for New York).

SAŠA STANIŠIĆ: Sometimes I do. But I leave the outline pretty soon.

JOSÉ MANUEL PRIETO: I do it in a very loose manner because it is not always followed, nearly always a few steps are skipped. But it depends on the story. There are books that are thought about so much that they're more or less outlined inside your head and you follow that guide.

CRISTINA GARCIA: I never outline. I don't know, it could be my own perversity but whenever I set out to do something, I completely sabotage myself. For me it's best just to work organically and always slightly in the dark about my own characters.

STEPHEN KING: No. Never.

SUSAN CHOI: No. Not so far.

MEHMET MURAT SOMER: I work with outlines. Detailed, well-calculated, almost scene-by-scene or chapter-by-chapter plotted outlines. I love that part more than writing! It feels like completing jigsaw puzzles or filling in the large Sunday crosswords. And I believe writing a thriller, a somewhat criminal case to be set and solved, needs to be calculated from the start. It is essential for me to put in the details, which will become useful in the following chapters, to build the suspense, to develop the characters with their reasons to be explained somewhere toward the end. I approach my writing as an "inspired" engineer, which, in fact, I am by education.

RABIH ALAMEDDINE: No. I was trained as a mathematician and an engineer, so I usually can keep spatial things in my head.

GLEN DAVID GOLD: I speak as a guy with the following experience: four unpublished, bad novels and one published novel and one on the way. So my experience with success is both limited and theoretical. I don't know how potable any of this is. But as of now, two weeks from turning in no. 2 (of the good ones), I never outline. When I sold the second book, I needed to write one before I'd done the actual drafting, and my wife called the experience "putting a baby in high heels and lipstick and shoving it onto a street corner." That outline ruined the book I was going to write. It was like trying to type with a graveyard taped over my computer screen. I ultimately had to abandon the book and start over.

NELL FREUDENBERGER: No.

RODDY DOYLE: No, I don't outline. As I go deeper into the book I jot down plot points so as not to forget them. But I don't enslave myself to them.

CURTIS SITTENFELD: I sometimes feel my way into a chapter or section, but once I have a few scenes, I do create an outline. Usually, a few words correspond with an entire scene: I'll write, "Lee's parents arrive at school," and then the scene itself ends up being twenty pages. I pin the outline on a mini-bulletin board that I can prop on my desk beside my computer. Basically, I know the one important thing that will happen in a scene, but almost nothing else. If I created more detailed outlines, I fear I'd rob myself of any spontaneity, but if I didn't do an outline at all, I'm pretty sure I'd write myself into a corner. I believe that the success or failure of a novel almost always hinges on structure—everything I know about structure, I learned from my grad school adviser, Ethan Canin, and it's the biggest educational gift anyone has ever given me because it gave me control over my own writing—so I try to also have a sense of the structure within the whole book, across all the chapters.

ALEKSANDAR HEMON: No. I set the limits. I have a vague idea of the direction or sequence of events that I follow only to see where that would take me. I think of the book or story as a space. I enter it, spend time in it, arrange the furniture, paint the walls, get out, leave it to the people who will live there.

TAYARI JONES: Nope. No outline. I worry that if I have the plot points set out ahead of time, I will start aiming for them. In other words, if I know what's going to happen next, the reader will too.

AKHIL SHARMA: No.

CLAIRE MESSUD: An outline for me is usually a list of items on a piece of paper. Perhaps because it's such a flimsy thing, I have, up until now, followed it fairly closely; although it would be more honest to confess that the list has, upon occasion, changed along the way.

GEORGE PELECANOS: I do not outline. I discover the book as I'm writing it.

PAUL AUSTER: Very, very sketchily. No more than a list of events, often described in one or two words. And the only reason I bother to make these lists is to keep the order of information in my head, but the story is already there inside me, and so when I write down the words *New York*, for example, or *the bedroom*, I know what is going to be happening in that passage.

RODRIGO FRESÁN: Little to none.

SANTIAGO RONCAGLIOLO: I work with rough outlines. I don't make a lot of plans because the story always thwarts them. Sometimes, by sticking to an idea that you think is quite good, you wind up drowning the rest of the novel. I usually have a clear understanding of the music I want, and I try to adjust the plot to it, not the other way around.

TASH AW: I do outline, but I never follow them closely—if at all. Outlines are just the flimsy scaffolding that holds up the early part of the novel, and the detail often expands to bring it all crashing down. I once read that Iris Murdoch knew every single scene, down to the characters' tiniest gestures, before she even started writing a novel—a very depressing thought indeed. Writing needs to be surprising, writers need to be surprised. Otherwise the whole process is dead before it even begins—like coloring by numbers.

CHRIS ABANI: No. I hold everything in a nice mush in my head.

YIYUN LI: I don't outline in detail. I know the approximate shape of the novel and that is about it.

RICK MOODY: Never. Books that are outlined often read as though they are outlined, as though events and personages contained within are subordinate to an outline, and that is a philosophical approach that is anathema to this writer. I think the characters should, as far as is possible, have total liberty. Liberty, in fact, is an essential part of composition. Or at the least the illusion of liberty. I have no story that I am supposed to tell. And I cannot write the novel in my head. So I will allow this one at hand to meander where it will, and then I will figure out what it is that my subconscious wishes to say in the rewriting phase.

YAEL HEDAYA: I don't outline. Wish I could, but I have the concentration span of a two-year-old. I'm beginning to seriously suspect I'm ADHD.

GARY SHTEYNGART: The last novel I completed had a total of thirty-six plot points. My protagonist balked at about half of them, and I had to accede to his demands. Then some of the medium to minor characters got pissed off as well, so I had to turn things around to please them. Why do people compare writers to God? We are entirely at the mercy of the wankers who storm across our pages.

HOW DO YOU KNOW THAT A SET OF EVENTS OR PLOT POINTS WILL HOLD THE WEIGHT OF A NOVEL?

COLM TÓIBÍN: If you don't know how a novel should be structured and how it should unfold, then give it up, go to law school. So there's no "how do you know." You know. It's called talent. Most people don't have it, just as I cannot draw or play the trombone.

CHRIS ABANI: Experience.

TAYARI JONES: Sadly, you don't. You just have to see if it works.

ANDREW SEAN GREER: Instinct and reading reading reading other novels.

ALEKSANDAR HEMON: I don't. I write until what I write becomes a novel, until the structure can sustain its own weight and I can remove the scaffold and get out.

RABIH ALAMEDDINE: I don't. I actually never know whether a novel is going to work until maybe three-quarters of the way over, and this is one of the terrifying things for me about writing. Now I've written four books—three novels—and you'd think that I've become a little more experienced, but no, I still don't know—like the book I'm writing now, I really have no clue whether I'll be able to do it and I'm so terrified most of the time. Even as I'm talking now, my heart starts beating faster and I'm so terrified that I won't know what to do with it.

JOSH EMMONS: This is unanswerable until the novel is complete, at which point some readers may judge its narrative action sufficient while others will say it's not enough. This is partly because there's no established minimum or maximum amount of plot for a novel. In Beckett's

The Unnameable, nothing happens, and yet even its detractors agree that it's a novel.

JENNIFER EGAN: I don't. That's why I don't outline until I've already made an instinctive stab at the action of the book. The successes and (more often) failures of that first draft help to give me a sense of what I need to do to improve the book.

DINAW MENGESTU: I tend not to write with that much of a concern for plot. If the characters are well-defined and have an integrity of their own then I tend to trust that they will be the ones to carry the weight of the novel.

SUSAN MINOT: You don't, until you write it. A gauge might be that if those points can hold your interest as the author, you should be able to convey that interest to the reader.

SANTIAGO RONCAGLIOLO: I only know once I'm writing. And I often ask myself that question much too late. Either way, I can always make up new pieces to the story to continue writing with a certain amount of coherence. I've written soap operas, so I'm trained for it. My problem isn't in creating a plot, but rather in determining which story line I want to recount when, and which one relates to what I want to say at a given moment. I take a lot of other factors into account to make that decision.

NELL FREUDENBERGER: Unfortunately I think that's something you have to figure out as you write. You can always change the events of a story, and make the plot fit the people; it doesn't work the other way around.

GLEN DAVID GOLD: Having a workshop of like-minded people who will read drafts.

RODRIGO FRESÁN: Who knows?

STEPHEN KING: I just do. I've been wrong (*Rose Madder*, for instance), but rarely.

SUSAN CHOI: I don't think there's any way to know until the draft has been written and read. Wonderful novels have been written whose "events" or "plot points" are on close examination almost nonexistent. It's about the writing.

RICK MOODY: I don't.

YAEL HEDAYA: I only know in retrospect.

PAUL AUSTER: You don't. You have to start writing, and after a while you discover if what you have is something worthwhile or not.

ANN CUMMINS: Trial and error. Through each draft, I jettison plot points and events (and characters) that aren't holding the novel's weight, but sometimes I bring a discarded idea back in if I begin to understand its relevance.

JOSÉ MANUEL PRIETO: I have a pretty good idea of the novel, what will happen within it. Those turning points, which constitute the pillars of the arch that holds up the story. But I can move them at will through the length of the story. Another important thing is the moment when each appears in the narrative, which doesn't exactly coincide with the time it occurs.

CLAIRE MESSUD: You just know. It's like music. It's visceral.

MICHAEL CHABON: I have never even thought of it in those terms; I'm not sure I really understand the question.

HOW DO YOU DECIDE HOW
TO BREAK UP THE NARRATIVE?

STEPHEN KING: Instinct.

JENNIFER EGAN: Instinct initially, and then just by seeing what works and what doesn't work in the execution. Often I'll try something else that also doesn't work, and then I'll try again. For me it's always a combination of, or dialectic between, instinct and analysis.

RICK MOODY: Generally speaking, I don't think of what I do as involving *decisions* because I like the idea that the important novel-writing problems are solved somewhere lower down than in the part of me responsible for decision-making. I incline in the direction of the notion that some part of the aesthetic process is automatic. Art that has the automatic as part of its presuppositions seems to me more organic, more genuine.

NELL FREUDENBERGER: I think I'm a pretty conventional writer of chapters. They seem to have natural endings, and I know when I reach them. I try not to make any chapter too long because most of the novels I admire have short chapters.

AKHIL SHARMA: When it gets boring for me. When it gets boring for other readers.

COLM TÓIBÍN: I walk a lot and think about this and I often get ideas when I am sad on airplanes or lying in bed being lazy. I know this before I begin. When to stop. When to start again. It's crucial.

EDWIDGE DANTICAT: Based on what's going on in the plot.

RODRIGO FRESÁN: It's not a decision. My narratives and my narrating styles come broken from the factory. My stories and novellas are for simultaneous assembly and disassembly. Abrupt changes, sudden ellipses, earthquakes and storms are the norm. Again: *2001* and "A Day in the Life."

TAYARI JONES: Every chapter ends with the end of a scene, but not every end of scene makes a chapter. I think of a chapter as a segment of the story that explores a theme. Once I have run out of gas for that idea, the chapter is over.

JONATHAN LETHEM: I find I'm less and less interested in headings, epigraphs, section or chapter breaks or names, or even white space between paragraphs to indicate a pause. (In fact, I have to work harder and harder to remind myself to begin new paragraphs and sentences sometimes lately.) I prefer a sense of oceanic immersion, a total and complete dissolving of the apparatus of boundaries around the material, or imposing the act of constant reentry—I'd rather have the reader fall into the work like a bottomless pit. Knowing this is probably excessive and unpleasant, I then back off and offer a few handholds and guideposts.

GLEN DAVID GOLD: Trial and error. Just had that question myself a couple of weeks ago. I had three stories I was telling at once. Should they be in thirty-page chunks so that a reader would have a chance to get lost in each story? Or ten pages so that they didn't forget the other two stories? Which one gave more momentum to the book? I tried it in thirty-page sections, and after showing it around, everyone thought the book was longer than it was. I was asked to shorten it. So I turned it in again with the same page count, but the scenes were now ten pages long. Everyone thought it moved a lot faster and wondered what I'd cut.

ALEKSANDAR HEMON: All those decisions are local. That is, it depends on the particulars of the book or the section. There are no case studies to be presented. Writing is nothing if not solving problems you've created for yourself. There are no outside solutions or methods.

MICHAEL CHABON: Truly, by the seat of my pants, on the fly. I just feel my way along to the next important thing. And try to avoid car rides or bus rides.

CHRIS ABANI: Intuition and experience; also trial and error.

DINAW MENGESTU: Breaking up the narrative tends to happen fairly organically. I know when a chapter ends by the sense of closure the last line brings for me. Of course afterward I often find that I have to go back through and condense or rearrange the sequence of certain chapters for structural reasons. I like narratives that aren't arranged in a chronological order—stories that loop back in time, or jump across years, decades—all of which makes breaking up and arranging the narrative a difficult but wonderful process.

YIYUN LI: I don't know if I make the decision consciously.

RODDY DOYLE: As I go further into the book and become better acquainted with the characters and, in recent books, the narrator, decisions as to when to stop one line of the story and start another, how much to give the reader—all the big and small decisions—begin to make stronger sense.

SANTIAGO RONCAGLIOLO: I'm a satirical writer up to a point. Usually the first version of what I write is much too cartoonish and hurried. I mold the narrative atop that first version, trying to make it more plausible, the atmospheres more nuanced, the characters more complex. When the voice or the story line doesn't give me the room to do it, I abandon the project.

SUSAN MINOT: Either there is an overarching scheme (flashback to present to flashback) that decides the structure, in which case you just go by instinct when one needs to switch back to the other, or there is no overarching scheme and you simply go by instinct without it. I do throw in some guidelines for myself, hidden ones. In *Monkeys*, for instance, I first conceived of having twelve stories in the book and each story would take place in a different month. That was an organizing scheme. Some of the stories eventually melted together and I ended up with nine. But they are all still in different months.

HOW DO YOU DECIDE WHO IS GOING TO TELL THE STORY?

CLAIRE MESSUD: There are lots of ways to decide, including trying out different points of view. But the fundamental question is what story it is you want to tell. Once you figure that out, you know who needs to tell the story. Because just as any picture has a vanishing point, so too every story is defined by its perspective. Three of us can spend the day together, and each of us will have a different story of that day. Same with three hundred people—everyone will have a different story. So if you know what your story is, then you've figured out who has to tell it.

PAUL AUSTER: This is the biggest question a novelist faces—first person or third person. You must ponder long and hard before you come up with the answer.

JENNIFER EGAN: That's an instinctive, gut judgment. If I find myself having to *decide* something like that, it's a sign that things aren't evolving naturally and may not work at all.

RODRIGO FRESÁN: There are not a lot of problems in that sense. Usually it's an omniscient first-person singular that I like to call—à la

Beckett—"last person." One that works as narrator and narrative subject at the same time. All that I have to tell, in reality, always happens inside the head of the person who is telling and living and dying to tell it.

STEPHEN KING: The story tells. Or, sometimes, as you approach the book, the narrative voice starts to speak. In the new book, there are a dozen or more points of view. I was delighted. It's been years since I worked on a narrative canvas this broad.

ALEJANDRO ZAMBRA: At the moment of making a decision for the story. They're inseparable decisions. Only this narrator can tell that story. I can't imagine *A Man Asleep*, by Perec, in the third person. It would be a very different book.

CHRIS ABANI: Trial and error, usually. The voice that rings truest after a couple of lines is the one I go with.

ANDREW SEAN GREER: I always know that. Each story I pick up is by necessity about a certain person. I may decide to work in third person, of course, and move even further out to omniscient, and that is a very difficult decision that takes much trial and error. It's all about writing the pages, hundreds of them, to find the right thing. You never get it right the first time, though you always think you will.

COLM TÓIBÍN: I work mostly with third-person intimate, and that person sees everything and knows everything and everything is from that person's point of view. I decide this out of fear. I would much prefer to write *As I Lay Dying*, but I don't have the talent.

DANIEL HANDLER: That always comes to me right with the story, for better or for worse.

YIYUN LI: I am not a first-person writer so I know the story will be told by different narrators. And since they are all very important, they all have a turn to tell their stories.

MICHAEL CHABON: That is the most important thing of all. I try to answer that, of course, in the very first sentence. Past tense or present; first person (and Watson or Humbert) or third; omniscient or limited. But I also try just to let it happen how it seems to want to happen. It's a consciously unconscious decision, or maybe an unconsciously conscious one.

RICK MOODY: He or she proposes to tell it.

SUSAN CHOI: This usually isn't a decision; I've only ever found one voice, per novel, that worked. I've never thought, Hmm, which of these two perfect voices should I choose?

EDWIDGE DANTICAT: Sometimes the story starts out with a character and it seems obvious that it's that character's story and he or she should tell it. Other times, I try different points of view before I find the right one.

GLEN DAVID GOLD: Currently I'm a fan of third-person omniscient. It seems to have the most room for monkeying around. The next book could well be different, though.

NELL FREUDENBERGER: I don't find characters whose voice I can sustain very often, and so whenever I find one, the decision is pretty much made.

T COOPER: The more I get to know my characters and the story, it just becomes evident who should be telling it. It's just something that I trust will make itself apparent, and if it doesn't, then I don't force any-thing; I will usually try out different approaches, and if one's not work-ing, I can tell pretty quickly and will make adjustments to try something else.

RODDY DOYLE: The story always starts with the character. In a way, there's no decision. If there's no character there's no story.

SANTIAGO RONCAGLIOLO: When I'm pondering a story, several po-tential first paragraphs occur to me. When I really like one of them, I know that I have the embryo of a novel. The plot provides the chronol-ogy of events, but the first paragraph sets the tone, the persona, the rhythm, in short, the voice. The narrator is the voice I always feel most comfortable with, but I have no way of discovering it until after I've be-gun writing a bit.

TAYARI JONES: I often try a story from several points of view. I end with the character who can see the most. This is usually a character who is an outsider in some way. Whomever is least invested in the values of the story can give the most rigorous examination of it.

SUSAN MINOT: Mess around with it. There is a lot of initially try-ing first person then switching to third person. It is a way to feel you are getting inside. I stick with the first person if the perspective is crucial and if the person's language is important to the telling of the story.

YAEL HEDAYA: I don't. It just happens. I know this sounds juvenile, but this is how it really works.

DINAW MENGESTU: I seem to always know the narrator's voice as soon as the story begins. I've only written in the first person, and I suppose it's because I'm always trying to figure out just who the voice in my head really is.

A. M. HOMES: It's not a decision so much as an evolution.

IS THERE A PARTICULAR WAY YOU APPROACH NOVELIZING REAL EVENTS? HOW?

ALEKSANDAR HEMON: Even if you tell someone about what happened to you today, you are transforming a "real" event into something else. So I retell the story of a "real" event to someone in writing and I allow for embellishments and exaggerations and I respect the logical space of the story.

NELL FREUDENBERGER: Fictionalizing real events almost never works for me. There's a lot of my own life in my stories, but I have to sort of trick myself into writing about it. Most of the time I start with a character who's distinct from me in terms of sex, age, or nationality and try to write from that unfamiliar perspective. I think fiction has worked best when you don't discover what you have in common with your characters until you're deeply involved in their stories.

DANIEL HANDLER: I think about who would be upset, and then decide if I care if they're upset or not, and change things accordingly.

TAYARI JONES: My first novel, *Leaving Atlanta*, is a coming-of-age story set against the backdrop of the Atlanta child murders of 1979–81. I was ten or so when this happened and two of my classmates were among the thirty children who were killed. When it came to novelizing this event, I had to let go of the historical weight of the moment. I had to let the daily drama of the characters play out. I had to bring the mundane to the fore and leave the history as the backdrop. In other words, the key to writing real events is not to overprivilege the "real."

JONATHAN LETHEM: A most particular way: I exaggerate, heighten, compress, and distort them to make them more interesting. Most real events are pretty vague, especially around the edges, compared to the sorts of things I want to put into my books.

ANDREW SEAN GREER: Avoid having characters run into historical events or famous people. When you do that, you abandon character.

SUSAN CHOI: I have a very ad hoc approach to it, though I've used real events in everything I've written. Each book seems to evolve its own set of rules. With *American Woman*, my main character had significant basis in the life of a real, still living, individual, and there I decided I'd only use facts that had been previously reported, and the rest I'd make up. This wasn't really logical; it was to assuage my guilt. I didn't want to be guilty of exposing information that had never been exposed about this person. But no reader was going to know what in my novel was based on real reportage and what was imagined by me; there was no logic to my system. It was only for me. With *A Person of Interest*, I borrowed from a number of real-life cases but my rule was that my case—the case against Professor Lee—had to have its own internal logic. This meant that many things I liked from real life couldn't go in—they didn't mesh with the logic of the case I was creating.

SAŠA STANIŠIĆ: With a lot of respect for the historical "truth" but at the same time with a lot of trust in fictionalizing that "truth."

JENNIFER EGAN: I'm dreadful at novelizing real events. In fact one of my biggest weaknesses is that I can't seem to write from my life at all. I need to make all of it up—or *think* I'm making it up. This may be one reason I like to write as—and about—men; the separation from my own life is freeing and fun. A strangely dead feeling comes over me when I feel I'm moving into writing about my own life or experience, and it's hard to write with any joy in that state.

RABIH ALAMEDDINE: I usually start with a real event, if you want to call it that, but it's not necessarily a real event that happened to me. I'm a natural liar. I'll embellish things. When I write something, even if it's a real event, in my head it has changed so much to make it a good story that it's no longer a real event. The idea is to tell a fabulous story—and I use the word *fabulous* in both meanings.

RICK MOODY: There's no particular way. In general, I have had no hesitation about including "real," or so-called real, events, because this has always been part of the fiction writer's palette. I guess that I include them when it makes sense for the story. There's no use including "real" events just for the sake of it, or because you imagine "real" events lend credibility to the narrative. Often what seems "real" feels more artificial once enclosed between covers. So unless an event feels like it's germane to the story you might as well leave it out and make something up. Sometimes making things up is more difficult, it's true, but laziness should never be a rationale for inclusion or noninclusion.

STEPHEN KING: You have to twist them, echo them, mirror them.

A. M. HOMES: I think of Richard Nixon—and I'm not kidding. I think of events such as Watergate, and writers such as Don DeLillo, and I look to see how they do it.

RODDY DOYLE: There's no particular approach. It depends how central the event is, or how historically well known—how much one can mix invention with generally accepted facts. I try to visualize my character there, watching and listening—photographs help, and music.

CRISTINA GARCIA: Sometimes I'll just simply change the gender, which alters everything. Everything falls into place differently and can't be said in the same way, and then before you know it, the real-life event that triggered it no longer matters. Sometimes gender will do the trick. Other times—and I'm thinking in particular of the mother in *Dreaming in Cuban*, who's based on my mother—there I just start throwing everything at her, you know, a hairnet and a wandering eye and orthopedic shoes and anything to physically distinguish her from the real person who inspired her.

SANTIAGO RONCAGLIOLO: I always start from real emotions and experiences because I think that gives the narrative a lot of force. But the act of writing consists precisely in distorting those facts through fiction, injecting them with lies, until fantasy overtakes reality. The truth is never enough. That's why I write novels.

CLAIRE MESSUD: Again, it's like music—visceral. I don't include many real events in my fiction. When I do, they're snatches or partial elements of distorted versions of real events. I have a code of ethics for this that probably wouldn't make sense to anyone else but makes sense to me. That's just how it is.

AKHIL SHARMA: I try not to be hurtful to relatives who might recognize themselves in the book. Still, the "real" events that happen in my fiction happened to me and so I feel that I have a right to write about my experiences.

CHRIS ABANI: I am not the best person to answer this question, as I don't believe anything is real outside of the imagination.

JOSÉ MANUEL PRIETO: I would say yes, in an obtuse manner, taking weight off real details, to say it like that, taking them to a higher level of abstraction. That, I believe, is fundamental. And that, sometimes, is given by time. But if not a lot of time has gone by, then it is better to get close from sort of far away, forget a lot of what is known.

MICHAEL CHABON: Yes, by memory. Which is inherently a fictionalizing tool.

RODRIGO FRESÁN: No. But I try to have those real-life events be as unreal and unlikely as possible. The concept of reality as something credible is sadly overrated. A day doesn't go by without reality slapping us with something that could not or should not happen but does anyway.

T COOPER: I have no idea whether I'm successful or not, but in general, I just try to seek out unexplored corners of things that happened in the past. I try to get into the dusty corners and attics and look around for perspectives and voices and moments and flickers of the kinds of moments that don't end up in the history books or most people's perceptions of how a particular event or period went down.

YIYUN LI: I would use the events as a frame but the characters should be born out of my imagination.

ADAM MANSBACH: Not deliberately. But I find that my fiction tends to want to do one of two things with real events. With events of historical significance, it wants to invent alternate versions, and illuminate unseen corners, explore the way what is in the history books ripples out to affect ordinary people in unknown ways, far from ground zero. This desire was the impetus for the anthology I edited with T Cooper, *A Fictional History of the United States with Huge Chunks Missing*; we asked contributors to help us break up the hegemony of the way history is written by versioning it.

When I'm drawing from real life in quieter ways—making use of something that happened to me, or a story I heard that piqued my imagination—my impulse is usually to make things darker and weirder than they were, to tease out dormant, perhaps imagined, conflicts and tensions and motivations. For example, in *The End of the Jews*, the main character, Tristan Brodsky, has a friendship with a professor named Peter Pendergast, a Boston Brahmin type. Pendergast becomes his guardian angel: his machinations keep Tristan out of the war, help him win awards, etc., but Tristan nurtures a deep resentment toward this man because he doesn't respect Peter's work and feels like Peter is using him to advance a social agenda, make himself feel better by bringing a Jew into the mainstream. It pits Tristan's ambition against his conscience. In real life, my grandfather, who was a lawyer, had a WASP mentor who got him jobs, used him to integrate clubs that didn't admit Jews, etc. But my grandfather spoke of this man only with the greatest love and admiration. Which is less interesting.

IS THE STRUCTURE OF A NOVEL USUALLY A CHOICE, OR DOES IT JUST HAPPEN?

PAUL AUSTER: I've always believed that the content of a book creates its form. You discover how to do it in the process of doing it.

MARIO VARGAS LLOSA: I believe every writer has a style, a method, idiosyncrasies, personal story. In my case, my novels follow a process that always begins with a lived experience. Something I saw, something I heard, something I experienced, something I read. And that forms images in my memory that little by little turn into a stimulus to fantasize from those images. A long time passes sometimes between the stimulating lived experience and the point I start working.

But when I start working I am usually very confused and I start writing with a nebulous idea of what I want to do, a character, or situation, or trajectory. I never begin to write before doing a few outlines, overall trajectories of what a character's development is from this point to that one, then how these trajectories crisscross. That gives me at least the minimum comfort to begin writing.

Now, when I begin to write, the first version of what I write is very chaotic—a kind of magma, confusing—but even this gives me a sense of comfort I don't have at the beginning. Then I begin to rewrite, which is what I like. It's what gives me pleasure and when I can work with more enthusiasm—with the knowledge that the story I want to tell is there in the raw material.

And then I work a lot on structure, points of view, on chronology. Generally I even do a third revision where I work much more on language. That is more or less the process that I've followed for all the novels I've written.

CLAIRE MESSUD: It's some inexplicable combination of the two. How do you build a sandcastle? Same thing.

ADANIA SHIBLI: At the outset, it may appear as if it just happens, but I'm certain that unconsciously it does not, that it is structured, that it pours out throughout a long period, slowly and persistently, every day, until the work is finished.

CRISTINA GARCIA: It usually begins to suggest itself in the second or third year of a novel. I'm still writing pretty messily at that point. Other times I need to impose a structure, even as I'm aware that it could change.

CHRIS ADRIAN: It is generally an overconsidered choice, and precedes any progress on the more important things like what actually happens in the story.

ALEKSANDAR HEMON: Nothing just happens. At the very least, you recognize the structure in the mess you've written. That's what editing is supposed to do. I make all the choices and decisions. There is no other agency in my writing.

RICK MOODY: It happens.

MICHAEL CHABON: It starts out just happening, and then sooner or later you realize that you have been making a choice.

SAŠA STANIŠIĆ: With me—it happens. But I've heard rumors about writers who know exactly what to do and how to do it from the beginning.

COLM TÓIBÍN: It comes after rhythm, and then after character and it is an aspect of plot. In my books, nothing just happens. If that started, I would go to law school.

DANIEL HANDLER: It's a choice.

ADAM MANSBACH: I tend to want to have a certain kind of structural symmetry, strike a certain balance between different voices or plotlines or time periods or whatever I'm juggling. I tend to know what that symmetry should feel like before I begin. The specifics of how it's achieved may change, but the conception of the symmetry itself, I seem to hold on to, if that makes sense.

RODDY DOYLE: Always a choice. Often a late choice. For example, the shape of *The Woman Who Walked into Doors* came to me late in the second year, of two. I had the writing, but not the structure that would bring it properly alive.

DINAW MENGESTU: I think it's a mix. The structure of the novel asserts itself to some degree as soon as you begin writing, but I think you also have to put your own critical skills as a reader to use to make sure that it's a structure that actually works.

GLEN DAVID GOLD: Early on, I don't think about structure. It's all playtime and experiment and question marks. But after a while, recess is over and it's time to impose, artificially and horribly, something recognizable. That's often painful but it's exhilarating as then I know what the book will look like.

EDWIDGE DANTICAT: I think sometimes it's a choice and sometimes it just happens based on what the story's doing. It all depends on the story.

RABIH ALAMEDDINE: My first two novels' structures were determined even before I started. For the second one, I wanted to write a tribute to Calvino, a novel of first chapters, and I was interested in what would happen if the same person couldn't go past the first chapter. With the first line I wanted to reflect the chaos of the time, so the book had to be chaotic. This one, like I said, took five years just to get an idea of what the structure is. And once I got the structure—once I understood that it's a book on storytelling, I determined the structure.

NELL FREUDENBERGER: I've only written one. I wished at the time that the structure was more elegant, but it did seem to be determined by who the characters were (and therefore which parts of the story they could tell) rather than by any preconceived design of my own.

STEPHEN KING: With me, narrative is instinctive; structure is strictly maintained. Structure gives form.

SANTIAGO RONCAGLIOLO: It tends to be an outgrowth of the subject and the plot. Therefore, it arises naturally while I attend to other problems.

RODRIGO FRESÁN: I begin with a very slight sketch of the scenery and then see what happens. Generally I work in three modes or parts.

That's the frame of reference. What happens is that each of those modes is another thing. The key is in trying to surprise myself while writing. Make me feel a bit like a reader.

SUSAN MINOT: Nothing gets put down unless my pen puts it there, so I would say it all is a choice.

JOSÉ MANUEL PRIETO: For the three novels in the Russian trilogy it was a conscious choice because structure is very important for all three. For the first, the *Encyclopedia*, it is the organization as a detailed dictionary, in alphabetical order; for *Nocturnal Butterflies of the Russian Empire*, which is organized as correspondence, but they really are long reflections, the draft of a long letter the main character will write at some point after the last page; and for *Rex*, the annotated text: the novel is organized in twelve comments, etc.

SUSAN CHOI: I sometimes make choices at the start, but whether or not they're honored by the book seems outside of my control. I "chose" to make *A Person of Interest* a very plot-driven, forward-moving, present-tense novel, and look at how much of it takes place in the past, and is elliptical.

A. M. HOMES: It's a process—so the material, the story in part dictate the form.

DO YOU WRITE IN SEQUENCE?

COLM TÓIBÍN: Of course I do. Is there another way to write?

HARUKI MURAKAMI: Always in sequence.

RODRIGO FRESÁN: No. Absolutely not.

JONATHAN LETHEM: I'm religious about it. "In sequence" seems to me fiction's law, just as in life time's arrow has us, for better or worse, completely moving in one direction. The reader will turn pages in sequence, so what advantage could there ever be in alienating myself from this fundamental structure of engagement with the story as I make it? I can't see one.

TAYARI JONES: I always think I am writing in sequence, but I often end up moving things around.

RICK MOODY: Not always.

ANDREW SEAN GREER: I do. I can't imagine any other way to do it—how could the end of the novel echo all of the imagery and symbolism of the last three hundred pages unless they are already written?

CHRIS ADRIAN: Almost never. . . . I generally bounce around in different places, and then the last few months of work is putting the different pieces together in this weird Ikea furniture process. It is generally the hardest part of the whole thing, and usually about as pleasurable as putting together nonmetaphorical Ikea furniture.

SUSAN CHOI: I did with *A Person of Interest*—I wrote it straight through, from page one to page four hundred or so, as if it were a serial I had to deliver at the end of every working day. I'd never done this before and I don't know if I'll do it again, but it was certainly my favorite way I've ever written anything.

CHRIS ABANI: No, I write like a moviemaker. I write scenes and then edit them together.

ADAM MANSBACH: Yes. In the sequence in which the words and chapters are going to appear in the book, rather than in chronological sequence. Sometimes it would be far easier to skip ahead, or move according to chronology, but I can't. I have this conviction that you can't leapfrog, you've got to know everything that's happened before the sentence you're writing. Often, that's utterly untrue, but I hold on to it anyway.

STEPHEN KING: Yes.

AKHIL SHARMA: Yes.

JENNIFER EGAN: Generally yes, even if the sequence is out of sequence. Because at least with a first draft, I'm writing as if I were reading: seeing the action unfold over time and hopefully being surprised by it.

ALEKSANDAR HEMON: Sometimes. But that does not mean that the book is being created in sequence.

YIYUN LI: Yes. I am very bad at jumping from chapter to chapter and I have to write in sequence.

DANIEL HANDLER: I write in rough sequence, occasionally skipping ahead.

EDWIDGE DANTICAT: I do write in sequence, but if a scene feels too menacing or too big, I'll skip right to it to remove the feeling of having a mountain ahead to climb. Also having written the "big scene" sometimes informs the scenes that come before it.

NELL FREUDENBERGER: For the most part I do, except that I sometimes have an idea for a scene or conversation that comes later in the story. With my novel and a couple of stories, I've had an idea about how they would end once I got to the middle. I wrote those endings as soon as I had the ideas, and in each case I didn't end up changing them drastically.

PAUL AUSTER: Yes. Sentence by sentence by sentence, from the first word of the book to the last.

RODDY DOYLE: Yes, although I often mess with the sequence once I have it down.

MICHAEL CHABON: Always. Can't even imagine skipping around. When I have (rarely) tried to do it, I felt nauseated and unable to proceed.

DINAW MENGESTU: I tell myself that I'm writing in sequence, but as a novel takes shape, inevitably it turns out that chapters, pages, paragraphs, and some sentences need to be picked up and moved to someplace more fitting.

JOSÉ MANUEL PRIETO: Not necessarily. I can first write a scene and later what preceded it. But afterward the job of making both fit together is very delicate. I always remember that Vladimir Nabokov wrote in large cards he stored in a shoebox and then moved them fluidly throughout the body of the text. Same with Proust, who famously glued in pages and pages of extra text just before publication. Nowadays we use the "insert" function in our word processors in much the same way.

SUSAN MINOT: I think it's safe to say never. For very short stories I might come close to it.

T COOPER: Yes. I don't know why I can't do it any other way, but my brain just needs to do everything in sequence—especially when several years of history are covered in the narrative in addition to the usual changes that you want to take place in your characters' lives.

CLAIRE MESSUD: Yes.

A. M. HOMES: Mostly.

AMY TAN: Pretty much so. So much of a story for me is about movement so I have to write in sequence. I do go back and I might insert
things that may not have been part of the story. Always, the book
changes.

ANN CUMMINS: I always think I'm writing in sequence until I come
to the dreadful dead spot where I have no idea how to continue. Then I
put the chapter or character or whatever aside, work on something else,
and go back to the first material after I've gotten a little distance and can
usually see possibility and relevance better.

WHAT NOVEL'S STRUCTURE DO YOU
MOST ADMIRE? WHY?

FRANCISCO GOLDMAN: I love books that have a complex, seemingly
effortless elegance and simplicity to their structures that always totally
eludes me. Ishiguro's *Never Let Me Go*, for example, the relentless inevitable journey to death—recounted almost like a classical myth—in a
story paradoxically filled with light. I love, for similar reasons, the narrative structures, even if they seem more elaborate, of Orhan Pamuk's
Snow and Saramago's *The Year of the Death of Ricardo Reis*. The structures
of Gabriel García Márquez's novels, from *Chronicle of a Death Foretold*,
One Hundred Years of Solitude—well, just about all of them are astonishing. I would never even try to do something like that—I think I prefer,
if only because it's all I'm probably capable of anyway, looser structures—
but I love studying and trying to dissect the way those novels are put
together.

AMY TAN: The structure that I very much admired while writing *The Joy Luck Club* was *Love Medicine* by Louise Erdrich. It's a book of linked stories set in a community, like what I was working on.

SAŠA STANIŠIĆ: The not-boring one.

AKHIL SHARMA: *War and Peace, Ulysses.* The ability of these books to keep so many things in play simultaneously is supernatural.

JOSÉ MANUEL PRIETO: Joseph Conrad's *Lord Jim* is one of the ones I admire the most. The novel is narrated by someone who knows what the story is but is not the main character. That gives the narrator a very comfortable distance, it allows for a friendly first person, with an intimate tone, but from a narrator not directly involved in the events. It's the way Fitzgerald's *The Great Gatsby* or *Doctor Faustus* by Thomas Mann is told. Also, since the narrator has the whole consummated story at hand, he can move around at will within it, at first tell something about the future, then the past, etc. That gives it a favorable density, makes it more complex.

CLAIRE MESSUD: I'm not sure I can answer that with a single answer. I admire Peter Carey's *Oscar and Lucinda.* I admire Thomas Bernhard's *The Loser.* I admire Proust's *In Search of Lost Time.* I admire David Mitchell's *Cloud Atlas.* I admire Marilynne Robinson's *Housekeeping.* I admire Italo Svevo's *Zeno's Conscience.* I admire Joseph Conrad's *Under Western Eyes.* And so on. Almost each time someone writes a novel, they reinvent the novel's structure; which means there are a lot of different versions to admire.

TAYARI JONES: I love *The Sound and the Fury.* I love the different voices speaking about the same events. Also, I love that you can read it backward.

ALAA AL ASWANY: I would answer this with a very beautiful sentence of Giangiacomo Feltrinelli, my publisher in Italy, who said, "I only know two kinds of novels: the epic novels and living novels. I only publish living ones." I admire the living novels: even if the structure is problematic, I don't care. I will give you examples from two great novelists. One of them is, I believe, the greatest novelist ever known, Dostoyevsky. In structure and form, his novels were not really perfect, sometimes were not even organized, but because of the power of the art, you just don't care about this. What you get is much more profound than the form. And I will give you another example, one of the greatest American novelists, Henry Miller. Miller wrote what you could call a novel without any form, a compilation of autobiography and fiction. He kept writing about what happened to him, and sometimes interspersed poems, quotes from Dostoyevsky, or Spengler, you see, but still he wrote masterpieces.

YIYUN LI: This is a hard question. I don't know. *Doctor Zhivago* comes to my mind, as there are several threads interwoven very nicely in that novel. But I don't know if it is the structure that I admire or simply the complexity of the novel.

RODRIGO FRESÁN: I suppose *Slaughterhouse-Five* by Kurt Vonnegut (where the lack of structure is the theme) and *The Dream of Heroes* by Adolfo Bioy Casares in that it's a novella where the whole book is about trying to remember a story from another night.

CHRIS ABANI: There isn't one novel, but I like novels that risk nonlinear narratives and break form, and take language risks too.

COLM TÓIBÍN: I love John McGahern's *Amongst Women* for its use of telling and then showing, its ability to sum up and then slow down. I love Joyce's *Ulysses* for how it developed and changed and became more interesting the more of it he wrote. I love Nadine Gordimer's *The Late*

Bourgeois World for the sheer perfect simplicity of its structure. I love anything by Conrad for the risks he takes with structure. *The Portrait of a Lady* is as beautifully structured as Chartres Cathedral. I wish more American novelists would study Henry James.

SUSAN MINOT: I have always admired the structure of *To the Lighthouse*. It is original and delivers the material in the most elegant and subtle way.

DINAW MENGESTU: *Herzog* by Saul Bellow is pretty high up there. It's a deceptively simple structure, but when you read it again you see how he's able to jump across decades while still keeping the reader firmly grounded in one moment.

RODDY DOYLE: I've always loved the shape of Joan Didion's novels. I love the way phrases and events are repeated, slightly altered. I also love the structure of Joyce Carol Oates's *Black Water*—again, it's the significant repetition. Repetition as novelty. I loved Flann O'Brien's *At Swim-Two-Birds* when I was a teenager, and still do; it broke all the rules. They're today's choice.

CRISTINA GARCIA: I love the structure of Anne Carson's *Autobiography of Red*. It's a prose poem, really, but I love the way she did it. I thought it was extraordinary. I loved Sebald's *The Emigrants* when he did those four novellas. His use of collage and kind of faux-documentary techniques— it was outstanding. I love Virginia Woolf's *Mrs. Dalloway*, which to me is almost like one of those conch shells you can stumble upon in Key West, once in a while . . . just sort of the circularity of it, the round-robin point of view. Those are just three but I could go on and on.

ALEKSANDAR HEMON: *Austerlitz* by W. G. Sebald. Because all of his aesthetic and structural choices are at the same time ethical choices. The structure therefore looks not only inevitable, but necessary.

RICK MOODY: *The Good Soldier* features a structure I admire. The contemporary novel is at its best when displaying fragmentary consciousness and multiple·points of view. Ford's novel is perhaps (not to mention *The Sound and the Fury*) the best example of this modernist suppleness with respect to point of view. I also very much admire the structure of *Pale Fire* by Nabokov. Structure in Nabokov is almost always very appealing. The entire tradition of the European novel, if we were going to make crude distinctions, is much more finely attuned to structure than is the American novel. The twentieth-century American novel is often notable for its plodding, graceless, and brainless approach to structure.

SANTIAGO RONCAGLIOLO: Mario Vargas Llosa's *Aunt Julia and the Scriptwriter*, because as the plot unfolds, the structure becomes the subject of the story. I don't normally enjoy gratuitous pyrotechnics by an author, but in that novel, that extraordinary craftsman created a perfect narrative.

SUSAN CHOI: *The Age of Innocence*, because it's perfect. Not an unnecessary word, and nothing missing.

CURTIS SITTENFELD: I think *The Line of Beauty* by Alan Hollinghurst is pretty much perfect, structurally and otherwise.

NELL FREUDENBERGER: I admire the economy of J. M. Coetzee's novels, especially *The Life and Times of Michael K*. Michael's story seems to divide itself neatly into three discrete parts, and yet Coetzee finds a way to introduce the voice of another character—someone morally compromised and therefore closer to the reader (at least to this reader)—without sacrificing the elegance of the book's structure. I think I'm mentioning *Anna Karenina* too often, but I admire the opposite thing in Tolstoy: the sprawling quality of the novels and long stories. I think that's because he's a completely loyal servant to character, and he'll make any leap (no matter how distracting) in order to further illuminate the people he's describing.

DANIEL HANDLER: *Madame Bovary* has a gorgeous structure, inventive but not show-offy, carefully constructed but with lots of room to maneuver.

MEHMET MURAT SOMER: Structurewise, my all-time favorite is Honoré de Balzac. He created a complete and vast picture of the France of his time. A secondary character in one novel is the protagonist of the other, a shop that people pass by in one book becomes a different novella with its own story. I love this. When reading them, finding these little connections and references gives me joy. As respect, I try to do the same: create my own Istanbul. There are shared characters even between *Champagne Trilogy* and the Hop-Çiki-Yaya thrillers, sometimes just cameos.

RABIH ALAMEDDINE: I like Calvino a lot because he valued structure so much, but he uses so many different ones. I don't know that there's any novel's structure that I most admire. I believe the structure is part of the novel itself and for a lot of people it's secondary. In some ways, when it's a great book, you don't even realize that there's a structure. Like when somebody asks you "What's your favorite sentence in a book?" If it's a great book, you really don't remember what that sentence is. You're just reading the entire thing. You're taken in first by the novel itself.

ANN CUMMINS: I admire novels where structure reflects content. Like Michael Ondaatje's *Coming Through Slaughter*. It's a kitchen soup kind of a book with lists and songs and poetry. It's jagged, like jazz, which is great since it's about Buddy Bolden, the great New Orleans cornet player. Doctorow's *Ragtime* is another such novel. It's structured like a rag.

MICHAEL CHABÒN: *Pale Fire*, I guess. Also tough to overlook *Cloud Atlas*. The effortless formality of them.

STEPHEN KING: Hard to say, but *The Raw Shark Texts* is very cool. Why? It challenges traditional narrative structure in a way that advances the story; Hall isn't merely showing off. There's actually a little flip-book shark in there! It attacks the reader!

Chapter 4

CHARACTER AND SCENE

DO YOU TEND TO IDENTIFY WITH ONE
CHARACTER IN YOUR NOVELS MORE
THAN THE OTHERS?

AKHIL SHARMA: I do. But I am willing to abandon this character if he doesn't work for the novel.

CHRIS ADRIAN: I tend to afflict multiple characters with my own faults and insecurities.

JOSH EMMONS: One character will usually appeal to me more than others because they're either just like me or nothing like me, depending on where I fall in the self-love to self-loathing continuum while writing, or simply because they're the protagonist and so command more of my time and focus, but I try to fully and democratically identify with all of my characters. Even the unlikable ones. Especially them. The better we understand why someone behaves badly or unattractively, the more convincingly we'll render them on the page. Characters come alive in all their maddening complexity when their motivation is apparent to readers, which requires that we both understand that motivation and adopt it ourselves.

YAEL HEDAYA: I try to be fair. Democratic. Unbiased. But the truth is that there's always more of me in a certain character, and people who know me well always say, Oh come on: she's you. Totally. Even if I myself don't see it or insist on denying it. There's always the character that gets more of my chromosomes than the others, the poor thing.

ANN CUMMINS: Actually, for *Yellowcake*, I auditioned characters I thought it would be fun to embody. When I was a kid, I had very lively make-believe friends, all of whom I found much more interesting than me. As a novelist, I just feed my childhood appetite for playing. I'm drawn to wicked types. I do find that in the process of developing characters, I always end up liking them, even the villains. They become very human for me.

GLEN DAVID GOLD: Emotionally? 100 percent. Literally, i.e., physical details and such . . . not so much.

SAŠA STANIŠIĆ: I like and dislike them pretty much all the same. Of course some of those ghosts are kind of more important than the others, but I never fool myself into giving them too much reality-credit. They are my inventions, I am their king and dictator of their life and death.

NELL FREUDENBERGER: In stories or a novel, I think you can only write from the point of view of people with whom you identify. The other characters may be in there, but you can't use them to tell the story.

RICK MOODY: In the end, I identify with all of them. But I often imagine, at the outset, that there's going to be one I like more than others. These preconceptions can quickly be scuttled in the compositional process. Characters I have believed to be *villains* often exhibit heroic qualities, and the *heroes* are often very flawed. I find something about failure incredibly human and moving and so characters that others think of as *losers* are often the ones to whom I am most sympathetic. I have to work hard to love the sheep who do *not* go astray.

FRANCISCO GOLDMAN: Ideally all kind of equally, no?

CLAIRE MESSUD: Perhaps I tend to identify more with two or three characters in any given novel. It's hard to say. Sometimes I don't care for much about a character; but that doesn't mean I don't identify with them. I don't know that I can answer this question accurately, because I think identification of some kind is essential to the creation of a character.

ALEJANDRO ZAMBRA: Yes. I need that identification while writing. I don't deny or battle against it. In the two novels I've published there's a character who, in a manner of speaking, listens to the music I listen to. But the music I listen to is very diverse and very common. It's the music a lot of people listen to. Meaning that the identification is individual as well as social, with the group. If the character is like me it's because he's like a lot of people. Like everyone and no one. At times they make decisions I did not make and live a life I have not lived. At times they represent nostalgia for a road not taken. Which doesn't mean they stop being ordinary.

RABIH ALAMEDDINE: Yes, usually the narrator. And even though at times, like in this latest book, there are other characters that are probably closer to me as a person than the narrator. But I usually tend to use a first-person narration, so by the time the novel gets going, I'm usually fully identified with it.

MICHAEL CHABON: Only when it's a first-person narrator.

CRISTINA GARCIA: There are characters that are so fun to write that I become kind of partial to them. And weirdly enough, they're the characters who are the most buffoonish, the over-the-top Cubans, which is ironic, because they're the same people who drive me nuts in real life, but I have a fantastic time being in their skin when I'm writing about them. I'm thinking, for example, of the Fernando character in *A Handbook to Luck*. He's probably my most recent favorite character.

STEPHEN KING: Usually.

JONATHAN LETHEM: I've almost always explicitly split my character-istics, my emotions, my anecdotes, my opinions—and with them, as-pects of identification—among several characters. And yet of course there often ends up being one with whom identification is strongest. Most inevitably, the first-person narrator, when I've used one.

SUSAN CHOI: No—I tend to love them all, even the bit players.

JOSÉ MANUEL PRIETO: I think it is almost inevitable, there's always someone that attracts you more, who you feel more sympathy for, more empathy, whose motives you know better or can better imagine. But the difficulty is exactly moving from that zone, toward characters different from you, be it due to gender or lived experience or age. That is the ma-jor challenge.

DANIEL HANDLER: I tend to like my female characters more, but I'm not sure that's identifying.

ADAM MANSBACH: I try not to. I think it's crucial that you be equally invested in each character—to go back to the chess metaphor, writing a novel is like playing a game against yourself, and you've got to flip the board after every move, and look at it from the other perspective. I find that readers, at least mine, are obsessed with the question of autobiography, and so I often find myself explaining that there is not one character in a novel who is me, but rather that they all are. You've got to imbue characters with as much humanity as you can, and so they all have to come out of you, on an emotional, psychological level, no matter how different from yours their minds and biographies are. More than anything else, I think that is what I love about writing novels: because of the central imperative to understand your characters, fiction is an immensely humanitarian endeavor, despite its inherent isolation and the enormous ego necessary to do it.

RODRIGO FRESÁN: No. But usually they tend to be writers. So a certain identification is inevitable.

MEHMET MURAT SOMER: I don't, but most of my readers believe I do because the Hop-Çiki-Yaya thrillers are written in the first-person narrative. Naturally, my observations, thoughts, and feelings are in the text, but they are filtered through many fictional devices. Even some critics pointed out that my approach to all my characters in the *Champagne Trilogy* is distant and restrained.

TAYARI JONES: Yes, but it isn't always the main character. I actually find that I write better if the main character is interrogating my own point of view.

ALEKSANDAR HEMON: No. I am every character in my books. Some I spend more time with, as they spend more time in the book. I spent years figuring out what Flaubert meant when he said: "Emma Bovary— c'est moi." He became Emma Bovary while writing the novel. You become everyone in your novel.

A. M. HOMES: It's always a mix; I identify with different aspects of the characters and am equally interested in those I feel very little identification with.

JENNIFER EGAN: If I do, it's often a peripheral character—never the actual protagonist. For example, the character in *Look at Me* who is most like me is the nerdy academic, Irene, who is hardly the focus of the novel. That said, I also tend to identify with all of the characters in my novels, at least to some extent—in other words, I don't think I can really write about someone at all unless I identify with them in a fairly deep way. And that includes people we might call "bad." I'd go so far as to say that the job of characterization in fiction is to make every character identifiable—known to the extent that labels like "good" and "bad" no longer really apply.

COLM TÓIBÍN: The third-person intimate through whose eyes the world is seen; or the first-person narrator. No one else much.

SANTIAGO RONCAGLIOLO: No. All the characters represent me and my personal conflicts in one way or another. But some receive more attention because I find it easier to reproduce their voices in a realistic manner, or because of structural necessity.

DINAW MENGESTU: Since I'm writing in the first person inevitably I'm spending more time in the head of a single character, which doesn't necessarily mean that I identify with that character more. It does mean, however, that I inhabit that character more fully, that their voice continues to linger in my head long after I've stopped writing.

RODDY DOYLE: Half my books have been written in the first person, so, yes, I identify with the narrator. I have to, in order to find the language I need to drive the story, and the geography and humor, etc. My first book, *The Commitments*, was more of an ensemble piece, but I still let one character, Jimmy Rabbitte, do most of the seeing. It was his book.

EDWIDGE DANTICAT: Yes. Usually the main character. Perhaps because that's the person I know the most about.

T COOPER: I identify equally with all of my characters, even when one seems to be more "like" me in some ways. I feel as though liking or identifying with one character more than others would leave those others open to the possibility of not being as rich and three-dimensional as any character I might identify with more closely. I always find it odd when people ask me, or even just assume, that one character is more "autobiographical" than another; I feel it's my job to care for, identify with, and ultimately render all of my characters with equal depth and levels of identification.

YIYUN LI: No. I think that would be unfair for the other characters.

CHRIS ABANI: Not really. The characters I write about, while obviously related to me, are often furthest from my true life.

ANDREW SEAN GREER: Yes, and I try to make him the villain.

HOW MUCH DO YOU DRAW FROM YOUR OWN LIFE WHEN CONSTRUCTING A CHARACTER?

MICHAEL CHABON: Heavily and consistently but in oblique and stealthy ways.

FRANCISCO GOLDMAN: In my first novel, Roger is obviously autobiographical, though there is a great deal of fiction in that character. Now I am making a novel out of Aura's life and death, and so "I" am there, but in the end I can only say what I want to say, I can only make the kind of novel that I like and that she liked, by fictionalizing. I tell lies about myself and discover truths, about myself and maybe about Aura and about us, if not the truth.

PAUL AUSTER: Very little. But there have been times when I've used events from my own life in my fiction. Nothing of any great consequence, but nevertheless small details and memories sometimes creep in.

DANIEL HANDLER: Probably more than I think I do.

JENNIFER EGAN: Very little. As I said before, involving my real life tends to trip me up. I'm at my best when I'm pulling it all out of my own mind.

ALEKSANDAR HEMON: I like to invent lives that could have been mine. Which is to say that some characters' lives are at the same time similar and entirely different from mine. My life has hierarchies that are fundamentally different from the hierarchies in my books. But drawing from your own life to construct a character in no way guarantees that the characters are going to be alive.

HARUKI MURAKAMI: It depends.

SANTIAGO RONCAGLIOLO: A lot. I need to write about something familiar to feel comfortable with a text. I once tried to write a novel set in 1930s Germany. I didn't even make it to the fiftieth page: I didn't know how the characters spoke, what they thought, how they made love. A disaster. I usually begin with personal feelings and I dress them up and put makeup on them with imaginary details. Thus literature becomes an exercise in exhibitionism and, at the same time, of modesty.

CHRIS ABANI: I draw all emotional resonance from my life, but little else.

NELL FREUDENBERGER: I don't usually write about places I haven't been. I try to describe things I've actually seen, and if they're impossible to see in person, I try to look at a picture. I think all writers draw from a limited number of emotional events or obsessions that come from their own lives, but it's probably best if those can emerge accidentally rather than deliberately. I think writers should only write about things they don't understand, since the writing is a way to figure out what things mean.

RODRIGO FRESÁN: Lots. But, generally, I lend them tastes and hobbies rather than biographical facts.

EDWIDGE DANTICAT: Sometimes I try to imagine how I would respond to something to determine how a character should act or react. I infuse a lot of my own emotions into my characters. I also borrow physical and psychological traits from friends and family members.

STEPHEN KING: Everything starts with me. Even if I'm trying to mimic someone from real life—Dick Cheney in the new book was a touchstone for one character—it obviously comes out of my imagination.

CHRIS ADRIAN: A great deal in some ways, and not very much in others. I think I spend a lot of time making some aspects of characters deliberately more grotesque than I am grotesque or my life is grotesque, but occasionally I make a studied effort to make them less grotesque than me.

CLAIRE MESSUD: Madame Bovary, c'est moi. How much does anyone draw from life? You can only know what you know. In creating the emotional underpinning of a character, inevitably you draw from what you have experienced and seen; but does that mean you are drawing from your own life, or from life in general? I don't know.

ANDREW SEAN GREER: Very very little, though I try to keep people in mind when I am drawing characters that are difficult to picture.

SAŠA STANIŠIĆ: Eighty-five percent.

ALEJANDRO ZAMBRA: Everything. What I've seen, what I've lived. In the first drafts I even use real names (in *Bonsai* I forgot to change the names of three or four secondary characters). The places I mention are places I've lived in. I think it's not necessary to invent so much. And, on the other hand, it would cause me lots of difficulty. I couldn't create a scene in a city I don't know and I know very few, to tell the truth.

TAYARI JONES: I set most of my work in Atlanta, a city I know very well. I pull from these insider details constantly. I do it to make the story more real, but also to preserve my memories of a rapidly changing city.

COLM TÓIBÍN: Very little, and then, slowly, everything. This is because a novel is a thousand or two thousand details. Through the emotional and physical details the world becomes known. You tend to use what is deeply familiar, or even better, what is hidden from you and discovered only as you work—memories, traumas, key scenes, fears.

T COOPER: Very little. I may do the requisite putting oneself into a particular situation and seeing how I might feel, what I might say, do, etc. But I'm not particularly drawn to writing autobiographical stories— perhaps I'll feel differently when I've lived longer.

ANN CUMMINS: I don't consciously draw from my own life, though I think some characters have come into being as mouthpieces for me. This is especially true in the first-person stories in *Red Ant House*. In *Yellowcake*, my father did inspire one character—the aging, ailing, and crotchety former uranium miller, Ryland Mahoney. Like him, my father was a "right to work" guy, very proud, but also smart and loyal. Like Ryland, my father had a long, debilitating illness, which was very traumatic and difficult for the family. His struggles—and my mother's—inspired the novel.

AKHIL SHARMA: Enormously. It is hard to know if a character is acting in a realistic manner unless you can test it against your own experiences.

YAEL HEDAYA: Most of the drawing is done subconsciously. When I was younger, I did everything possible to conceal my life, distance myself from my characters, but lately I find that I have no qualms about exposing myself. I mean, I've worked so hard creating characters who are total strangers, don't I deserve being a character myself? So I'm experimenting. Splicing myself, re-creating, or just plain blabbing and confessing (the book I'm working on now is all in the first person, with multiple characters, all talking a mile a minute, going on and on, shamelessly). Maybe it's because I really long to go back to therapy but can't afford it. So I'm giving myself sessions through my writing, and enjoying it tremendously.

YIYUN LI: I don't draw much from my own life. I think I would draw from my observations and my memories of other people.

JOSH EMMONS: Emotionally, I draw everything from it when constructing characters because passion and fear and happiness and jealousy and anger are the same for everyone in kind, if not in degree, so to write persuasively about someone's panic at the sight of their family being threatened you have only to remember how it felt to see something/one you valued in jeopardy, and then to adjust that memory's intensity accordingly.

RODDY DOYLE: At one level, not at all; none of them are me, or attempts at me. At other levels, I do draw on my life, or my version of my life, to get closer to creating the fictional characters, to make them convincing. I've used the geography of the area I live in, school experiences, as a student and teacher, my recollection of pain and how I tried to deal with it, grief, happiness—all of it, really. Although I've no interest at all in writing about myself.

JOSÉ MANUEL PRIETO: That is inevitable also: any character is a collage of the people you know, gestures, words, attitudes. Only you know, really, what your characters are made of. I almost never copy someone directly, but only a few details, features of various people.

A. M. HOMES: Not much. I am truly a writer of fiction, I work from my imagination.

DINAW MENGESTU: I think you're always drawing on your own life to some degree or another. My characters don't live the same life as me, but they are the sum of my experiences and my thoughts.

RICK MOODY: I think it's useful to start with life drawing, but to feel free to depart. After all, what does it mean to *know* a person or to imagine you do? A person's character is a collection of tendencies, as a quark is a set of probabilities with regard to location or velocity, and if you have not seen this person in *all* possible situations, you have not known the person. Accordingly, we can make predictions about a character, but in truth we don't know how he or she is going to act in all circumstances. In the construction of narrative, despite what Nabokov has to say on the subject, the characters can occasionally behave in a way that is out of character. In fact, this may be when they become interesting. It's important to allow for discovery, for surprise, for adventure in the construction of character, and to avoid shutting down such thoughts as: *he wouldn't really act like this.* The only time you really need to worry about credibility in character, I suspect, is when you are writing dialogue. Then you really want to work carefully, diligently.

HAVE YOU EVER CONSCIOUSLY USED A FICTIONAL CHARACTER TO DRAW A PORTRAIT OF A REAL PERSON? WHAT DID YOU LEARN?

ANNE ENRIGHT: Never—I don't think I could. (Good question!) So wherever they come from it is not from other people's work—that would be like eating someone's chewed food.

STEPHEN KING: Yes. Sort of. What did I learn? Huh? What is all this about learning?

DANIEL HANDLER: I've learned that some people will find themselves in anything.

YIYUN LI: I wrote a novel (a failed first novel) that had one character that was a portrait of a real person, and I think the novel failed for that reason. (There were four other characters constructed out of my imagination and they were all fine.)

RABIH ALAMEDDINE: Yes, yes. What did I learn? Everybody believes that a good fictional character is three-dimensional and rounded. If that's true, then a real person is one hundred dimensional. We're all a lot more complex than we let the world see, and we're all a lot more complex than even we know.

HARUKI MURAKAMI: Sometimes I do. Nobody notices it anyway.

SANTIAGO RONCAGLIOLO: I've tried it, but human beings aren't interesting enough. I've always had to change them a lot, and add on characteristics of other human beings, so that they can work in fiction.

ALEKSANDAR HEMON: No.

CHRIS ADRIAN: In *The Children's Hospital* a number of the main characters' superiors were based on my own superiors as a resident. I learned that it complicates your interview for a job when the person interviewing you has recognized herself in your writing.

NELL FREUDENBERGER: I'm trying to do that now for the first time, and it's really hard. So far I've learned that you have to love someone (at least a little) in order to write about them, but that loving characters is dangerous, lest you make them too admirable, or their paths through life too smooth.

ADANIA SHIBLI: Yes, I sometimes do, but these characters I take from paintings only, and turn them into what may be like a living character in reality. This is amazingly magical in blurring fiction and reality, something that I discovered at the early stages of my childhood, and since then has been one of the most precious joys for me in life.

SUSAN CHOI: Not consciously, no. But of course this happens all the time.

RODDY DOYLE: I used real figures from Irish history, but once I had them opening their mouths and talking, they became as fictional as the fictional characters.

TAYARI JONES: I have tried to "use" real people in my fiction, but by the time I am finished writing, it isn't that person anymore. I can use things that a real person did. I can describe a house that a real person really lived in. However, to try and presume to know another person's true motives, thoughts, or feelings is the height of arrogance.

YAEL HEDAYA: All my characters are fictional, but if a pathologist did a postmortem on them, he'd probably find they have the organs, not to mention genes, of real people.

MEHMET MURAT SOMER: Yes sir! I plead guilty! I love to incorporate or encode some real-life people or gossip in my novels, usually as leitmotivs, side stories, or one-liners. I even used anagrams for certain names in *Champagne Trilogy*. It was kind of a puzzle for a close circle of friends. They said they enjoyed it enormously. Perhaps they lied to my face.

AKHIL SHARMA: No.

COLM TÓIBÍN: My father and mother were very useful to me, even more so when I was not conscious at first of what I was doing. When I became conscious I did it even more. I never learn.

EDWIDGE DANTICAT: No. Or maybe I don't understand the question. I've used real people to create fictional characters, yes. It's not as easy to do as it sounds.

RODRIGO FRESÁN: Yes, in *Kensington Gardens* I wrote extensively about James Matthew Barrie, the author of *Peter Pan*. I learned that I'll never attempt it again.

JONATHAN LETHEM: I've never done it directly, no. I always use bits and pieces, so all my characters have real DNA in them, but only in a Frankenstein way. Plus, they're all made out of other people's fictional characters, as well as real people. And they're all partly me, if I'm interested in them. I only broke this principle once, quite recently, to gratify a specific request by someone. It amused me to try, and the result was pretty charming to the novel in question—but then, my friend is pretty charming. Oddly enough, after doing it once, I was immediately compelled to use the same person again, so I built a short story around him, with which I was also very pleased. He comes out so differently each time, I may use this person again and again, who knows? Maybe I could even populate a whole novel with different versions of him.

JOSÉ MANUEL PRIETO: No, to be honest I've never done it, they're always a mix. What I have done is blend real characters with characteristics from fictional characters.

CLAIRE MESSUD: No, I haven't. Colm Tóibín once said you can either take the characters from real life, or the story from real life, but you can't have a story with neither, and it doesn't work so well with both. I certainly have taken the shell—that's to say, the narrative events—from the lives of people I do not know, or barely know, and have felt free to create characters to fit those events. But I haven't knowingly done the inverse, which is to say, taken people I know and created scenarios for them; or if I have, they have been transformed by the scenarios into people I didn't know. Writing transparently about people I know doesn't interest me.

A. M. HOMES: Yes, but only very minor characters. I learned that my friends like it when I use their names in a story.

JENNIFER EGAN: The character of Moose in *Look at Me* has some pretty strong similarities to someone I love a lot, and it was very hard to write him as a result—I tended to overindulge him, and he needed reining in at every turn. What I learned from that experience is that, indeed, I'm pretty lousy at using people I know, but that with hard work, I can do it if necessary.

FRANCISCO GOLDMAN: In my first novel, I wrote about my mother by creating a mother who was in every way the opposite of my real mother—in every way. My mother somehow saw through it, deciphering this portrait of herself by inverting every aspect of her fictional doppelganger, and she didn't like it. Read that way, it wasn't an unflattering portrait—my real-life mother, for example, never had an affair, while her fictional counterpart did—but still she felt violated. And she complained also that now everybody who read the book would think she was like the fictional mother, that that comical harridan and snob was the real her! I learned that you should if possible write novels without mothers in them. But it mostly isn't possible.

I think, by the way, that this ethos fiction writers develop in the United States—abetted by publishers' fears of lawsuits—that it is reprehensible to write about characters whose real-life models will recognize themselves, even if the portrait is not necessarily negative, is mostly laudable. (I am also mostly in favor of trampling on all pieties, so I am on both sides of this question at once, not without confusion.) It isn't always possible to avoid exploiting real people to make fictional characters, especially if you're not a writer like, say, Borges or Calvino—writers I, of course, revere—who seem to draw more purely on intellectual and poetic imagination. But in Latin America this ethos doesn't exist. Contemporary Latin American writers—including writers some North American readers and critics lavish praise on and probably regard as great and pure literary artists who couldn't possibly resort to such low literary villainy—draw from real life and savage recognizable people in their novels all the time! Maybe this reveals how tendentious or naive some of our ideas about literary "purity" actually are, I don't know. In Latin America, anyway, people don't necessarily expect a writer not to be a scoundrel too. But sometimes I've been shocked by the way people I know have been transparently depicted in novels—portrayals that I consider cruel and unfair, even in one or two novels written by good friends of mine. If you rebuke such a Latin American writer for this in any way, they accuse you of having lost your sense of humor, or of not understanding the nature of fiction. They also benefit from living in cultures where defamation suits of the kind practiced in the United States have little chance of prospering.

RICK MOODY: I learned that it doesn't work very well.

WHAT MAKES A CHARACTER COMPELLING?

CLAIRE MESSUD: What makes a person compelling? The same things make a character compelling. One thing I feel it would be important and revolutionary for the American reader to understand is that niceness will never make a character compelling. Niceness is not compelling.

JENNIFER EGAN: To my mind, contradictions—irreconcilable personality traits. Consistency is deadly in literary characterization, as in real people!

A. M. HOMES: The depth of their humanity, a sense of what they are struggling with.

MEHMET MURAT SOMER: When it comes to people, evil without a reason is compelling for me. But when it comes to fictional characters, I perceive the superficial ones to be more compelling. No depth of thoughts, feelings, behaviors . . .

MICHAEL CHABON: To write? My favorites are irritable, accurate ranters who tell painful truths in scabrous language. George Deasey in *The Amazing Adventures of Kavalier & Clay*; Inspector Dick in *The Yiddish Policemen's Union*.

CHRIS ABANI: The journey they make toward some realization or transformation. People care about people, so that's what we all care about.

CRISTINA GARCIA: I think there's a level of blind self-love in buffoonish characters and a level of delusion and a certain amount of wellmeaningness that I find incredibly touching. I find optimism very touching and these characters are very optimistic. I'm not like that at all myself.

RICK MOODY: Unpredictability.

JOSÉ MANUEL PRIETO: That they're inevitable, that it seems as if they can't act another way, and at the same time their impenetrability, the mystery that emanates from them. In the same way a person that we can't "read" completely, but we find fascinating, from what they say, from what they lived, from what we can learn from them. I, for example, learned a lot about my character in *Nocturnal Butterflies of the Russian Empire*, V., who taught me something I didn't know before sitting down to write the book. In a certain way, I haven't stopped thinking of her since then; that character is inexhaustible to me in its enigma.

JONATHAN LETHEM: Contradictions.

ANDREW SEAN GREER: Contradiction and energy on the page. But sometimes a character never does come to life, and it is the writer's job not to let the reader know—ALL the characters should be alive, even the ones you don't love as much.

ALEKSANDAR HEMON: The story or the book the character is in. The interaction with the world around him or her.

YIYUN LI: That is very hard to answer. For me, if I read a novel and a year later still remember the character that makes him or her a compelling character.

JOSH EMMONS: Most compelling characters want something. They want revenge against the white whale that took their leg. They want sex with nymphets. They want to get married. They want to destroy the round gold embodiment of all the world's evil. They want to find someone who isn't phony. They want to live purely and adventurously as a knight errant. They want to be flattered by their dissembling daughters. They want to get back home from the war. They want to solve the crime. They want to survive after waking up one morning as a dung beetle. They want to know if their partner is cheating on them. They want fame or riches or enlightenment or food or alcohol or the right pair of trousers. They want to climb a mountain or get down from a mountain. They want a different husband or racial justice or regime change. In short, they want what they don't have (or think they don't have), and their efforts to attain that thing make them both interesting and sympathetic. While there are exceptions to this rule, characters content to stay where they are and do nothing whose fascinating reflections or other attributes make them compelling, it's generally true.

FRANCISCO GOLDMAN: Too too many ways to answer this. The ways in which a character can be compelling are probably as infinite as the novel's capacity to go on surprising us actually turns out to be. I realize that sounds very optimistic, but today I have been rereading my friend and former student Rivka Galchen's *Atmospheric Disturbances*, and it makes me feel that way.

RODDY DOYLE: Life. A sense that he or she lives and is very aware of that.

STEPHEN KING: Either you're amazed because you see yourself in that character or because he's completely different. Like the serial killer in Joyce Carol Oates's *Zombie*. But usually, yeah, it's identification. More "I'd do that" than "I'd never do that."

HARUKI MURAKAMI: If you are any good as a writer, you can do it naturally.

EDWIDGE DANTICAT: Memorability. Something about the character that you can't forget. A third eye. Twelve fingers. A missing limb. Idiosyncrasies.

YAEL HEDAYA: I think it's a mixture of hyperrealism, the feeling you get, as a reader, that you actually know this person, or even better (or worse, sometimes) that this is actually YOU, but also magic realism, not as in the name of the genre, but in the magic that this realism creates in the reader's and writer's mind.

NELL FREUDENBERGER: Not the objective facts about his life, I don't think. I think it's the character's voice, by which I mean his way of looking at the world.

COLM TÓIBÍN: The rhythms of the sentences.

ANN CUMMINS: In two words, veracity and unpredictability. Those two go together. I hate reading about ho-hum "typical" characters who say predictable, generic things and don't seem real. A character's language must reveal her or his personality, and the personality must reveal distinctive human traits. A writer might start creating a character as a problem-solving exercise, creating the character's background, family situation, social life . . . but a character doesn't become compelling until problem solving drops away and the idea becomes organic, fleshy. For me, it's a matter of embodiment—really trying to crawl under the skin of a character. If the character isn't real for the writer, how can he or she be for the reader?

SAŠA STANIŠIĆ: When his actions are shameful or painful.

DANIEL HANDLER: Placing them in compelling circumstances.

RABIH ALAMEDDINE: Good writing. If the character is well drawn, the character becomes compelling. I can't say more than that. In my opinion, sometimes a novel tips over when a character becomes too well drawn, when you know everything, a lot more than you need to know, about a character. A character becomes compelling when there's enough mystery that the reader can fill in some blanks. In this way, the reader and the writer create the character together.

TAYARI JONES: I find that seeing what compels a character makes her compelling. I tell my students, We love characters when we see what they love.

SUSAN CHOI: The same infinite range of things that make humans compelling. There's no pat answer to that.

T COOPER: If I have a strong reaction to a character, I know I'm on to something (whether as a reader or writer). I've been told by several people that the character of Esther in my second novel isn't "likeable." Again, I've always found that to be such an odd comment, like, are we supposed to "like" every character we come across in a novel? Does that make our reading experiences better? I feel like I've done my job if a reader is having a strong reaction to a character. Nobody or no thing can be all good or all bad—it's just life—so to me a compelling character is one that feels alive because he or she is multidimensional.

AKHIL SHARMA: Situation, style, characterization. Madame Bovary is interesting because the style makes us care and remain with her.

GLEN DAVID GOLD: Desire. Experiment with this sometime: make up the most odious person you can imagine. But give him or her something he or she really really really wants. Insta-compelling, I bet.

SANTIAGO RONCAGLIOLO: Knowing that I could be like him under his circumstances, especially if he faces emotionally extreme situations. Deep inside, we search for a piece of ourselves in every character, because in the end, we don't care about anybody else.

RODRIGO FRESÁN: Who knows?

RIVKA GALCHEN: I was reading a lot of "confessions" when I wrote my novel, and I think that reading helped me understand how interesting it is to have someone be wrong about himself. One can almost think of that as what character is made up of: one's very particular way of being wrong. That's what tends to interest me in a person, in a character. There's *The Confessions of Augustine* (which often verge on being a complaint), *The Confessions* (where Rousseau seems to be willing to confess to anything except for fathering five children none of which he supported or acknowledged, each of which he immediately handed over to state care) . . . also Werner Heisenberg's *Physics and Beyond*, a kind of intellectual biography (which in fact reads like a roundabout defense of his decision to stay in Germany through the war), . . . also rereading *The Interpretation of Dreams* (which you can't help but see as Freud's most—primarily unintentionally—autobiographical work, full up with warped guilt and denial). Those books all read like mysteries that weren't labeled mysteries. Really, really good and frustrating mysteries.

HOW DO YOU GET TO KNOW YOUR CHARACTERS?

COLM TÓIBÍN: They are just words. I try to write carefully and truthfully.

ALEKSANDAR HEMON: I spend time with them. But knowing a character is not a relevant issue. The simplest characters are the easiest to know. The issue is loving them. What I strive to achieve is loving my characters regardless of what kind of people they might turn out to be. Once you love them you become them.

DINAW MENGESTU: As soon as a character enters the page they begin to take shape in my mind. I'll find myself spending plenty of quiet hours thinking of them, wondering who they are, what they would say, where they come from, and how they would react to certain situations. Sometimes that means writing scenes that in the end don't really work or that must be cut but that nonetheless provide a little bit more insight into how the character functions.

TASH AW: By writing them. I try and think about them as much as possible beforehand, in the planning of the novel, but familiarity invariably comes with the actual time spent with them, i.e., in the writing of the novel.

ANDREW SEAN GREER: Having them speak.

TAYARI JONES: I write to know them better. By the end of the novel, I know so much more about them that I have to go back and rewrite the opening chapters.

JOSÉ MANUEL PRIETO: The same way we get to know a person in real life: gradually. It is not something you can open up and have presented to you at once, but is shown bit by bit. That's my experience.

MEHMET MURAT SOMER: I am their creator. Without knowing their story, their background, their motives, I don't dare to create a new character. And when I create one, I am the father, the mother, and the God of it all.

YAEL HEDAYA: We spend a lot of time together. Sometimes in complete silence, sometimes engaged in conversation. Since I never know what I'm going to write in advance, for me, every word I type is a revelation, another thing about my character that I had no idea about. I can be writing a sentence about this character or another, who I just described eating lunch or having sex, and in the next sentence I'll suddenly mention (without even knowing that this is what I was going to say) that the character is in a rush to beat traffic and make it to the cemetery on time, although her mother would have hated that she even left the house on such a rainy day, and I'll be saying to myself: Oh, so her mother just died. Interesting.

JOSH EMMONS: As my characters move through their world and make choices—yes to steamed broccoli, no to Tantric sex—I gradually learn their likes and dislikes and phobias and frustrations and excitements until I know them well. I like to begin with a nearly blank slate and then pile on attributes as they're revealed in situations.

CLAIRE MESSUD: You listen to them. You watch them. You wait for them to unfurl.

PAUL AUSTER: By living with them in my mind for a long time before I start writing. Composition is one thing—it can take months or years— but preparation is another, and I've always lived with my books for years before I sit down to write them.

MICHAEL CHABON: Sometimes a little at a time; sometimes right off the bat. Sometimes, alas, never.

NELL FREUDENBERGER: I write many hundreds of pages that I don't use.

STEPHEN KING: I watch what they do and how they talk.

CHRIS ABANI: I talk to them, try to imagine them, and sometimes there are some method-acting techniques that I apply. It takes time, but mostly I learn to listen to them and not to my own ego.

AKHIL SHARMA: Time. Writing a scene over and over. The characters are not set. I make them based on what I am able to do and what I need the characters to be.

JENNIFER EGAN: I need to hear them, kind of literally, odd as that sounds. If I can't hear them talk, then they're not alive in my mind.

T COOPER: An exercise I used for my first novel (and to a lesser degree for my second) was a simple one, but I found that it really helped me to get to know my characters before attempting to write about them. There were four main characters in the book, and for each, I wrote their names at the top of a page and just wrote and wrote and scribbled and sketched, brainstormed and vomited out all the details about them I could possibly conjure. Down to the kind of soft cotton boxers they wore in high school, how it felt when they intercepted a note from their best friend to another friend who said they were ugly. How they talk, what they look like, what music they like, sports they're good at, secrets they have, food allergies, how they'll die, what their relationship with their mother was like, and so on. I just try to come up with all of this (admittedly) embarrassing material I wouldn't want anybody to ever see, nor would I ever want actually ending up in the novel—but to me, it's important to know all of these details about my characters before putting them in motion in the narrative.

HARUKI MURAKAMI: Living with them.

SANTIAGO RONCAGLIOLO: As the story advances, the structure requires that they take certain predetermined actions. Then I ask myself, why would this person do this? Often, the reasons lie in his past. Other times, in his relationship to the other characters. Either way, creating them and getting to know them are one and the same.

FRANCISCO GOLDMAN: By working really hard until the illusion of their existence becomes an obsession.

EDWIDGE DANTICAT: I sometimes cut pictures out of books and magazines, pictures of people who might look like my characters so at least they can have a face for me. Once I know their names and the place they were born, I get to know them more or less as I write about them.

RODRIGO FRESÁN: Spending too many hours a day with them.

RODDY DOYLE: Slowly.

RICK MOODY: When stuck with trying to understand a character, I have in the past *interviewed* him or her. This works best if you then avoid using any of the material in the interview. Does he like area rugs or wall-to-wall? Has she ever tried to get a coworker fired? To what extent is he willing to fudge numbers on his taxes? It's really *fun* to ask a character these sorts of questions, and the experiment also helps you know well the idiosyncrasies of that person's voice. Voice is to character development what the makeup and the outfit is to actors, the thing that legitimizes the intent to create, the thing that obliterates the artifice.

SUSAN CHOI: By writing the book. That's it. I don't do exercises, create fake diaries, fill imaginary closets with clothes, whatever. I just do the writing and if the character doesn't make sense to me, I revise.

HOW DO YOU KNOW WHAT TO DRAMATIZE AND WHAT TO SUMMARIZE?

ALEKSANDAR HEMON: I don't know what that means.

STEPHEN KING: Dramatize the really good stuff.

CRISTINA GARCIA: I deal with that more instinctively than intellectually, by paying attention to where the heat is in the book. I move toward the heat, move toward where things are getting molten or changing suddenly. And I actually feel no obligation to summarize much, honestly, or to fill in the blanks or the in-betweens. I think that if you do those scenes well, the rest will suggest itself, and the reader can conjecture and participate.

CHRIS ABANI: I try to avoid summary. I leave that for the Cliffs-Notes.

RICK MOODY: Through trial and error.

TAYARI JONES: For this, I imagine that someone is telling me the story. If I would zone out, then that is something that would be summarized. If it is a part of the story where I would say, "Wait! Tell me exactly what happened!!!," then that is the part I dramatize.

COLM TÓIBÍN: I knew this when I was five by listening to people at home and then trying, when they were listening to me, not to bore them.

SUSAN CHOI: Instinct. Usually, when I read a draft, I can feel where the method is wrong—where the scene needs to unfold or where it's unnecessary.

RABIH ALAMEDDINE: Instinct, usually. I tend to think that I dramatize, in some books, everything. In others, I tend to do both—it's instinct for the most part and I want to end this stupid "show, don't tell" bullshit. I think that's one of the stupidest lines that's ever been said. I mean, a good description can tell and can tell so well that it'll—*tell* stories, for crying out loud! Most of the great storytellers tell you, they don't show you, they tell you that this is a hero and you believe it is a hero. They don't have to show you every single thing he does to make you know he's a hero.

PAUL AUSTER: A question of pacing and rhythm.

SAŠA STANIŠIĆ: I sense it.

HARUKI MURAKAMI: Take your time to revise a draft. Then you will know it.

JONATHAN LETHEM: In writing I always skip the parts I'd skip as a reader—physical description unenlivened by emotional affect, dull transitions, functional explanations that I'd rather pick up inferentially from dialogue and situation. On that principle, I'd probably skip anything I thought I was obliged to "summarize." A well-paraphrased conversation should be as vivid and engaging as a version written out in dialogue, for instance.

DANIEL HANDLER: I tend to dramatize everything and then go back and summarize the boring bits.

ANDREW SEAN GREER: That is always the question. It has to do with pacing and the heat of the scene. Some scenes may verge on sentimental, so you cool them down by summarizing them or rushing them. Some may be too subtle for the emotion to show, so you have to dramatize them. It does not necessarily correspond to the "important" scenes in a book.

RODRIGO FRESÁN: Certain intuition that the years give you and, above all, reading.

EDWIDGE DANTICAT: I take what feels like the "bigger moments" and make those into scenes. If I have a series of events that don't need to be drawn out, I summarize them.

JOSH EMMONS: The common rule of thumb is that you dramatize crucial action—slow down to concentrate on and make the reader experience what's happening to the characters—and summarize what is rote or unexceptional—the boring but necessary information needed to bridge one time period with another—so that Pip's first day with Miss Havisham lasts for twenty pages and his years as Joe's apprentice are over in two. But really it all depends on what your story is. If instead of concentrating on Pip's inheritance and belief that he is Miss Havisham's intended son-in-law, the narrator of *Great Expectations* had wanted to depict the trials of a working man in mid-nineteenth-century England (as George Eliot does with infinitely finer results in *Adam Bede*), he might have sped over the boy's song and dance in front of a love-scarred old woman and then dwelled on the young man's struggle to master a trade. In other words, the emphasis of your story will determine which episodes should be rendered in scene and which in exposition.

YIYUN LI: I don't know if I consciously decide what to dramatize or what to summarize.

NELL FREUDENBERGER: When writing starts to feel like a chore, I think it either means you're on the wrong track, or that it's time for some summary. A lot of times I compress scenes I've written into a sentence or two, but often it's necessary to write something before you can know you don't need to dramatize it.

AKHIL SHARMA: I try to create felt experience in my fiction and so this forces a reliance on scene.

ANN CUMMINS: I'm a big fan of putting work aside to cool, returning to it after a time (preferably after I've begun to forget what I wrote, which is probably easier for me than most because I have a bad memory), reading it and noting my attention. If my attention lags or I grow bored, I know the pacing is off, which usually means the material needs work too. Then I might change two pages of dialogue to one paragraph of summary, and vice versa.

GLEN DAVID GOLD: I don't. I screw that up all the time. My readers tell me I went on too long here, too little there. "Should be in scene" is one comment, "could be two sentences" on the other hand. I'm still learning.

CLAIRE MESSUD: Again, the music. You follow the formal necessities of the music.

RODDY DOYLE: It's the decision of the moment. I don't have a general response or solution.

FRANCISCO GOLDMAN: Maybe I sometimes get this wrong, but my own sense of it is that this is as particular as one's own sense of humor. I try to do the unexpected—the expected bores me but maybe sometimes you have to at least give the illusion that you are doing the expected. Like mixing lots of off-speed weird stuff with fat eighty-mile-per-hour fastballs over the middle of the plate.

A. M. HOMES: Again, it's not something overt—it's part of the process, part of the act of being a writer, over time you practice these skills.

MICHAEL CHABON: That is a tough one. I'm not sure, after all these (almost twenty-five) years, that I really do know, yet. I still dramatize what could easily be summarized and summarize what must be drama-tized, all the time. Especially the latter. Usually if I start feeling really really down on what I'm writing, that (lack of scene) turns out to be the reason.

WHAT MAKES GOOD DIALOGUE GOOD?

GARY SHTEYNGART: You have to read aloud every sentence of dia-logue you write to make sure someone can actually say what's between the quotation marks. False dialogue seems to be the norm in half the books I read these days. Try listening to the dialogue in *The Sopranos*, or another show or movie that rings absolutely true, and writing some of it down to see how it looks on the page.

RODRIGO FRESÁN: I'm one of the worst dialogue writers I know. The day I find out, I promise to put it in practice.

TAYARI JONES: Good dialogue is something that you wouldn't mind overhearing. The key, I think, is to let the people talk about hard and difficult topics. Never let anyone walk away from a conversation. Make them stay in there and deal.

ADAM MANSBACH: It's got to be true to the characters, and revelatory in as many simultaneous ways as possible—of mood, of character, of plot, of place. It's got to ring true without being overly slavish to the boring and inarticulate ways people often speak in real life. Effectively inarticulate dialogue is hard to write, but when done right, it's beautiful. By the same token, clever dialogue is easy, but also easy to overdo. Good dialogue has to be stylized without appearing stylized, succinct without feeling perfected. It's got to have a self-propulsion, a rhythm, that comes from within, and interlocutors' tempos have to be beat-matched, blended. I think humor is crucial; even in a tense, dramatic, emotional scene, or a violent one, dialogue can and usually should have elements of humor. I don't mean punch lines, or slapstick; I mean that the subtle ironies and nuances that make lines memorable are usually dependent on humor in a broader sense.

DANIEL HANDLER: Nobody but nobody will believe me on this, but the best dialogue sounds not at all like human beings talking in real life.

CRISTINA GARCIA: Good dialogue of one character is not interchangeable with another character. In other words, it's good if you can recognize an individual character, if you can recognize the peculiar poetry of that voice. Even in mundane utterances there's something about them. I think good dialogue comes from a good sense of rhythm, essentially.

AMY TAN: My notions of good dialogue have changed. I think less is better. I read my books over again and I think, "This needs to be cut entirely or put into a narrative, or summarized, just not written in dialogue." Good dialogue is nothing excessive. It doesn't try to be clever or too witty or spin out a joke too long. I like dialogue that doesn't have too much "he said, she said"—too much "he said, rolling his eyes," or "she said, raising her eyebrows." . . . I think in a first-person story it's excessive sometimes when your character is noticing gestures too much. Less is definitely more.

CHRIS ABANI: It has to be realistic and reveal character psychology. It must never be used as a device for loading information.

JENNIFER EGAN: I think the most obvious thing is that logical dialogue—in which each utterance responds directly to the one before it—is pretty dead on the page. Real conversation isn't logical; it's chaotic, interruptive, and often circular. Rarely are people responding directly to what's just been said. Don DeLillo's dialogue is really helpful to look at with this in mind; he's a master of the elliptical exchange. So is Robert Stone. David Mamet too, though his version is more overtly aestheticized.

ANDREW SEAN GREER: When the characters each are trying to get something from the other but must not talk about it.

CLAIRE MESSUD: There's a craft book by Janet Burroway that has a very good section on dialogue. Dialogue, as she points out (and as doubtless many others have also pointed out), needs to be doing as many things as possible. Ideally, about half a dozen things. If dialogue is only doing one thing, or even only two things, it's not good dialogue.

ALEKSANDAR HEMON: The music of it.

DINAW MENGESTU: There are a lot of supposed ways to make dialogue good, but for me the strength of almost any dialogue is determined by how convinced I am of the characters who are speaking. If a character feels completely real and fully formed to a reader then they have the liberty to speak and act in the most bizarre or particular manners.

MICHAEL CHABON: It's appropriate to the scene, milieu, education, intention, context, and style of the character; it has a rhythm; it *sounds right*.

JOSÉ MANUEL PRIETO: The inexactness of what is said, reproducing the spoken vagueness and the approximate quality of verbal communication between two people that supposes, always, a quantity of nonverbal information that alters and modifies the sense of what is said. If you try to be too specific, in other words, if you try to put that nonverbal information in the text of the dialogue, it weighs it down, doesn't work, and seems unnatural.

COLM TÓIBÍN: No rule for this, just good rhythms. A little can stand for a lot. But then, see Ingmar Bergman, a long speech can be the best fun.

ANN CUMMINS: Not all lines need to be zingers. In fact, very few do. Most lines of dialogue need to sound like they come from real humans with real issues. A zinger in the right place, though, makes all the difference. When a character is ripe for speaking a surprising but revealing line, or a scene's emotion is at its peak, the zinger is like an arrow hitting its mark.

MEHMET MURAT SOMER: Wit! Feelings! Reason . . .

NELL FREUDENBERGER: People usually don't listen to each other, even when they're supposedly having a conversation. That's what makes dialogue fun to write, and also, I think, good. Obviously dialogue is precious, and it should never be used to convey information. Everything a character says should tell you something about who he or she is.

A. M. HOMES: That it's like double-word score in Scrabble—you say one thing, but it works two ways.

JOSH EMMONS: A subtle blend of nature and art. Dialogue should sound plausible—the reader should answer yes to the question of whether that character would speak those words at that moment—without being a direct transcription of what a character would actually say, because most people use a range of nonverbal cues to augment their speech (facial expressions, hand gestures, intonations) which, coupled with the shorthand and fragmentary way in which people actually talk, especially people who know each other well, make totally naturalistic dialogue almost impossible to understand.

HARUKI MURAKAMI: I have not given thought to what is "good dialogue." It's just bread and butter for a novelist.

SUSAN CHOI: Instinct again. Good dialogue often bears no resemblance to how people actually talk. You have to see how it works on the page.

FRANCISCO GOLDMAN: A Saul Bellow–like ear, music, brilliance, and comedy, a Junot Díaz–like ear, music, brilliance, and comedy, a Roberto

Bolaño–like ear, same plus his mad sexy daring and desperation, which can bring even his lovers' dialogues closer to Beckett.

RICK MOODY: A nice sense of the colloquial, a little bit of ungrammaticality, comic timing.

EDWIDGE DANTICAT: Wit, humor. Unexpected quips. A sense that if people were really brilliant, or really smart or really funny or really annoying, they'd speak that way. Good dialogue does not go on forever and not every question is answered.

YIYUN LI: I don't know if I know the answer to this question!

GLEN DAVID GOLD: I don't know. Big beginner's mistake is to have characters ask questions that other characters answer. Also, I think dialogue is fun to write, so I end up always cutting it down later. I think you should finish a scene with two characters talking and you should want more. "Should should should." Damn me.

RODDY DOYLE: It should seem very real, but be even more immediate and clear than real. It should be entertaining when, in reality, it mightn't be. It should be sharp, even—or, particularly—when not very articulate. It should be hard work but should never look as if it was.

STEPHEN KING: It rings true in the mind's ear.

SANTIAGO RONCAGLIOLO: Narrative tension. A novel incorporates external actions—walking, eating, kissing—and internal actions—convincing, doubting, deciding—which are reflected through dialogue. Good dialogue uncovers characters' inner worlds without slowing down the narrative.

T COOPER: There is nothing worse than bad dialogue. And you just know bad dialogue when you hear or read it. Beyond that, I don't know what makes good dialogue good; I just know it when I see it. There's probably a very tiny, delicate bone in the ear that is uniquely tuned to parse good dialogue from bad. Honestly, it's an ear thing, and listening to how people really communicate helps. But it's not everything, because good dialogue doesn't always capture *precisely* how real people talk. It's closer to that than anything, but it's not quite that alone. It's capturing how people talk—plus something else, but I don't know what that something else is.

RIVKA GALCHEN: It helps to notice that oftentimes people don't really listen to each other; they just kind of volley comments back and forth, more following up on their own last comment than on whatever the other person just said. Also that people's words wander off track after whatever distraction, an itchy elbow, a preoccupation with the mortgage, an opinion about a passerby's haircut. So the element of chaos there—to capture that, I think, can make for great dialogue. Also, that age-old trick, irony. When one person in the dialogue (or the reader) knows something that the speaker doesn't—(No, Oedipus, she's your mom!)—that adds dimension to the words. And lying—lies make such great dialogue! Because it's nice to learn what lies a character wants to tell, and to whom. And then there's the nice anxiety of wondering whether they will get away with them.

DO YOU BORROW DIALOGUE FROM CONVERSATIONS YOU HAVE OR OVERHEAR?

SAŠA STANIŠIĆ: Rarely. People don't talk that strange like I'd need them to do for my work. And if they do, they are drunk and don't make much sense.

PAUL AUSTER: Very rarely, but it has happened. Usually things that strike me as comical. For example: the story my wife once told me about going to the local bagel store and trying to order a cinnamon raisin bagel and garbling the words so that what came out of her mouth was "cinnamon Reagan bagel," and the man behind the counter shot back at her: "Sorry, we don't have any of those, but I can give you a Pumpernixon."

TAYARI JONES: Every now and then. I often overhear things that would be great in a story, but not a story that I happen to be writing. I have tried to shoehorn it in, and it was a disaster.

CHRIS ABANI: All the time. Like most writers, I am a shameless thief, a magpie of sorts.

ANDREW SEAN GREER: Rarely.

NELL FREUDENBERGER: No. Real conversations are almost always much less interesting than the ones in fiction.

ALEJANDRO ZAMBRA: Always. I have very little imagination. Maybe I have, in its stead, a good memory, or good involuntary memory. Then I grab on to what I've heard: the phrases, to say it that way, that have passed the test of life. Phrases that have existed, that have been used to bring people closer or farther apart.

DINAW MENGESTU: No, but I've often overheard snippets of conversations and thought, "That's brilliant," but I could never make it work in a fictional dialogue because no one would believe people talk that way.

DANIEL HANDLER: I eavesdrop constantly and take notes, and then arrange the sentences I overhear—or, likely, mishear—into a more interesting arrangement.

CLAIRE MESSUD: I've been known to.

JOSÉ MANUEL PRIETO: No, I don't think so. In fact, it is easy to imagine a conversation between two people. If you really concentrate, you can "end up there" and, in consequence, "listen" to what your characters are saying. Only in that sense, then, do I "copy" or use what I hear in a conversation.

RODDY DOYLE: Not really. The odd phrase.

STEPHEN KING: My mind files away stuff that people say that sounds good to me. Like "Stick it up your ass and rotate." It leaps up and bites your nose.

FRANCISCO GOLDMAN: Thrilled when I discover one worth filching.

ANN CUMMINS: I do have bits of remembered dialogue in my head. Sometimes those bits even become the kernels from which character begins. I don't go around writing down the interesting things people say, though. Most of my dialogue comes when I'm in a story. It grows out of the characters engaging with each other.

JENNIFER EGAN: Not consciously, but I note good snippets of dialogue, sometimes literally, and I think they may stay with me in an unconscious way. I guess I try to train my mind to hear certain aspects of dialogue so I can replicate them—in spirit—on the page.

MEHMET MURAT SOMER: Yes! Yes! I even take notes when I have a potential one. Old people are a real treasure for me. There are many sentences or sayings of my late grandmother . . .

SUSAN CHOI: I don't think I ever have.

AKHIL SHARMA: No.

COLM TÓIBÍN: No.

ALEKSANDAR HEMON: No, but I borrow the music.

AMY TAN: Yes. And the snippet doesn't have to be a completely marvelous Confucian aphorism. It just has to be this revealing piece that shows something about the character.

SANTIAGO RONCAGLIOLO: All the time. And from movies, books, newspapers. But I also steal facts, attitudes, effects. I'm really a big plagiarist, but I remain within the legal limits.

EDWIDGE DANTICAT: Very often. I'll borrow a line or two and see where it leads me.

MICHAEL CHABON: On occasion, if I can remember. I'm not a good note-taker.

A. M. HOMES: Sometimes.

HARUKI MURAKAMI: Never. A real-life conversation is boring.

DESCRIBE THE SCENE YOU'VE FOUND MOST DIFFICULT TO WRITE. WHY WAS IT SO HARD?

HARUKI MURAKAMI: Skinning a man alive. Too bloody. You could even laugh while you are writing about skinning a man.

MICHAEL CHABON: The Seder scene in *Wonder Boys*. A whole bunch of disparate characters; a lot of simmering tensions and crosscurrents; a long, prescribed ritual to get through and to perceive through the eyes of a stranger.

COLM TÓIBÍN: The death of the father in *The Heather Blazing*, the death of the sister in my new book. I could not write these scenes without fully feeling them, seeing them, and I ended up, even as I rewrote, crying uncontrollably and not being able to look at them for days. Then I went back, all steeled up, and did what I had to do. This is not a business for softies.

CLAIRE MESSUD: Alas, I'm not sure I can pick out that most difficult scene. Lots of them have been difficult—some because of insecurity about historical fact; others because of the presumptuousness of the undertaking (e.g., writing about 9/11 in *The Emperor's Children*); others because I was struggling, listening like a safecracker, to get the exact emotional vibrations of a scene. There are so many things that can make a scene difficult to write. Beware the scene that is easy to write.

JOSÉ MANUEL PRIETO: Sex scenes, maybe, but on the other hand I don't have many. It's difficult to not end up with something vulgar or pretentious.

ALAA AL ASWANY: It's not the scene that matters, it's the novel itself. What is terrible is when you are looking for the novel, but can't find it. This has happened to me many times, especially in the beginning of my career, because I didn't have enough experience. I often have projects for novels, many projects and ideas, and I keep thinking about them for hours, and sometimes for months, waiting for that feeling, for something to click. The moment I have it, I know I must follow my feeling. I do not invent novels, I discover them. The novel exists in my heart and my mind before it is written.

RICK MOODY: For a long time, in writing *Purple America*, I shied away from the fact that I was going to have to describe a nuclear blast. I imagine many writers would say the most difficult scene for them to write was the one in which they killed a cherished character, or perhaps the scene in which they tried to depict *love*, and I suppose I have wrestled with those kinds of scenes. But for me the scene that was most memorably difficult was this description of the nuclear blast. I think I wrote a great deal of the book before admitting to myself that I was going to have to do it. I remember talking with Jo Ann Beard, a good friend (and a great writer), who really encouraged me. I felt like I didn't have ownership of the material, and so I didn't know how to go about it. Finally, I decided that everyone has a nuclear blast lodged in his or her subconscious, and I didn't need to summon the *actual* blast (there are not so many people who know firsthand about *actual* nuclear blasts) so much as I needed to summon the one in the American unconscious.

DANIEL HANDLER: All the scenes that have been the most difficult for me to write have turned out to be unnecessary. I think I had trouble writing them because somewhere in my brain I thought they were useless. I'm trying to listen to that part of my brain more.

EDWIDGE DANTICAT: I find crowd scenes very difficult to write. It's a challenge for me to keep track of what my characters are doing plus what the rest of the crowd is doing. I once wrote a scene in *The Farming of Bones* where a mob was attacking my characters. I had to write a general scene of two people being attacked by two other people, then layer in more and more of the mob in revision.

JONATHAN LETHEM: I don't usually feel very hidebound by race or class or sex, and I've written whole novels from a female point of view, but I do remember coming to a strange impasse in *Girl in Landscape*, the first time I wrote a scene in which no men appeared at all—two women out for a walk in the desert having a conversation. Perhaps the absence of other human markers also left me feeling isolated with this problem—

how could I trust myself as a witness to a scene in which I'd eradicated the male point of view completely? The feeling went away after I launched myself into the material problem of making the scene work.

MEHMET MURAT SOMER: Usually when there are some technical details I want to put in, I go slow. With caution. The most difficult to write, though, was a scene in *The Gigolo Murders*. My then-editor found it too graphic and let me rewrite it several times. After the third, it was boring and difficult. In the end, we cut it.

AKHIL SHARMA: I can't think of one. They are all hard and they are all easy. It is the overall book that is hard.

T COOPER: I think the most difficult scene I've had to write thus far was a pogrom scene when one of my main character's daughters is raped and murdered by an anti-Semitic mob and his wife is beaten and forced to watch. The scene is based on a real event—the Kishinev pogrom of 1903—and as preparation, I did a significant amount of research about it. I read an academic text that pretty much recounted what's known of the event and how it went down, hour by hour. I looked at a lot of photographs and read some other accounts of it from different perspectives. When I sat down to write my scene, which takes place during the pogrom, I wrote it all in one sitting, and I just let myself go to the most gruesome and horrible places, and I went about it in the most matter-of-fact way.

I was a wreck after writing it, and only after I'd read parts of the passage aloud several times to audiences did I recall how hard it had been to write the scene in the first place. Somebody in the audience one time started hyperventilating and crying when I read from one of the more violent parts, and she got up and left the room rather quickly. For some reason I'd gotten really far away from the fact that even though it was presented in a matter-of-fact way (because the character describing it was being matter-of-fact about it), the events themselves were still brutal and crazy and, worse, totally based in reality.

I was so disconnected from the moment of writing that scene, that I must've been in some sort of trance when writing it, because it took reading the passage aloud to an audience upward of a few dozen times for me to reconnect with the fact that it had taken so much out of me to write it in the first place—and that it was damn depressing to hear. I'd never had anything like that happen to me before.

YIYUN LI: In this novel there is this scene where a woman, a mother, has to give up her young child, as well as her marriage, for a higher calling. It's the most difficult scene for me to write, as, naturally, as a fiction writer, I questioned her a lot, and each question seemed to be damaging the scene a little more.

SAŠA STANIŠIĆ: I once wanted to write a scene where two clouds bitch around about the sun. It was the worst idea I ever had. I had no clue what dialect clouds speak in and what their problems with the sun would be. I am not a very talented meteorologist either. But I fought really hard to invent something funny. Nothing in there was funny, though. So I gave it up.

RODDY DOYLE: I honestly don't remember.

TAYARI JONES: In my first novel, one of my favorite characters willfully gets into a car with a murderer. It was hard to write because it was difficult to make it plausible. Also, I didn't want Rodney to die. I wanted things to work out for him. It is the only time I have cried while working on a book.

GLEN DAVID GOLD: Hmm. Most difficult? About halfway through *Carter Beats the Devil* there's a scene where Carter is going to get information from his old friend Borax. It took me eighteen months to write. With, admittedly, about a seventeen-month gap during which I was doing no writing at all. It was a perfect storm, an overdetermined set of explanations: 1) I knew the scene would mostly be exposition, so that was no fun; 2) to write it, I would have to know the entire conspiracy plot; 3) I had to have confidence that I was right; 4) when I wrote that scene the rest of the book would be downhill from there, sort of "solved," if you know what I mean. Also: massive crisis in which I wondered whether writing fiction wasn't just a symptom of dealing with unresolved childhood traumas. (It is, turns out.) So, I got out via therapy, changing my life, skipping ahead to a different scene, and coming back. And then I decided I needed to surprise myself so it wouldn't just be exposition. I was in the library in the stacks and I decided I would throw an object into the scene based on the first book I grabbed. Which, no kidding, turned out to be the history of the guillotine. So there was something to break up the exposition, surprise me, and also hang the rest of the scene on.

ALEKSANDAR HEMON: I forget the process. Once I've written a story or a book I usually forget how it really came about, except in the most general terms.

YAEL HEDAYA: The hardest scenes to write are sex scenes and death scenes. On the one hand, I want to be hyperrealistic, on the other, I don't want to overdo it. The problem with sex and death is that if you're going to be hyperrealistic then there's no way you're going to avoid overdoing it. Sooner or later you're going to have to get graphic. Writing in Hebrew also presents another challenge. Modern Hebrew is still very young and it's constantly evolving. It's hard to find the right register. And it's a very user-unfriendly language when it comes to sex. You're either archaic and ridiculous or pornographic and promiscuous. Same goes for death.

One of the hardest scenes I ever wrote was the death scene in *Accidents*. Shira, the main female character, is in a hospital room with her aging father when he dies. This scene is not only based on but almost an exact replica of my own father's death, and it took me almost seven years, and one book in between, to be able to handle this, fictionwise. I needed what I saw and felt during those horrifying, mystical moments to go through a very complex, secret, recycling process in order for me to be able to write something true to reality, yet containing the magic of fiction, rather than just be a therapeutic exercise. I needed to lose the rawness and pain, I needed to FORGET, in order to be able to create. Still, I cried when I wrote that scene.

ANDREW SEAN GREER: Scenes of confrontation and honesty, because they are so damned corny. I find dialogue in them desperately hard to write—easy to get lines down, harder than anything else to get right. It's so easy to be glib in dialogue. But that is a waste of a reader's time. The important thing is for each line to matter—and that's very hard for me.

NELL FREUDENBERGER: It was a crowded, dynamic scene in which something needed to be publicly revealed about the main character. I'm most comfortable when I have two people talking in a room; managing a lot of moving bodies is a challenge for me.

DINAW MENGESTU: The most difficult scenes for me have revolved around two people talking. In one instance the main character of my novel is trying to begin a romantic relationship with a woman from a different economic and racial background from him, and over the course of their very quiet conversation the deep divides that separate them begin to slowly emerge.

RODRIGO FRESÁN: I don't remember any in particular.

STEPHEN KING: Mass meetings in *The Stand*, I think. Why was it so hard? Low emotional gradient. I thought the aftermath of Gage Creed's death in *Pet Sematary* would be hard, but it was strangely easy.

FRANCISCO GOLDMAN: I have been procrastinating on it for weeks.

A. M. HOMES: The stabbing scene from *The End of Alice*. I cried while I was writing it—it was so brutal, so awful, and so deeply dark. When I finished writing that book I felt like I'd fallen into a black hole, the most challenging work I've ever done, but very very dark.

HOW IMPORTANT IS HUMOR?

STEPHEN KING: It's great when it works.

T COOPER: It's one of the most important things. Both in the writing, and *especially* when it comes to sending your writing out into the world and getting responses and reactions to it. The whole writing and publishing process is going to be more easily weathered and navigated with a healthy sense of humor.

RODDY DOYLE: Very—and its absence is vital too. It's a bit like every other tool—how and when to use it. And only use it if it happens to be one of your tools. There's literally nothing worse than humor that isn't.

ANNE ENRIGHT: If you have to ask, you'll never know.

CHRIS ABANI: Essential. No one likes a sourpuss.

ANDREW SEAN GREER: What? Depends on the book!

ANN CUMMINS: Humor can oxygenate a serious story. It allows the reader to come up for air. In the best novels, heaviness and lightness work together to create lively (as opposed to dank and sludgy) narratives.

CLAIRE MESSUD: Indispensable.

RICK MOODY: It's essential! I recognize that comedy is very particular in cultures and subcultures—you have only to watch a few screen comedies to experience this. Therefore, to pursue the comic is, I think, to marginalize your writing somewhat. But work that has no comedy in it feels to me pretentious, dull, formulaic. This is one reason, I suspect, that George Saunders is such an important writer. He is the very quintessence of a writer of well-made short stories in some respects. But the comic register in his work is very unpredictable, very anarchic, and it makes the epiphanies, for me, that much more sublime. The same is true, in different ways, in the work of David Foster Wallace. The funnier his work is, the better I like it.

SAŠA STANIŠIĆ: The most important thing.

YAEL HEDAYA: Very important. Even though I'm not considered a funny writer, my writing does contain humor. Sometimes cynical, or subdued. Sometimes my writing is even funnier than I intended. When readers tell me they found this or that scene funny, or actually laughed, I sometimes get upset. Laughed? Out loud? I mean, here I am busting my chops writing something that I, personally, think is very somber and deep and some readers actually found it funny?

MEHMET MURAT SOMER: I value a smile more than lots of things, and every day I try to get a little more joy out of life. Humor helps a lot, especially when dealing with the bitter things in life. It's not easy trying to survive as a hedonist.

JOSH EMMONS: In fiction, as in life, humor should be used liberally, at least when appropriate, because it makes more bearable the painfully serious subject matter of most art. Better also to use it consciously and confidently, so that your comedy is intentional rather than accidental. We've all grieved for Charles Dickens when encountering Oscar Wilde's observation that "it takes a heart of stone to read about the death of Little Nell and not laugh."

TAYARI JONES: I tend to write about hard topics, like child murder, infertility, betrayal. Yet I always have a fair amount of humor in my writing. I think that every story should contain the full range of human emotion and that includes humor. I always feel that if nothing funny happens in the story, there is something important that has gone un-examined.

ALEJANDRO ZAMBRA: There must always be a hint of it, a shade of humor. Nicanor Parra says that "authentic seriousness is comic," and I agree. I think the narrator must always preserve that minimum space, that almost imperceptible distance that allows him to narrate. A dash of irony that saves us from complete silence.

COLM TÓIBÍN: You mean jokes? I hate jokes. I have no interest in hu-mor. Irony maybe. Or wit. Or vicious laughter.

AMY TAN: As I write more I have more humor, and my humor changes with each novel. It can be ironic, or more like slapstick, or sometimes intentionally very funny. I find that I say things and people more often call me a funny person. And I wonder why that is. I have a brain disease and I think it ate away at something called "think more seriously" and it inflamed an area called "be irreverent."

ALEKSANDAR HEMON: Depends what you are writing. But I've al-ways wanted to accomplish what Nabokov thought Chekhov was doing.

Chekhov, Nabokov said, wrote sad stories for humorous people—you could not see their sadness unless you had a sense of humor. And, for the record, I do find the notion of "comic relief" entirely stupid.

RODRIGO FRESÁN: Very much. I tend to distrust books without even one smile in them. Again, blessed be Kurt Vonnegut.

DANIEL HANDLER: Without humor all is lost.

EDWIDGE DANTICAT: Super important. Though I am not funny myself, I love humor. It's good for balance, especially with darker and heavier subjects.

GLEN DAVID GOLD: I don't think there is anything else. All of my favorite writers know how to make me laugh out loud.

A. M. HOMES: It's essential, the funnier you are, the more serious you can be.

SANTIAGO RONCAGLIOLO: In my work it's fundamental, because I write about very difficult subjects: violence, loneliness, war, sex, death. Humor allows me to talk about those things without being unpleasant. At the same time, on the other hand, it emphasizes them once the text disappears. But I don't think I have a choice. My view of the world is plenty ironic. We Latin Americans develop a considerable amount of dark humor as a weapon of self-defense against reality, to the degree that I write with humor even when I don't intend to.

DINAW MENGESTU: Humor is one of those things that I wish I could do better. It can be used not only to make a reader laugh, but also to disarm them a bit. It lowers the reader's resistance to a character or scene and can make something tragic that much more powerful because of the contrast it creates.

YIYUN LI: Very important, I think.

NELL FREUDENBERGER: Not at all important! Funny writers suck! Everyone loves them, and gives them attention, and prizes, and money, and what's so great about being funny anyway?

MICHAEL CHABON: Not one bit. Just kidding.

Chapter 5

WRITING

HOW DO YOU MEASURE A SUCCESSFUL WRITING DAY? IS THERE A WORD COUNT YOU SHOOT FOR? AN AMOUNT OF TIME YOU DEMAND OF YOURSELF?

CLAIRE MESSUD: This has varied at different times in my life. At this point, a successful writing day is one in which I write. Period.

ANDREW SEAN GREER: I write three pages a day at home, four or five pages a day at an artists' colony. That's every weekday. I caution young writers against writing in long creative spurts in the way a coach would caution a marathon runner against only training in sprints. It's a three-year process, mostly, so the only thing to count on is consistency, not "inspiration." Inspiration seems to come when your ass is in the chair and you are typing. Though I do spend a great deal of time napping.

JOSÉ MANUEL PRIETO: I don't count words, I feel like it's been a good day when I nail down an idea, when I'm able to put it down in a way that satisfies me. I think six hours of work daily is ideal, something I'm not always able to do much because of job responsibilities. A good day, logically, can go on longer.

MARIO VARGAS LLOSA: A successful day of work is a day when I feel the story has progressed, and that it has acquired boundaries I have to respect. At the beginning, the material is very cold, very distant, and it feels almost dead. But when I feel like the story is beginning to move, when it has found an inner strength I have to respect, when I feel like I can no longer have a character do certain things, or talk in a certain manner, when that character has established a certain autonomy, that's when the work is stimulating. When you discover an innovative possibility that alters your initial plans, but gives the novel a dynamism, an energy that you had not anticipated. These surprises, which I believe come from the intervention of the conscious, the rational part of the personality, are for me the most stimulating moments of the work.

LAILA LALAMI: A good writing day for me is one in which I have successfully kept the world at bay—no phone calls or e-mails or visits—and managed to write two or three pages. I am scrupulous about keeping track of how much work I get done. I have a little notebook, and each day I write down what I have worked on (novel, short story, essay) and a word count. I try to write a thousand words per day when I am working on a first draft, but I don't impose limits on myself when I am revising. I usually also write down what I am reading at the moment, because it's always fun for me to go back many months or years later and find out what I was reading while I was working on a particular piece of prose.

CHRIS ABANI: I don't write every day. I couldn't. It would bore me to death. But I read every day and I think about the work I need to do and how to do it. Lying on the couch thinking through your characters is a very productive writing day.

JOSH EMMONS: I aim for three hours and five hundred words per day. Some people can write longer and produce more—there are graphomaniacs who regularly get down three or four thousand words by nightfall, who dream in complete paragraphs and give literary expression to their every passing thought—but most others, myself included, feel hollow and lethargic as we enter our fourth or fifth hour of writing, and so stop in order not to have to erase too much the next day. That said, certain days are better than others, so that on a Monday I might go from morning to evening and pile up a short stack of paper (or cover a long stretch of a computer file), while on a Tuesday I'll do nothing but pare down the previous day's work to a single hard-won, because not lost, paragraph.

HARUKI MURAKAMI: No good day, no bad day, in my case. I write almost the same amount every day.

CHRIS ADRIAN: If I get anything done at all, even if it's just a paragraph or two (and even if it sucks), that generally relieves the guilt of not writing for, like, twenty-four to forty-eight hours.

COLM TÓIBÍN: I push myself very hard some days and try to write two thousand words, working all day and into the night. But you can't do this much. It is very good for you, however; it gives your tone a sort of urgency and fluency that you can't get if you just write a sentence here and there throughout the day. I cannot imagine writing in a café. It would be like doing a long, slow, and difficult shite in the middle of a busy freeway.

SAŠA STANIŠIĆ: If I can watch a movie in the evening without thinking about the text I'm working on, then I was successful. Sometimes this happens after writing two lines, sometimes it doesn't after writing five pages.

MEHMET MURAT SOMER: My preparations for a thriller are in two phases. The first is creating, plotting, and solving the case arithmetically in my mind, or with some notes. This takes an indefinite amount of time. Sometimes it's very quick, sometimes months. Then comes the second phase, putting it into words and sentences, typing it up. . . . When I start this, I aim for five pages a day as a challenge to myself. I fall short most of the time, but it does challenge me.

JONATHAN LETHEM: I've become very firmly oblivious to word counts and page counts and clock-watching. The bad days require just as much involvement and energy as the good ones, so in the long game of writing a novel, I prefer to pretend not to notice the difference. I have only one rule, which stands in for all the others: write every day. I find that if I do that, the rest takes care of itself, and counting to "one" once a day is simpler than the other kinds of counting.

EDWIDGE DANTICAT: It depends on where I am in a project. For me the good writing days don't end. You'd sit there all day, all night if you could. A great writing day is when I start writing and it's light out and when I stop it's dark and I never noticed the change. I don't demand much of myself, but whatever comes that day. Sometimes it's five hundred words, sometimes it's nothing at all. Sometimes it's a whole chapter or story.

ALLEGRA GOODMAN: Now there's a question. I wish I could say— Oh, three thousand words. That's a good solid day's work for me. Or, I write a chapter a day, nine to five, with a lunch break at noon. Somehow my workday doesn't look like that. This is partly because I have four children and I write while they are in school, Monday through Friday, with interruptions, staff days, snow days, and sick days thrown in. My workday is short, and my work resists quotas. My novels do not pour forth easily and smoothly like cake batter—although I wish they would.

When I'm beginning a book, a successful day could mean outlining the characters' relationships on a large piece of paper. In the middle of a novel, a successful day means editing the previous day's work, and then adding two or three new pages. There is a point in a book where I begin to write more quickly, and then my big challenge is to slow down. I am quite impatient and I wish I could write the whole book at once. I begin opening my laptop at all times and trying to push forward. When I was younger I'd start churning out pages, but I don't let myself anymore, because whenever I rush, I end up tossing and rewriting. My desire to work quickly and effectively backfires and I end up making more work for myself. Ironically, eagerness can cause burnout and confusion. What a delicate balance between a successful writing day and a migraine. I try to hold myself to three or four good pages and quit while I'm ahead.

One trick I use to slow myself down is to start writing by hand in the middle of a book. I take an extrafine Pilot pen and ink in a good fifty pages on unlined white paper. When I was writing *The Other Side of the Island*, I drafted eighty pages in purple. The story was coming along well, and I began growing superstitious about a particular purple pen. I began to carry pen and manuscript everywhere in my bag. This is strange marsupial behavior on my part, as if I can keep my young book warm in my pouch. I grow protective, as my book develops. I'm afraid of losing my work, and I also fantasize that even when I'm running errands or taking care of kids, I can whip out my novel and continue, whipping up a few more lines the way knitters whip off another row of stitches. The sad truth is that writing novels is not much like knitting sweaters. I've never been successful at capitalizing on odd moments here and there. I feel strangely uninspired in the dentist's office or airport or on park benches at playgrounds.

Several hours of quiet writing at a desk. That's a good day's work. Three or four pages, but, really a single good page will do. An excellent paragraph. A new idea. I'll take what I can get. Revery alone will do, if bees are few.

AKHIL SHARMA: Every day is successful if I don't shoot myself, and if I behave in a loving manner to my wife and to all the people I should be loving toward.

AMY TAN: A successful day is when I've not been diverted by distractions like e-mail, when people haven't been interrupting. When I've been fully concentrated in my imagination. When I've been writing with the voice of what the novel should be, not inserting other voices. It's really a discipline—when I sit down at nine o'clock and work all day.

RABIH ALAMEDDINE: Is there such a thing as a successful writing day? I don't know about that. I don't think there is. Sometimes you think that you've done something great and then two months later, whatever you wrote that day is, you know, you look at it like *graaah*. There is no such thing, not in my opinion. A successful writing day is the day you look at your novel, the entire thing, and say, "Oh, this is not as bad as I thought it was."

TAYARI JONES: When I am feeling generous with myself, I hold myself to either time or word count. Never both. I think it's best to measure time because, really, all you can do is try. But sometimes, I am very hard on myself for not getting anything done. I try not to treat myself this way because it only makes me feel bad about myself and get even less done. A good day for me is two hours. Three hours is fantastic. But just one hour isn't bad at all.

GARY SHTEYNGART: Two to three double-spaced pages per day in the first draft, three to four in the second draft, five to six in the third. If I don't meet those requirements, I will not talk to myself for the rest of the day. The silent treatment.

JENNIFER EGAN: Depends. When I'm writing original material, I try to write a minimum of five pages longhand each day. That's not actually that much, and I can do it in an hour, but I can also sit there a LONG time not doing it. Once I'm in the editing phase, which is where I spend most of my time, I can conceivably do it all day, except that I almost never have all day. If I'm still early in the editing process, then I tend to measure success in terms of whether I've had some kind of insight or discovery—whether I've emerged in a slightly different place from where I began. Later in the process, when I'm really trying to work through material in a very directed way, I'll often have specific goals in terms of how much ground I want to cover in a day, or a week, and I'm pleased if I manage to fulfill those goals.

ALAA AL ASWANY: Until three years ago I had to work like any other dentist, so I had a very, very tough schedule. As a matter of fact, I woke up in the morning at six a.m. for years, and wrote from six thirty to ten thirty, six days a week, because I cannot write fiction for more than four hours, and then after this, I would be a dentist. But now I have a more flexible schedule because I have been getting good money for the last three or four years. I have been a bestseller in the West, and this means money. So I now have some colleagues working for me in the clinic and I can afford to be at the seashore three days a week, or four days a week, and only work as a dentist three days a week. I am in my best form as a novelist only in the early morning, and I love to wake up at six a.m. For some reason I can't write fiction during the day; I only write when I wake up very early. I can write articles, for example, during the day, but not fiction. And I cannot write fiction more than four or five hours; after this I lose concentration.

DANIEL HANDLER: I'm lucky enough to get to write all day, by which I mean, about nine a.m. until about three p.m. I like to think that I knock off work about the time everyone else knocks off work.

FRANCISCO GOLDMAN: I am happy to pour myself a tequila and say, that was an okay workday. Sometimes this might involve as little as some hours of seemingly futile rereading and rewriting, but you've sensed some solution on the horizon.

DINAW MENGESTU: I do keep a very loose word count idea in my head, but I'm definitely not tied to that. A good writing day is one in which I don't end up flinging myself against a wall or curled up on a couch in a state of nearly blinding frustration. On a good writing day the sentences come out easily, and I know when I'm finished that they are the right ones, whether there are hundreds of them or only two.

ALEKSANDAR HEMON: I write only when I have something to write. There might be long periods of not writing much, except for magazine and newspaper stuff. But when I am on a project, I just keep working until I'm done. Sometimes I miss a day, sometimes I work a little more. But thinking about it and being tormented by not writing and avoiding writing and writing crap—all of those are legitimate parts of the process. Once I start writing, I never write more than two or three hours a day, but I try to do it every day. When I edit and revise, I might work four or five hours a day.

GEORGE PELECANOS: I try to get five pages of manuscript a day. That is, in the first couple of months in the process. As I find the book, as I accelerate into it, it is not uncommon to write ten to fifteen pages a day. At that point I know where I am going and I'm in a zone. I've worked eight or ten hours straight behind the desk without food or drink and not even noticed the passage of time.

ANN CUMMINS: My life has two seasons: my teaching season and my writing season. I teach one semester every year, and I give that time to my students. Though I'll steal a little time for myself, I can't really concentrate on my own work when I'm teaching. But I always feel a little off during my teaching semester when I'm not writing. During my writing season, when I'm starting a project and don't know what I'm doing, or if I'm not inspired, I try to keep to word and page counts. When I'm in a project and inspired, I can write for long periods and any time of the day. I don't measure my days, though, by whether I've written or not. If I've been neglecting something, like yard work or exercise, and I choose them instead of writing, that's a successful day for me.

GLEN DAVID GOLD: I have no discipline, no routine, no standard amount of time I write, and no ability to stay focused. And yet I just finished a thousand-page manuscript that's pretty good. I guess I have drive instead. It ends up that I shift routines a lot—not because I want to, but because it's just how it works out. Six weeks of writing from eight till noon, a two-week break, ten weeks of all-day-all-night, a month break, a colony stay, then back to eight till noon. Right now it's breaking down into chunks that I need to get done: finish this scene today, finish two more scenes in the next three days, that kind of thing. It's more about bulldozing than anything else.

NELL FREUDENBERGER: I measure it with time. I work on fiction for three hours almost every morning. I can work on an article or freelance assignment, or do superficial revisions to a piece of fiction that's already pretty far along after I'm finished with that, but as far as writing new stuff goes, three hours is pretty much my limit.

PAUL AUSTER: I generally work between five and seven hours a day. If I can get one decent page out of that time, I consider it a good day.

RODDY DOYLE: I measure the day in words. If I hit a thousand, I'm usually happy. I divide the day into different projects, and usually spend about three hours on the novel. So a thousand is a reasonable amount of words, unless they're utter shite and I know it.

RODRIGO FRESÁN: If I'm able to reach my desk chair and sit and write that's already a good day. It isn't difficult for me to write. What I find difficult is SITTING to write. Once there, I try to not go below three pages per day (the average length of a magazine piece).

STEPHEN KING: Five pages and a little left over to start with tomorrow. Do five pages and word count takes care of itself. When those five pages are done, I'm done. Sometimes it's three hours. Sometimes more. Occasionally a little less.

SUSAN CHOI: When I'm struggling, and time drags, I shoot for a thousand words, or three consecutive hours trying. When the writing is going well I don't have to do that.

A. M. HOMES: There is no word count—when I was younger, sometimes I could write ten pages in a day, lately I feel lucky if I get one. Also, for me stories are slower than a novel, there's less room for error or wandering off in a story so you really have to stay on it. An amount of time I demand of myself? If it's not going well, I pretty much sit here until I can turn that around—I like a day that goes from seven a.m. to four p.m. and then a night shift from seven p.m. to ten. That's ideal.

YIYUN LI: A good writing day for me is either four hours of active writing or something—a critical scene or a difficult page—achieved.

T COOPER: For some reason, when I'm generating a first draft, I'm not very good at doing an hour here, an hour there, three hours the next day. I need long chunks of empty time with no interruptions stretching out ahead of me. If there's one thing to do, say, take the dog to the vet at four, and I have from eleven until then to work—I can't, and I'm miserable about it the whole time. That's why I seem to do such good work at writers' colonies when I'm generating a first draft of a book. I can do revisions and editing and journalism and even work on short stories in smaller chunks of time, but I really prefer a whole day or afternoon or night with no interruptions. A word count seems arbitrary to me, but I do have colleagues who live by it—even if it's a page-a-day schedule—and I admire the shit out of them for it, but it just doesn't seem to be my thing.

SANTIAGO RONCAGLIOLO: The truth is, I dedicate the first four hours of every workday to novel writing. Sometimes I manage five pages, sometimes not even one. Sometimes I just edit. Sometimes I get discouraged because I think that everything's wrong and I'll never be able to get it right. This sensation is more frequent during the first pages, because every line is crucial and establishes the course the story will take. But it tends to get easier as the writing advances, because it follows channels that have already been sketched.

MICHAEL CHABON: I try to get a thousand new words every writing day, five days a week. Fifty-two weeks a year. Try.

RICK MOODY: My minimum is fifteen hundred words, but I am secretly unhappy if I don't get over two thousand. It happens, because of how busy I am, that I don't get to write as often as I'd like. But when I am composing first drafts of things, it's as indicated above. The most I've ever accomplished in one day is three thousand words, and that has only ever happened two or three times. I am allowed to take as long as I need to achieve my minimum, and the sad truth is that it takes me eight hours to have two or three good solid hours of writing. And yet I do feel, on the good days, that the time not spent writing is somehow being used productively, despite appearances, because I think there are limitations on what the imagination can do. When I have been at Yaddo, the artist's colony, I have often been there with a novelist named Joe Caldwell, who never fails to walk to town from the Yaddo campus, despite the fact that there are many people who would be willing to drive him. He says he gets his best ideas on those walks. According to this strategy, time wasting may be a very important part of novel writing.

SUSAN MINOT: If words got on the page and I feel good afterward. That's a good day. I've never counted words. Never enough time.

YAEL HEDAYA: This is a painful question. For me, a successful writing day is any day in which I've managed to plant myself in front of the computer and not budge for at least five minutes. I know this sounds pathetic. But I mean five minutes without surfing the Internet, checking my mail, or playing solitaire. Five minutes without self-inflicted diversions. A whole hour would be nice. Two or three or even four, truly miraculous. I am the queen of diversions. If they're not imposed on me from the outside, I create them. God forbid I should hop out to get something at the drugstore. Chances are, I'll come back six hours later with loads of stuff I don't need and a guilty conscience. I become intimately involved with the cosmetic counters and home appliance stores when I'm writing. I tell myself I'll be inspired there, I tell myself I deserve a little break, and I end up forgetting all about the inspiration because there happened to be a sale on bathroom mats or antiaging serums. But I don't have to actually leave the house in order to escape my computer.

Since I work at home, I have no shortage of diversions. I find myself jumping out of my seat every so often to make myself a cup of coffee (my sixth or seventh or eighth) and on the way to the kitchen I put a load in the wash and then remember I need to look for a sock that got misplaced the day before, so there I am in my kids' room, picking up toys from the floor, when the phone rings, and I promised myself I'd let the voice mail get it, but how can I? What if one of my kids is sick and it's the teacher calling? What if I've won something? Lost something? So I answer the phone, of course I do, how can I not? and by then I'm already sitting down having my coffee in the garden, chatting on the phone with whoever it might be (and I welcome calls, even from bothersome salespeople, when I'm writing), an orphaned sock in my hand, and since it's already noon and I'm getting hungry, I'll prepare myself something, and while I'm at it I'll start defrosting some chicken for the kids' dinner, and when I need a diversion from my diversions, I'll go upstairs to my computer, sit down again, with the *So where was I?* look on my face, and I'll work for about three minutes straight feeling very committed and proud of myself, before I start feeling really tired, and I mean REALLY tired, so I'll lie down for a few minutes, I'll even set the alarm clock to ring in an hour, but how can I nap when I'm feeling so guilty about wasting my workday? Well, I can, and I'm in a deep sleep when the phone rings, and it's the teacher.

HOW RIGOROUS ARE YOU
ABOUT MAINTAINING A SCHEDULE?

ANNE ENRIGHT: My children dictate my schedule—I have done vast amounts since they were born because they keep me from my desk and make me impatient to get back to it. I don't count words so much any-more, or note beginnings and endings. I work on several things at once, so there is always a file to open and no such thing as a blank page. I like working. What discipline I have comes from the fact that I don't do any of the other things I am supposed to do. Housework, per-sonal administration—everything else goes to hell. My husband cooks. We don't starve.

ANDREW SEAN GREER: Extremely so. It turns out that talent is not as important as willpower for a novelist. It is like training for the Olympics—you really have to do it every every every every day. Not in one ten-hour caffeine-inspired stint every Friday night. Every day.

COLM TÓIBÍN: I finish everything I start and I always feel guilty about not working hard enough but I am not rigorous.

T COOPER: When I'm writing, deep into writing a first draft of a novel, I'm a schedule fascist and very selfish and structured with my time. When I'm at a colony, and even if I'm at home working on edits for a deadline or whatever, I have a set schedule of waking, getting some cof-fee and food in me, working for three or four hours, having another cof-fee or a snack, and then doing another five or six hours before taking a break to exercise or listen to music or get some business done, whatever. And if I'm on a roll, sometimes I like to work through the night until

I'm exhausted and collapse into bed around three or four in the morning, and then get up late the next morning and do it all over again.

DANIEL HANDLER: I don't know what else to do with my day.

RABIH ALAMEDDINE: I am not rigorous at all. I am one of the laziest, most undisciplined writers you'll ever come across.

AMY TAN: I'm terrible at the schedule. I have so many distractions in my life. They are very seductive. I have to decide which things are necessary for my life. I might have a crisis going on and then I go for days without writing, although every single day I'm in the novel, thinking about the novel. Every night before I go to sleep I think about the novel. I think about every observation I've had that day, about the structure of the novel and so on.

MEHMET MURAT SOMER: Not much, recently. Previously I was working in a more disciplined way. Now there are many more things attracting my attention, especially on the Internet. I really should disconnect, even cut off my high-speed connection altogether. With any kind of Internet surfing, I end up either on deep, very specific intellectual details or porn. And believe me, sometimes it's far more satisfying than the planned five pages.

STEPHEN KING: Plenty. I'm a fucking drudge.

SAŠA STANIŠIĆ: Not very much. Which is a good thing about being a writer.

DINAW MENGESTU: I try to write every day, but inevitably that becomes impossible the more I travel. When I do have clear stretches of uninterrupted time, though, then I tend to wake up and write every morning with as few distractions as possible.

EDWIDGE DANTICAT: Not at all. Life often intrudes.

GEORGE PELECANOS: Very. I don't think you can leave that fictional world, not even for a day, when you are hard at it. It becomes very difficult to find your way back into "the tunnel" if you walk away from it. I don't believe, as others do, that you should put a manuscript in a desk for a few weeks and come back and look at it if you don't like it or it has become problematic. You rarely like it and there are problems damn near every day. You have to work through it or the book will not get done.

JENNIFER EGAN: Never enough, it often feels, but I try not to get too stressed out about the days when I fall short. One thing I've learned is that it's what you do *over time* that really matters, and not the fruits of any particular day. If one of my kids is sick, so be it—I'll lose a day and read *Treasure Island* to him instead.

YIYUN LI: When I am in the middle of a project I try to maintain a rigorous schedule.

RICK MOODY: Not very.

HARUKI MURAKAMI: I work constantly.

SANTIAGO RONCAGLIOLO: Very, because it's very difficult to reconnect yourself with a story that you've put aside for too long. But I've become less obsessive. I'd rather allow a story to breathe for a few days than continue forward at full speed and reinforce an error.

CHRIS ABANI: Ha! Schedule? I write for focused spurts. The rest of the time I think, which is more important than actually putting words on paper.

NELL FREUDENBERGER: I'm pretty rigorous now, but I was much less so when I had a full-time job.

JOSÉ MANUEL PRIETO: I can't be rigorous, my job as a professor doesn't allow it. I always have interruptions: preparing classes, grading exams, etc. Those distractions I find very maddening, but when I can, I look for a way to start work at the same time every morning.

TAYARI JONES: I'm not. And it shames me.

PAUL AUSTER: I'm not militaristic in my habits. Some days I wake up early, some days I wake up late. But I always work—and always manage to put in my hours.

A. M. HOMES: I like to have a schedule, I like to go to work every day. But I am also a single parent and that's a HUGE job and I take it very seriously.

RODDY DOYLE: I'm very disciplined, although I sometimes take on too many other projects. I'm just a boy who can't say No. At this stage I hear myself moaning about this before I actually start moaning, so I don't trust the sincerity of the moaning.

ALEKSANDAR HEMON: I try to be disciplined, but I don't beat myself up if I feel lazy. In fact, if I feel like not writing, I try to understand that as a signal—perhaps I should think a little more about what I am planning to write.

CLAIRE MESSUD: Again, it depends what the surrounding circumstances are. A good period in life is one in which there is a pretty rigorous and utterly regular schedule. The clichés are alas true: such tedium is indeed the writer's friend.

JOSH EMMONS: I'm very rigorous except when I'm not. Writing every day is a good idea and the goal of hundreds and perhaps thousands of writers, and I subscribe to it in theory, but when it's impossible—when family or work or traveling or depression or illness get in the way—I forgo it and try to forgive myself (as with everything, sadly, dangerously, this gets easier over time and should be kept to a minimum).

TASH AW: I'm pretty strict with myself. I don't have a choice—without a routine I'd waste the day on YouTube, or just reading in bed. Writers always talk about their routines in a way that suggests there's a kind of magic ritual involved, but the reality is, I suspect, pretty prosaic for everyone. If you're really interested in just how humdrum my routine is, here it is: at 8 a.m. I turn my computer on and make myself a cup of tea. I read what I wrote the previous day—a kind of warm-up, if you like. I like to be at work before I'm fully awake, so that my head is full of my novel by the time I reach for coffee (9 a.m.-ish). This way, I'm also less prone to distraction. Then I write, make tea, write, etc., until about one p.m. Then I have a swim, or walk, or pay my bills. From 3 p.m. to 7 p.m. I write again. I do this five days a week. On Saturdays I write in the mornings but not the afternoons, and on Sundays I do neither. I like to think of writing as any other job, with proper parameters, otherwise it all gets out of control: I either work all the time or not at all.

RODRIGO FRESÁN: I've never been able to keep a schedule or writing program. Each book imposed its own rhythm and time. Or its lack of rhythm and time.

MICHAEL CHABON: As rigorous as I can be with four kids and a lot of ancillary stuff, side-projects, a column in *Details* magazine, and so on.

AKHIL SHARMA: Not at all. I have enough problems without adding to them.

SUSAN CHOI: When I'm in the midst of a project I try to work five days a week, and it's pretty easy to do that. When I'm between projects I try to do the same thing, and it's almost impossible. Without a project there's nothing to provide continuity, nothing feels compelling—but the problem is that without creating some sort of false continuity, a new project never materializes. So I try to fake myself out, and force myself to work on ideas I know I'm not going to stick with, in the hopes that the real idea will emerge.

CURTIS SITTENFELD: Like a lot of people, I find adhering to a schedule easier on some days than others. But I think it's very important, and when I teach, I tell my students that they should schedule writing times with themselves—this is especially true if they work full time—and write them in a calendar and treat them the way they'd treat an appointment with another person. Even if you can set aside only two hours a week, that does add up. And obviously, if you wrote one page a day, you'd have three hundred sixty-five pages in a year—plenty for a novel. I once heard a woman describe herself as a "binge writer," and I've sometimes been this way myself, but think it's not ideal because if you go away from your manuscript for a long time, you sort of lose touch with what you've written and you also quit thinking about what comes next during all the time in the day you're not working on it. It's like running only once a month and trying to go for ten miles.

RIVKA GALCHEN: I'm kind of a defender of maintaining a really boring life, of having the same habits every day; that's what works for me. Since life is inevitably kind of exhaustingly interesting if you pay the least bit of close attention to it, it makes sense to cordon off an area for repetition and reliability. Like: I know I write best in the morning, and the coffee shop in my neighborhood opens up at seven thirty and getting there around opening time lends the structure to my writing day. I like to sit there, eat my two cookies with my tea, and feel my job is to write. For much of working on my first novel, I only had until ten thirty a.m. to myself, and then had to teach or attend to some other obligation, but that was still a lot of time, but only because it arrived so predictably. And my particular coffee shop is perfect for me—no Internet, no music, the same-ish handful of morning regulars. I find it so, so comforting. And even if I think I have no ideas that day, I try not to luxuriate in that depressed feeling, and instead try to just write something, anything, even something bad, figuring it'll somehow help me write something better another day. For me, this kind of plodding regularity is the only thing that brings out the ghosts. And there's no good writing without the ghosts. (In order for me to like something I've written, I need to get to that place where it doesn't feel like it's me writing, but instead me transcribing, which sounds moronically antique—even to me—but, there you go, somehow it still seems right-ish.) But I can't just go about my life and wait for haunting, it needs to be called to, and regularity is (again, for me, probably not for everyone) a kind of séance. It's kind of like those people who keep a little shrine in some corner of their home. You've got this little shrine, and you tend to it in all these really prosaic ways: dust it, give it its daily incense, occasionally a sifter of brandy, a cigar, whatever seems likely to appeal to the spirit. And sometimes the shrine looks not haunted at all, even kind of childish and pathetic, but the space is there, ready, for whenever the spirit comes. So, well, that's how I think of habits, that they tend to a little shrine of time.

WHERE DO YOU WRITE? HOW IMPORTANT IS YOUR WRITING ENVIRONMENT?

PAUL AUSTER: I don't write at home. I have a small apartment a few blocks from where I live and do nothing there but my work. A Spartan environment, nothing to do in that space but sit at my desk and write.

ALEKSANDAR HEMON: Anywhere. Home, coffee shops, visiting friends, on the train. The only places where I can't write are peaceful writers' retreats. Peace and quiet make me sleepy, and after a few hours of writing I want to see people, go to a bar, play soccer. Writing makes me more engaged and interested in the world and the last thing I want to see after writing is a quiet pond or a poignant sunset.

NELL FREUDENBERGER: I've always written at home until this year, when I was lucky enough to get an office in the public library through the incredible Dorothy & Lewis B. Cullman Center for Scholars and Writers. I'm looking for another office space for next year now. I'm not too picky about what it looks like, or even about noise, but I really need a door that I can close.

HARUKI MURAKAMI: Quiet room. Decent desk. Hopefully, music of Telemann. Early in the morning. No work after sunset.

ANNE ENRIGHT: I write where I can. Time is much more precious to me than space.

JOSÉ MANUEL PRIETO: I can write more or less anywhere. As long as there are no interruptions. I work well in hotel rooms. I work badly in my office at the university. It's something that varies.

RICK MOODY: Sometimes in my office, but more often in bed, and the good thing about writing in bed is that you can find a bed almost anywhere. There are motels everywhere that offer them, sometimes on the cheap. I like writing in bed because I like lying down while I work, and I like lying down while I work because I think imagining is very close to dreaming. Sometimes I can do the two things nearly simultaneously. I can, that is, write a couple of pages, put the computer aside, sleep, wake up, and write a couple more pages. This is the best kind of work—when all of life, basically, is about putting words down on the page. Or sleeping. There's nothing else I really want to do all that much, except maybe play guitar and sing.

CRISTINA GARCIA: Right now I'm subletting a place in Los Angeles, so I don't have my things around and I'm feeling a little bit displaced. But generally I like to work in my home office. The only books I have there are my books of poetry. A wall of poetry. It's really important for me that they're nearby and I have easy access to them.

CHRIS ADRIAN: I seem to favor small closetlike rooms, or actual closets, lately.

JENNIFER EGAN: I can write pretty much anywhere—one of the advantages of writing by hand. Sometimes being away from home is helpful, so I'm not tempted by the Internet or the ten thousand unfinished household chores I feel responsible for. But generally I work in my home and office, which is quiet and light—my two main requirements, though God knows I wrote for years and years without much of either one.

FRANCISCO GOLDMAN: Usually at home at my desk, but I live now in a succession of borrowed homes and so I work at borrowed desks. I am restless; sometimes I need to move around. For example, where I live now in Mexico City is on an avenue that runs around Parque México and that actually used to be a racetrack, and if I am feeling really restless, I can take my notebook, write in a café awhile, walk restlessly into Parque México to pace, and then dart back into another café a little bit farther along the avenue, and so on, until I've traveled the entire loop, and am back at my front door. I used to work a lot as a journalist, sometimes in war situations, which required lots of hard travel and weird hours and long stays in airports and hotels, and so I got used to being able to write just about anywhere. Sometimes I need noise around me, which acts as a kind of wall, a sound-proof wall of noise, and helps me concentrate, while the silence and loneliness of my apartment can feel like an overwhelming horizonless desert.

EDWIDGE DANTICAT: I have an office at home and I write there, but when I'm in the middle of a project and it's going well, I can pretty much write anywhere.

ADANIA SHIBLI: I usually write in my bed, from the morning until late in the afternoon. It is very important that the room be facing the southeast, so as to have the sun lighting up the room. Sometimes, in places I arrive to and have no way to rearrange them, I follow the sun and go to the room in which its light is most present. In winter times I don't write much, but if I have to, I try to arrange the lighting to somehow remind me of the sunlight. Light, in my case, is very important for being able to write.

ANDREW SEAN GREER: I think there should be nothing magical about a writing environment or else you will think "I can't write without my magic coffee cup!," which is ridiculous. That said, I need solitude, silence, a window, and the promise that no one is going to knock on the door.

COLM TÓIBÍN: It doesn't matter where as long as it is private. I write only on the right-hand-side page of an A4-size hardcover notebook using a throwaway fountain pen. I do little (and sometimes big) rewrites on the left-hand side of the page before I start typing.

GEORGE PELECANOS: I write in an office in my house. I cannot write on the road or in hotel rooms. I have to be in my spot.

DINAW MENGESTU: These days I tend to write only at my desk in my living room, but in the past I've been surprised at how flexible I can be when needed, or when fully immersed in my work. Some of my best writing moments were on a series of long train rides all across Morocco in a cabin stuffed with strangers and barely enough air.

JOSH EMMONS: I've moved ten times in the last five years and so don't have a fixed spot in which to write, but I like small quiet rooms with uncluttered walls best. Public parks and coffee shops and libraries aren't bad, but the temptation to eavesdrop or watch other people (or animals or grass growing) can be powerful, so I generally work at home.

RABIH ALAMEDDINE: I tend to write at home. That's the only thing. I'm not very good at writing in cafés or anything. Where at home? It could be my bed, it could be anywhere. I have a writing chair, which I barely use, but it could be on the sofa, it could be on the floor. I've done it this way for my back, where I'm lying on the floor and my legs are up in the air, and no, I was not having sex.

MICHAEL CHABON: I have a very nice office behind my house in Berkeley, which I share with my wife, Ayelet. It is lined with books and cool stuff to look at and just now got some crazy Arts and Crafts movement wallpaper. But I can work pretty much anywhere, it doesn't really matter that much. Airplanes, hotel rooms, doctors' offices. As long as I have an iPod and a comfortable chair.

YIYUN LI: I write at our dining table.

SANTIAGO RONCAGLIOLO: I have a very small studio, like an office, without a television or music or a telephone, that I've been decorating with little toys that I bring back from my travels. It's like a personal toy room: a private space, quiet, bright. I warm up my food in the microwave and spend the day there.

ALEJANDRO ZAMBRA: Every time I have tried to create an adequate writing space, the result has been a blank page. For example, the beach: on one occasion I got a house at a resort and lost the first few days trying to create, in a foreign place, a place of my own. I ended up so tired

I spent the rest of the time lying on the sand, thinking about a book, but also observing the rare end-of-summer beachgoers.

Generally I write at home, but the work is never continuous. I never spend more than an hour sitting because I'm pretty hyper. I let myself, also, get interrupted; I answer the phone and e-mail, sometimes I listen to news on the radio. It usually happens that a word or dialogue gets mixed into what I'm writing. I really like those interferences, I believe they are somehow necessary.

I'm not a fan of silence. I prefer the moderate sounds of loved ones moving around, or the music played by the neighbor, who, from a distance, seems to have rediscovered the speed metal of his youth.

MEHMET MURAT SOMER: At home, in Istanbul, usually in my library room, at the desk with my favorite music on. The music changes from operas of G. F. Handel to Amy Winehouse, with occasional stops at Andy Williams or swinging bossa nova tracks according to my mood. But I have written in very odd places as well. I'm afraid wherever I have my laptop, I can write.

YAEL HEDAYA: I write at home. I don't have a studio or anything, but rather an alcove on the second floor. I share my work space with my three kids, my eight-year-old boy-and-girl twins and my three-year-old, who abuse my computer with their games and stuff. I can never find my backup CDs because they're in a pile with SpongeBob SquarePants games. So, no, I don't have a room of my own, and actually, strangely enough, I'm fine with this.

CHRIS ABANI: I used to have rituals. Now I write everywhere and whenever I need to or can; airplanes, coffee shops, in meetings, in readings, on the bus, on the floor in the living room while I watch *Lost*.

AKHIL SHARMA: In my apartment, after my wife leaves for work. I have gotten used to writing when I am alone and when it is quiet.

RODDY DOYLE: I work in an office in the attic of my house. It's great—both remote and close. It's important but not vital. I could work anywhere. I've written in libraries and airports, and beside a swimming pool while my kids were learning how not to drown.

SUSAN MINOT: Ideally at a quiet desk. Though I can and do write on airplanes, in cars, in coffee shops, on ferries, on trains, on the floor, in bed. Of course it's nice to be in a pleasant environment if you are there for long hours, to have a window, or some space over your head. The most important element though is knowing you will not be interrupted. That is the necessary thing.

SAŠA STANIŠIĆ: Wherever there is no hard rock playing.

RODRIGO FRESÁN: Now, in a room at the top of a set of stairs with views of a hill and a forest. It's the best writing space I've had. I can't stand noise and, nowadays, they're cutting down some trees and drilling the rock to build an apartment building. So the best writing space I've ever had is on the road to becoming one of the worst. I've complained. But no one protects writers. Maybe that's why we're a species heading toward extinction.

DANIEL HANDLER: I have a nice office with the OED and music and tea, but sometimes I get tired of it and find a lousy café with nondistracting food and drink.

A. M. HOMES: It's not my writing environment that's so important but my general environment. I write best at Yaddo, the artist's colony, because there the rest of the world and the demands recede and I am able to get a depth of concentration that eludes me in my usual life.

CLAIRE MESSUD: I write on a particular pad with a particular pen. Beyond that, I can write in any number of places. There are elements of my writing environment that are important—for example, that any noise not be generated by my own progeny—but I'm basically pretty flexible.

ANN CUMMINS: I have a stand-up podium desk with a small laptop on it. It faces a green wall (which needs painting) in our house in Oakland. I like to walk around when I write, shake out the cobwebs. I need to be alone when I write, and I can't write if a TV is on or music's playing. I can write most anywhere, as long as I'm alone.

SUSAN CHOI: My writing space keeps changing. The most important thing for me is that it be private; I can't write in cafés or other public spaces, I just end up staring into space or eavesdropping on people. Currently I work in a studio apartment about a ten-minute drive from my home. It's bare bones but comfortable—table and chair, mushy couch to nap on, kitchenette for lunch or snacks, bathroom.

STEPHEN KING: A room upstairs. My writing environment doesn't matter much.

T COOPER: I want to be one of those annoying people who can just flip open his laptop anywhere—a café, on a train, at a library, on the toilet—and get a ton of work done, but I'm just not. I like to be at my desk, which has my comfortable chair, my model airplanes and photographs and all of my research materials on it. Or, it's so wonderful to have the opportunity to have a residency at a colony where there are four blank walls to hang my outlines and a completely empty desk for my computer, printer, books, and me. (Though one plane always goes with me—usually an F4U Corsair.)

AMY TAN: Ideally I would be writing at my desk at my home in Sausalito. If I put headphones on I'm able to write almost anywhere on a computer. I do also write in a journal—which is good for traveling when I can't have my computer. Like in the back of a bus.

HOW CONSCIOUS OF INFLUENCE ARE YOU
WHEN YOU ARE WRITING?

STEPHEN KING: Almost never. Although if I'm reading a powerful stylist like Cormac McCarthy or Jon Hassler, those rhythms sometimes carry over. You have to smooth that shit out later.

JONATHAN LETHEM: I think I may be a peculiar writer in the degree to which I am constantly, lucidly aware of influence at any given moment—usually a few of them at once. For that reason I've always felt it was pointless to imagine some kind of pure state where influence has been put to rest—instead, it is a companion and a fuel, an inevitable and rich environment in which the work is to be done.

COLM TÓIBÍN: You must be joking. I am conscious only of the sentence I am working on.

MICHAEL CHABON: Sometimes if I have been reading somebody with a pronounced, distinctive style all day I will note some echo creeping into my own writing. Usually I leave the other-tainted language in there until the next day, or week, when it tends to stick out like a sore thumb. Sometimes it's appropriate enough or close enough to my own voice that I find a way to work it in.

PAUL AUSTER: Early on, as a young man, I sometimes felt crippled by the writers I admired. But as the years have gone on, that is no longer an issue.

ANDREW SEAN GREER: Very conscious. I keep a few books around that I pick up when I want to soak them up. I am very particular about what I keep around, and they change from book to book. What never changes is *Lolita*, Proust, and Wallace Stevens.

YAEL HEDAYA: I used to be more conscious of influence at the beginning of my career. Now, I'm less so. I don't read as much as I used to, for lack of time and being too exhausted at night, so I'm not so influenced anymore. I actually miss being influenced because it was like being in love. It filled me both with hope and dread and I was on a constant influence HIGH.

SUSAN CHOI: If my work is going well, I'm not conscious of it at all, but if I'm struggling to find a subject or a voice, then everything I've ever admired and plenty of things I don't admire will elbow into the vacuum.

JOSÉ MANUEL PRIETO: Influences are felt or weigh you down more when young. As an adult or when a certain maturity in writing is reached, this is something that one may even play with. It's good, I think, to introduce certain tones or allusive quotes in the style of other writers, that make, for example, reference to how that person confronts certain circumstances. A dialogue in the style of Hemingway, for example. There's a chapter ending in *Nocturnal Butterflies of the Russian Empire* in which I absolutely consciously included a small dialogue in the Hemingway style because it was the kind of "rock" or "material" I wanted to use in that segment, so that it would shine with the same polish that Hemingway liked to give his books: with light braggadocio. My character looks at himself the same way; it is a voluntary "quote." Or then Proust's languorous style, the entwined prose of Nabokov, etc. But all that one tries to adapt into a personal style. *Encyclopedia of Russian Life* has, at times, the terse and tight style of Borges; it seeks that effect.

T COOPER: I don't think I'm conscious of it at all, and the reason I think that is because I can't even really figure out what this question is getting at.

AMY TAN: I can be very conscious of literary influence if I happen to be reading at the time and that's one of the distractions. I have to try either not to read or to shut that out. I have to immerse myself fully in my own voice and my own story. It's very easy to fall into the voice of another writer and then I have to knock that out later.

ALEKSANDAR HEMON: Writing always involves me in dialogue with other writers. Sometimes I quote them; sometimes I want to do what they did, sometimes the opposite. I never think that I am the only one involved in the text I am writing.

FRANCISCO GOLDMAN: There is the consciousness that you willfully incorporate—you're in some way in a dialogue with books that have come before you—and that is fine; and then there is the other kind that is an annoyance. These days, unlike when I was younger, I am pretty good at shrugging it off.

EDWIDGE DANTICAT: Not at all. Sometimes I want to scream out to all writers dead and alive in the entire universe, "Influence me, please."

YIYUN LI: Not conscious at all. But when I revise I would recognize things that could be traced to my favorite novels.

NELL FREUDENBERGER: Sometimes I write a sentence I think is brilliant, and then I realize that it's brilliant because I stole it (not the actual words, but the voice) from something I'm reading. Those sentences have to go (even if you're the only one who recognizes them) because you can never sustain someone else's voice. But I don't think there's anything wrong with being influenced; of course writers learn by absorbing what they read. The process is very slow and roundabout, at least for me.

SAŠA STANIŠIĆ: It depends on what I'm working on. Sometimes I think of myself as the only person in the universe dealing with a subject. But most of the time I'm stealing the ideas of others and trying to fool myself into "working in the tradition of Kurt Vonnegut. . . ."

CLAIRE MESSUD: When I'm writing I'm only conscious of the writing. Which is why nothing is better than to be writing.

SANTIAGO RONCAGLIOLO: The basic ideas behind my books have nothing to do with other authors, but rather with my own creative interests. But I constantly look toward other authors for artful touches or nuances to add. In a way, influences are like the colors on a palette: I use so many of them at once that it's hard to distinguish among them on the final canvas.

CHRIS ABANI: I wish the writers I admire could influence me. We should all be so lucky.

DANIEL HANDLER: Sometimes I'm conscious of it but mostly I'm conscious that I'll never know the half of what has influenced me. (I never understand the anxiety of influence. Of course you're going to be influenced by things, and you won't know what they are except perhaps occasionally. Some writers seem to get upset about this, which mystifies me.)

A. M. HOMES: Not conscious and not worried.

RODRIGO FRESÁN: Less so with time. I suppose that as years go by you're more influenced by your own self. A bad influence, perhaps, but conveniently nearby.

SUSAN MINOT: I'm pretty conscious when there appears another sound in my head if it's of another writer. Sometimes I listen to it and let it guide me and will see if I can use it to get at something particular of what I have to say and sometimes I banish it because it gets TOO loud and therefore isn't original.

RODDY DOYLE: Influence isn't something on my shoulder as I write. It's just me and the page—on the good days.

RICK MOODY: Worrying about influence, finally, is vain, because we are all influenced. There really isn't that much about me or my work that's truly unique, and I don't really *need* to be unique. I try not to think about what I'm doing. I just try to scribble down some more words, or perhaps to correct some of those I have already set down. It doesn't matter if there is influence, it doesn't matter what it all means. That's for critics and audiences to settle.

AKHIL SHARMA: Tremendously. I seek to be influenced. I wish I could be more influenced.

WHAT'S THE LONGEST PERIOD OF TIME YOU'VE LEFT AN UNFINISHED MANUSCRIPT REST?

HARUKI MURAKAMI: Once started, I finish it.

GLEN DAVID GOLD: Zero.

ANDREW SEAN GREER: A week or so. I do nothing else when I am working on something. I do not multitask.

JOSH EMMONS: I'm just now returning to a half-completed novel after a six-week break; I can see that some of what I wrote in a first-draft fever needs to go or be extensively rewritten, which is a nice perspective to have, though at the same time I feel a distance from the story that wouldn't have arisen had I not been away from it for so long. While it's usually a good idea to let at least a month pass between completing and revising a novel, I'm of two or more minds about the benefit of vacationing from it before it's finished.

NELL FREUDENBERGER: Only a month or two, in the case of things I went back to later. I've left many manuscripts to die, though.

RODRIGO FRESÁN: Varying times. Not very long. Generally, I nearly run to the printers. Letting a manuscript rest scares me a little. There's the danger that like an apple falling from the tree without anyone biting it, it ends up rotting on the ground.

FRANCISCO GOLDMAN: Many months. I don't recall.

EDWIDGE DANTICAT: Six months.

ANN CUMMINS: I'd say six months.

YIYUN LI: Eight months.

TAYARI JONES: Almost a year.

RICK MOODY: There have been stories that I have set aside for months. In one case, I can remember setting aside a short story for almost a year.

STEPHEN KING: A year.

ADANIA SHIBLI: Two years.

AKHIL SHARMA: Two and a half years.

CLAIRE MESSUD: Years.

DANIEL HANDLER: Years and years.

MICHAEL CHABON: Oh, years. Depends, really, on how you define "unfinished." I have all kinds of twenty-page starts sitting around on my hard drive.

COLM TÓIBÍN: With most of the books I write an opening chapter and leave it for a year or two years. And then I pounce on it and do everything to finish it even if I fail to finish it fast. With some of the short stories I write them up to the last few pages and leave them for a year or two.

CHRIS ABANI: Eight years.

ANNE ENRIGHT: I have come back to an unfinished fragment, very happily, after ten years—but this only works with short pieces.

PAUL AUSTER: My fourth novel, *In the Country of Last Things*, took me fifteen years to write. I started it when I was twenty-two and didn't finish it until I was thirty-seven. I would pick it up and then put it down again. Again and again. The intervals sometimes lasted for several years.

SUSAN CHOI: Fifteen years and counting. Though I don't think it's resting—I think it's dead. But you never know.

CRISTINA GARCIA: Right after *Dreaming in Cuban* I worked on something for two years that I never finished, so I suppose you could say that it's been fifteen years. For something I finished, probably the longest I've been away was six months.

A. M. HOMES: Well, it took me ten years or more to write *The Mistress's Daughter*, despite the fact that a hundred or more pages were finished in the first three months.

MEHMET MURAT SOMER: There are several on my hard drive. I don't know whether I will ever return to them. For some I have an inclination. Or they may rest in peace. Usually when I lay a piece to rest, I lose my interest in the material. I even forget the details I have written, including the names of my characters. I envy the writers remembering every sentence they've put on paper during their long careers.

RODDY DOYLE: Twenty-five years. It's resting in a landfill site somewhere. In fact, it's probably under a housing estate or a motorway by now. I usually leave "finished" or "nearly finished" work aside for months.

SANTIAGO RONCAGLIOLO: *Prudishness* had a few first chapters that lay dormant for a year until I discovered exactly what I wanted to do. I always save those aborted projects, but that was the only time that I took one of them up again.

SUSAN MINOT: Are we counting the ones that still are resting? I have stories that have been resting for thirty-five years and counting. . . .

YAEL HEDAYA: I don't think this ever happened. I mean, there are times when I'm working on a book and then there would be a few weeks, or even months, when I haven't made any progress or even looked at the text, but to me, this isn't considered letting an unfinished manuscript rest, just a hiatus or break from my work. For me, writing is sometimes more about NOT writing. I envy writers who just write. Who don't teach or have other jobs and can maintain a regular, vigorous writing schedule. My writing is just as chaotic as my life, but somehow, I don't know how, the book gets written. There are times when I complain that I'm not writing, that I haven't written in a while, but when I look at the text a month later, it actually expanded, so I must be writing even if it doesn't feel like I am.

JOSÉ MANUEL PRIETO: This has changed; now I work much faster than when I started. But in any case, it's a good idea to let the manuscript rest, forget it up to the point where you approach it again as if it were somebody else's work. And then all the inexactitudes, the vagaries, or better yet, certain behaviors by your characters that lack motivation, or stand in contrast to their character, etc., stand out.

ALEJANDRO ZAMBRA: I've abandoned a lot of manuscripts, but I don't feel nostalgic or frustrated about it. Those stories somehow reappear. Or: you had to do a lot wrong to later do less wrong. In any case, I sketch a lot. Most of the time what I'm doing is sketching: I write without destination until finding a clearing, hitting a vein, and toil until I give form to the novel or my failure.

ALEKSANDAR HEMON: Leaving the manuscript alone is part of the process. I call that "sagging." If I drop it for a while, it does not worry me. Something is still happening. So I never really have any unfinished manuscripts in my drawer. I finish almost everything I start. I think that it is very dangerous to organize your writing in terms of measurable production. One of the joys of writing is that it ain't a factory. You don't really have to do it if you don't feel like it.

WHAT DID YOU LEARN UPON RETURNING TO IT? WAS IT USEFUL?

RODRIGO FRESÁN: I have a finished novella (it's not the one I'm currently working on) and the truth is I'm afraid to go back to it. Afraid it will bite me like one of those dogs you leave locked inside the car without food or water.

AKHIL SHARMA: That the book was fine and I was driving myself crazy for no reason.

COLM TÓIBÍN: I learn nothing from what I write.

ANNE ENRIGHT: I returned to it when its moment came, and I knew how to proceed.

DANIEL HANDLER: It was useful not to publish it, yes. But all I've learned from work that I've set aside is that I was right to set it aside, and the few scraps that are useful to me are hardly worth the effort of finding them—it feels like diving into a shipwreck in order to find a few usable bolts and screws.

SANTIAGO RONCAGLIOLO: It was helpful, because beginning to write, even though I wasn't sure of what I wanted to do, was a way of activating my ideas. Once one part was written, the text became more of a concrete reality whose possibilities I could explore more easily in other writings and in movies.

MICHAEL CHABON: Often that has been the case with short stories . . . that I come back to them after a long absence and see at once how to complete them. It's never happened with a novel. Not yet.

MEHMET MURAT SOMER: Not for me. I'd lost my sense of speed and pacing, which I believe is essential in my thrillers. And while trying to elaborate and embellish it, I lost total interest in the material. It became "stale" to me. I, myself, flow more comfortably with "fresh material" at a page-turner pace.

CRISTINA GARCIA: I learned that I probably shouldn't have taken that much time off, because I've been having a hell of a time getting back into it! And now the whole enterprise is being called into question. For me, I need to have daily access to it.

ADANIA SHIBLI: I realized how "wise" it was to leave it, although as a person, I rarely make "wise" decisions; they are merely decisions. The wisdom of this decision lies in that this time out gave me the chance to realize and accept why I was not fully satisfied with the work, and more, what to do to continue working on it, rather than compromise on what I deeply thought was mediocre, and publish it, then move to the following text.

ALEKSANDAR HEMON: Yeah. You forget about certain things, find some other things annoying. You return to it more as a reader, sever some vain, writerly attachments.

EDWIDGE DANTICAT: It was very useful. After six months, I could see a lot of weaknesses anew. (I could also find some good things objectively.) It was like reading someone else's work.

NELL FREUDENBERGER: The thing I've let rest longest (and then returned to) was the first story I published. In that case, I learned almost everything about it after I returned to it. I think I knew who the characters were, and I had a very strong sense of where it took place, but I didn't know which parts of the story were the interesting parts—or what I needed to explore more deeply. An editor helped me figure that out, and I'm still grateful.

A. M. HOMES: I learned that the first hundred pages were fine and there was nothing about them that I would rewrite, which meant to me that, like it or not, I got the story right, and the fact that in ten years nothing about the experience or the emotion had shifted meant that I was on very solid ground to go forward.

CHRIS ABANI: I learned that I could lose two hundred pages and be left with a beautiful and necessary novella like *Becoming Abigail*.

STEPHEN KING: Don't do THAT again. Was it useful? No!

FRANCISCO GOLDMAN: Very useful. You see more clearly what has to go.

YIYUN LI: It was harder to get back into the manuscript, which perhaps was a sign that I should not have let it rest for the first time, but

I did it only because other aspects of life were too demanding, and there was no choice there.

RODDY DOYLE: It's always wise to set work aside for a while. It's a cliché because it's true: time is a great editor. You can reread the work without the silly enthusiasm or passion that went into its completion.

RICK MOODY: I'm never as bad as I think I am. Nor am I as good.

TAYARI JONES: It was very hard to get back into it. Part of it was just me beating myself up for not sticking with it. I don't know what I learned. Oh yes, I learned not to do that again!

SUSAN MINOT: It is always useful for time to pass not looking at your work. Sometimes something will be salvageable. But if you left it for a while, there was probably a reason for that. You lost interest.

CLAIRE MESSUD: Usually that it was no good at all. Or that I couldn't possibly return to it. But in my old age I am trying to accept that there is usefulness even in these realizations.

DO YOU READ YOUR WORK ALOUD?

AMY TAN: I do. And I should do it more often. Reading aloud gets me into the rhythm. Helps me tell where the novel's gone off in the wrong direction. Mostly it's for clunkiness, for getting a sense of authenticity.

SUSAN MINOT: When composing, I very much hear the words and how they sound in my head. I might mutter now and then, but it's not a regular practice.

JOSÉ MANUEL PRIETO: No, because prose written in fiction is not always work to be read [aloud]; the eyes can put up with longer time periods, subordinated sentences, that the ear can't. Also, prose read aloud or written to be read aloud tends to be more dramatic.

YIYUN LI: Not really. I can't bear to hear my voice.

COLM TÓIBÍN: Never! (or see below).

AKHIL SHARMA: Yes.

ANDREW SEAN GREER: I always claim I will, but never do, alas!

CLAIRE MESSUD: I read my work aloud in my head, if that makes any sense. Again, it's about the music. And then sometimes to my husband's horror, I read bits aloud to him. He hates it.

DINAW MENGESTU: I used to at first, and these days I can't stand to even think of hearing my words out loud.

RICK MOODY: I think this is very useful, if not essential, in the pursuit of good prose. One result of the computer age is this: people can produce faster. The prose sometimes *looks* acceptable, when digitally airbrushed, but it doesn't ring in the ear at all. I think of what we do as writers being consonant with an oral tradition, and so it should *sound* good. When it does sound good, I suspect, it looks even better on the page. Look at a writer like William Gaddis. Very difficult, yes, but also incredibly sublime as far as his ear goes. You can't write eight hundred pages of unattributed dialogue without having a perfect ear.

MEHMET MURAT SOMER: No. Not the novels. When writing film scripts in the past, I did. To test the speed, the breath required, the timing. . . .

ALEJANDRO ZAMBRA: Always. A phrase that cannot be said aloud, in a whisper or scream, should not exist. I can think of no better way to internalize rhythm, to test the wholeness of a paragraph, than by its interaction with silence. Also, for me it is a habit related to poetry writing. I don't believe we should demand less music from prose than from poetry.

GEORGE PELECANOS: No, but I print it out and read it off a page rather than off a screen. There is something about the words on the printed page that tells me whether or not I am on the right track.

CHRIS ABANI: Yes, all the time. This is vital to gauge rhythm, music, cadence, tone, and mood, and also to cut all the unnecessary words. I have so many of those.

JOSH EMMONS: No, but people who do say it alerts them to syntactical infelicities (if I read this aloud, for example, I might not use the phrase "syntactical infelicities").

EDWIDGE DANTICAT: I often read difficult passages into a tape recorder. The passages I stumble on while reading are often the ones that need the most work.

DANIEL HANDLER: Every single word.

GLEN DAVID GOLD: Yes. I find that it really helps me understand its rhythm.

PAUL AUSTER: Yes, both to myself when I'm alone in my workroom and also to my wife, about once a month.

ANNE ENRIGHT: I used to read everything aloud to my husband at the end of each day. He finally told me to shut up in 1993.

TAYARI JONES: All the time. I love it. It makes the story come alive for me.

ALEKSANDAR HEMON: No, but I always hear it in my head.

JONATHAN LETHEM: Yes, to myself as I work, and in sections to others to get a sense of what is and isn't working—hugely helpful at nearly any point in a project.

A. M. HOMES: For pace, rhythm, and to make sure a line works—but I never orate!

ANN CUMMINS: Yes. I whisper it while I'm composing, and I read a finished manuscript aloud before I send it off. If the "sound of it" is off, it's not finished.

SANTIAGO RONCAGLIOLO: Never.

RODDY DOYLE: Never.

RABIH ALAMEDDINE: Yes. It's both helpful and not. It is helpful because I find mistakes and stuff, but it's not helpful because a lot of the times I get lost in my own stories, so I think, "Oh, this is a great story that I'm telling," and it might be the most boring story ever.

NELL FREUDENBERGER: Almost never, although I admire a lot of writers who do. Grace Paley always did, and I think she was a writer with perfect pitch.

MICHAEL CHABON: Yes, I do. To myself, every so often to my wife. But not as often as I ought to—it's an incredibly invaluable editing tool. But time consuming.

RODRIGO FRESÁN: A phrase here and there. I find it useful in order to find repeated words. The computer screen fools and lies a lot. Like a mirror that hides—but does not eliminate—wrinkles and imperfections.

STEPHEN KING: If a passage is syntactically difficult, reading aloud is vital.

HARUKI MURAKAMI: Never.

JENNIFER EGAN: Reading aloud is a critical part of my process. I do it alone, but even more helpfully, I do it with a group of peers that meets regularly. We don't look at anything on the page; we just read aloud to each other and respond. I recommend this highly, for many reasons. One is, there is no better way to hear the music and rhythm of one's own prose than to read it to a group that has no written corollary to look at—to just hear your language hit the room. Often it's excruciating, and sometimes it's exhilarating. But it really helps you to hear the work in a different way. Also, in terms of getting feedback, there's a natural triage that occurs when everyone is hearing something at once, rather than reading it (or, more likely, skimming it) privately. Those immediate reactions tend to address the crucial things and dispense with the niggling unimportant things. By the time I publish a book, I will likely have read all of it aloud, in private or to this group, often many times.

T COOPER: No, it feels indulgent and I get uncomfortable any time I've tried, so if I'm trying to work out a particular line or section, I just do it in my head.

FRANCISCO GOLDMAN: On the phone to one or two friends, who probably aren't even listening, and hopefully when I'm not drunk.

CURTIS SITTENFELD: I always read my work aloud—I think I even read aloud my e-mails before I send them! (This is not to say my e-mails are works of art, alas.) With my most recent novel, which is five hundred and fifty pages, I read the entire thing aloud at least three times. This would take me about ten days of reading six hours a day, and I'd sometimes feel hoarse by the end of the day even though I hadn't left the house or talked to another human. But I swear there's no substitute for reading aloud in terms of avoiding word repetition, overly similar sentences or observations, and clunky rhythms. Plus, once I'm so familiar with a manuscript that it's started to become nonsense, it still makes sense when I hear it rather than read it.

YAEL HEDAYA: Absolutely not. Why would I subject myself to such torture?

HOW DO YOU MOVE FORWARD
WHEN YOU ARE BLOCKED?

A. M. HOMES: I am usually a bit like an air traffic controller: I have lots of things in the pipeline, art books, articles, films, plays, so when I am stuck, I simply shift to another format, another project. Long story short, I can't afford to be blocked, on any level. That said, I think there's a thing called writer's blank, which is different from a block. The blank means that in the depths of one's brain the soup is not soup yet, it's not ready to happen; writing novels is a process and to do it well you have to dig deep and it takes a while for that material to be ready and available for use—not that it's personal material, but just processing and preparing one's thoughts on a subject or character.

HARUKI MURAKAMI: I have not had any experience when I was blocked, so far.

ALEJANDRO ZAMBRA: My friend the Chilean poet Leonardo San-hueza says that the best way to overcome a block is to shave and then sit and await the aftershave muses. I've followed his advice. I don't always get results, but the image is more precise than it seems: I think it is good to concentrate on something else, and shaving requires absolute concentration. The risk is nothing less than cutting up your face.

ALEKSANDAR HEMON: I'm never blocked. When I don't feel like writing or have nothing to write, I don't write. Writing should not be a job. If it is a job, you are a hack. Besides, not writing is very important for writing.

RODRIGO FRESÁN: Throw myself down the stairs: no forward move-ment, I fall. The Law of Gravity never fails you.

ANDREW SEAN GREER: Sit down and keep going anyway. Again, willpower is the major force in finishing a novel. No block is permanent. But maybe I will change my mind about that!

SAŠA STANIŠIĆ: I don't believe in the myth of writer's block, and so I never have it.

PAUL AUSTER: Great patience is needed. I have discovered, after many miserable weeks and months of suffering, that when a writer is blocked it generally means that he doesn't know what he is trying to say. You have to go back and examine your motives, your intentions, what you are trying to accomplish. But the essential thing is not to force things merely for the sake of putting words down on the page.

FRANCISCO GOLDMAN: Lately—go out into the park and pace around and go to the next place with a table and coffee.

ANNE ENRIGHT: I don't do blocks.

TAYARI JONES: I just keep at it. I think it's a lot like using a pen that isn't working. You can make the scribbling motion and nothing happens, until suddenly it does. Who knows why. But it does. Thank the lord.

AMY TAN: There are many different ways. One is to put on the same music I had on when I was last working on the scene. Music is hypnotic. It aligns all the other senses of the imagination. So that takes me there. Another way is for me to go into my journals. In there are all kinds of observations and ideas that might prompt me or are exciting and get me thinking. Sometimes I wake up at two in the morning and that's when I write furiously and write ten pages. And when I wake up I don't recognize the writing but sometimes I look back and I say, Oh, this is good, this needs to go into the novel. And there are other ways—including having someone that's whipping you with a deadline. Deadlines are very effective.

AKHIL SHARMA: It's very hard. I've tried doing it by lowering my standards. This usually doesn't work because you end up producing garbage.

STEPHEN KING: Go for more walks. Don't take a book. Throw my mind on its own resources.

DANIEL HANDLER: I just write anyway, even knowing it's lousy. Ten pages of bad writing are more useful to me than giving up for the afternoon—let alone the week, or the year.

MEHMET MURAT SOMER: Ask my trusted readers, i.e., my agent and close friends for help. But, usually I don't get that "block" when writing. I get blocked on planning the plot and pace of events. A nice trip to someplace I haven't been before or a beach in the tropics, like Rio de Janeiro, usually helps a lot.

DINAW MENGESTU: I used to throw myself back into my work until I worked through the "block," and there is often a real benefit to that. You can see where you went wrong in the narrative the more you keep writing, but at the same time there is a lot of frustration and anger that can build up, so I try to balance that by reading heavily. I tend to find that when I'm really stuck, immersing myself in a few novels, old or new, tends to spur my imagination back to life.

COLM TÓIBÍN: I have never been blocked. I have been lazy or just been enjoying myself too much.

YAEL HEDAYA: I revise. I used to think 99 percent inspiration and 1 percent work. Now I know it's the other way around. Since I'm always blocked I'm always revising. I never start from where I've left off the day before. I always go back to the first sentence, just checking to see that everything's okay there, and of course I always end up cleaning things up a bit, expanding, branching out, pressing the ENTER key to move old paragraphs down the page and make room for new ones. Once I have a mass of material, say, over fifty pages, I move on to the next section. This is what I always tell my students. If you want to move forward, go back. Writing is not about leaping forward like an antelope, or some other fast, graceful creature. Writing is about moving like a crab. Sideways.

RICK MOODY: My approach is simply to move forward even when I don't want to.

JOSÉ MANUEL PRIETO: It hasn't occurred to me yet. Only the normal resistance of whatever the theme may be to be put into words and in a style of your own, but I haven't experienced what is known as writer's block.

EDWIDGE DANTICAT: I put the work away and start reading other books that have similar patterns. Often I find clues in other books as to how to unblock myself. Time itself helps too. I refuse to tell myself that I'm blocked. I tell myself either I'm not ready or the story's not ready.

GEORGE PELECANOS: I force myself to put something on paper.

SUSAN MINOT: Painfully, helplessly, dismally, doggedly, despairingly, hopefully. I keep chipping away at it, or banging the dead horse, or screaming into the darkness, or however you might put it. Something moves eventually. Blocks are really loss of the touch . . . you have to work at it to find it.

JOSH EMMONS: When blocked, I go over what I've already written and think about the narrative options and write drivel with the intention of cutting it right away and read my favorite authors and breathe mindfully to stem the panic that accompanies being blocked and knock off early and assure myself that this state won't last forever, that sometimes my unconscious is working hard without my actually writing and that this will be beneficial in the end.

GLEN DAVID GOLD: Hmm. I do an end run, trying in another part of the book. Or I give up for a while. Or I go back and figure out where the narrative went off the rails and try to go in exactly the opposite direction.

NELL FREUDENBERGER: Apart from taking a walk, just forcing yourself to sit at the computer (and then return to the computer the next day) is the only thing I think you can do. I do think it's very dangerous to go around telling yourself (or, god forbid, other people) that you're "blocked." I think it's probably a self-fulfilling prophecy.

ANN CUMMINS: Running or hiking is very important to my writing process. When I get stymied in my daily writing, I go for a run and can usually come back with a few ideas. I don't know that I've had writer's block, as in "no ideas." I've certainly looked at work and found absolutely no merit in it. I suppose that's a sort of block. Then I put it away and try to forget it. Sometimes I'll see merit when I return to it; sometimes not. I have had periods when I didn't have the stomach for writing—when I told myself I was done with it. I've gone as long as a year without writing. In retrospect, it was good. I didn't spend the year looking for material or anything. Maybe I was trying to feel a sense of wonder, the kind of wonder I felt when I discovered writing. It's good to remember that the act of writing, itself, can become deadeningly routine.

JENNIFER EGAN: I decide that I will write really, really badly for as long as it takes. My working title for *The Keep* was *A Short, Bad Novel.* I was writing dreadfully, and I continued to for many months. But even amid that dreadful material, there were some helpful impulses, which ultimately guided me through the novel. Being "blocked," for me, is about being unwilling to write awful stuff. If I can persuade myself that it's okay to write crap, then the block seems to disappear. And sometimes that crap seems to clear the way for better writing.

RODDY DOYLE: I don't think I've ever been really blocked. If things are slow or very unsatisfactory, I move to a different project, and come back to the problem later. I'll happily write crap, knowing it's crap, and edit it properly later. Often, we write six bad sentences before we get to the good seventh one. But we have to write the six first, before we recognize them and realize that the seventh is the true sentence. So, even the bad days are useful.

SANTIAGO RONCAGLIOLO: I do other things until I become unblocked. It's a matter of relaxing—but also of knowing how to distinguish between a brief creative block and a dead end, a story with no future.

YIYUN LI: Taking a break and writing a story, mostly.

T COOPER: Reading some nonfiction material that pertains to my work usually jump-starts my brain into a different gear. I'll get excited about some small detail and then motivated to work it into somewhere else in the manuscript that wasn't blocking me. Looking at books of photographs also helps, or even opening a favorite novel to a random page and reading for a few minutes.

CHRIS ABANI: I don't know what it means to be blocked. I think this is just a personality issue. Carpenters never get blocked, or plumbers (in fact, the very opposite). What I do is a job, and when you aren't precious, you go to work. Simple.

CLAIRE MESSUD: Any advice on that score would be most welcome.

MICHAEL CHABON: I just add words. Even bad words. Words that I know, as I type them, I will end up cutting. The point is to get to one thousand.

Chapter 6

REVISION

WHEN/HOW DO YOU SHOW A DRAFT
TO YOUR TRUSTED READERS?

PAUL AUSTER: I have only one trusted reader, my wife, Siri Hustvedt. She is my indefatigable companion and critic, and I trust her opinions completely. We have been living together for more than twenty-seven years, and I don't think there has been a single time when I have not taken her comments to heart.

EDWIDGE DANTICAT: When I'm totally done.

SAŠA STANIŠIĆ: Some chapters or paragraphs I even show immediately after writing them.

COLM TÓIBÍN: Oh dear. I hate to admit this and I don't do it as much as I used to. But I have a close friend and a few times I have read her long passages over the phone. I know that I should be shot for this and I will certainly do a long period in purgatory. I will try and make it up to my friend, but God will not forgive me. Sometimes I love finishing something so I can show it to her, so it makes me work. I have an agent, Peter Straus, who used to be my editor in London, and I show everything to him as soon as it is typed. And a few other friends who are not writers see chapters or new stories in early drafts.

STEPHEN KING: I only have one, my wife. Halfway through a book, I'll ask her to read it if she's willing. I want to know if it makes sense. Also, I listen to see if she laughs.

NELL FREUDENBERGER: I usually don't show it to anyone but an editor (or sometimes my husband) until I have something with a beginning, middle, and end.

RABIH ALAMEDDINE: I show it very early. I usually show before I've even finished, though it depends on which readers. Unless I'm in trouble, I usually don't show my agent anything until I have a final book. That wasn't the case for this book because I was in trouble early. And it took so long that I wanted to show somebody, particularly my agent, whom I trust. I wanted to show her that I hadn't gone crazy. But for the most part I show friends really early on. If I have thirty pages, I usually start showing.

T COOPER: After I have a very good first or second draft I ask my trusted readers to take a look at it for me. I don't like showing parts or sections, so I wait until I have something that feels representative of the entire project; that way the feedback will be more helpful for me, and I won't be disrespectful of my readers' precious time.

HARUKI MURAKAMI: When I feel the work is 98 percent done.

DANIEL HANDLER: I show pages to my wife when I have a considerable amount—maybe one hundred pages—and I'm suddenly insecure and need someone to tell me whether or not it's worth pursuing. When I have a complete draft I might pick a couple of people to read it.

ADAM MANSBACH: Generally, when it's as finished as I know how to make it for the time being. Which really means it's nowhere close.

GLEN DAVID GOLD: Remember those four bad novels? Wrote 'em on my own, showed them to friends, didn't pay enough attention to their screams of anguish. I wrote *Carter Beats the Devil* at UC Irvine's MFA program, and so I'm a workshop kid. I have a small workshop that I bring stuff to when it feels ready (and, like "jazz," "ready" is one of those things I don't know how to explain). I listen to their advice a lot but don't always follow it. For instance, a request that something be shorter might actually mean what I have on the page should be longer. But better.

FRANCISCO GOLDMAN: I have to be pretty much done.

ADANIA SHIBLI: It varies. Sometimes in a total state of uncertainty, other times in a total state of tranquility, I may ask one of my five trusted readers if it is possible for me to read one section to them. This in turn either brings back reassurance to me so I can continue work while having gotten rid of uncertainty, or unrest, and I go back to work without that tranquility. The shift in one's emotional state often leads to new and unfamiliar paths in writing and in language itself. But this only happens occasionally. Usually, after I've completed a second draft, I pass it on to the five trusted readers. Now there are only four, as one of them has died recently.

JENNIFER EGAN: I usually try to get to the point where I've solved most of the obvious problems that I can solve so that readers won't be simply telling me things I already know.

TAYARI JONES: I show drafts to different readers at different phases. My friend Joy is good at sorting out the good from the bad. She's gentle and encouraging, so she is asked to read early drafts. Other readers are more detail-oriented and I ask them to help out when I have done all I can do with the manuscript. It's really a team effort.

SANTIAGO RONCAGLIOLO: Once I'm done writing, I let the text rest for a few months or half a year. I go back and edit it and then I hand it over to my readers. And I wait until I've received all their feedback before considering it for a new round of editing. Criticism doesn't bother me. What really depresses me is when someone doesn't finish reading my work. Fortunately, it's been a while since that's happened.

ALEJANDRO ZAMBRA: I would like to be more disciplined in this regard, but I act impulsively. There are times when I work secretly, guardedly. But the trend is for me to bother much too much those reader friends, with very urgent attachments, with tedious telephone calls, or with sudden and suspicious visits. The worst I've done is wake up a reader to approve a phrase. I always reach out to people nearby and I think that the most basic thing is a sense of trust. I like that Ezra Pound poem that says, "I join these words for four people . . ." or that other one by Bob Creeley: "You send me your poems/I'll send you mine," titled, perfectly, "The Conspiracy." Two of those readers are poets, and I always listen attentively to their texts, so then it is reciprocal. The other two are not writers, so they perceive the inexactitudes absolutely on point, without getting stuck on "literary" problems. It becomes, like in the Pound poem, about four people, four people whose contrary opinions I would not be able to tolerate. I follow them blindly. Even when I don't agree, I force myself to validate the other point of view. To say it along with Pound: the opinion of those four people is more valuable to me than that of the whole world.

YIYUN LI: I show my readers a whole draft when I finish it.

DINAW MENGESTU: I only showed the novel to a few friends when it was almost done. They were people whom I trusted and had known for years; some were writers, a few were not. I think fortunately each one understood that I wasn't looking for advice on the novel itself, but really just a little assurance that I hadn't gone completely mad and that there was some merit to the work.

SUSAN CHOI: I really try not to show a draft to readers until it is complete and pretty clean. I don't want to waste their time and attention on the things I know how to fix; I need them to help me with the things I'm not sure how to fix, or that I'm not aware need fixing.

CHRIS ABANI: As often as they are willing to read them. My trusted readers have learned to run when they see me coming.

CRISTINA GARCIA: I usually do two or three rounds. And then I have different friends and different readers for those rounds, depending on how bad I think the manuscript is and of course people's time frames. So, I would say, do two or three rounds before finishing a manuscript, with friends.

RODDY DOYLE: I show it when I think it's finished. Although I'm less cautious with books for children. I have shown early drafts to my children and asked their opinions.

JOSH EMMONS: After I've finished and gone over a manuscript so many times that I can't see what needs to be fixed, I give it to a few people likely to be both generous and critical. It's best to find readers who will appreciate your work while also recognizing how it can be improved. With the manuscript I include a few specific questions ("Is character X developed enough by the time he does action Y?" and "Is the pacing off in scene Z?") and ask for general comments ("Are there any places where the drama feels like melodrama?" and "Should the flashbacks be spliced together or stay separate?").

ANDREW SEAN GREER: I show no one anything until I have finished a first full draft. It's not vanity—it's that I am too impressionable and any kind of comment—even "well that's nifty"—would throw me off and change the course of the book. Once done, I show it only to my editor and agent. Too many readers and I begin to write for a committee, instead of for myself. I have shown a draft to a close writer friend and said, "Please tell me whether to burn it." Of course he said the only thing you can: "You're crazy."

SUSAN MINOT: My editor might see some early pages of something long, but it would probably be most of the book by then. A book is too wobbly to show something early to anyone and expect helpful feedback. It's really up to me to create it.

RODRIGO FRESÁN: Nearly always, always to the same people. I give them the monster and take off running.

ALEKSANDAR HEMON: Seldom and only when I think it is pretty much finished. What I look for is their reaction to the text, rather than precise workshoppy advice. I test the text to see if the things I designed work.

JOSÉ MANUEL PRIETO: Once everything is resolved. I don't send out drafts of my books to be read. In reality, for a work that is well thought out and consciously plotted, it's almost useless to consider opinions from others.

RICK MOODY: I show things to friends when the prose is in a state that is nearly perfect, or, at least, as good as I can get it. I am too ashamed of my mediocrities otherwise.

YAEL HEDAYA: I don't. Though I sometimes have this terrible urge to show what I'm working on to people, I resist, because I know what I'm really looking for is not feedback, or God forbid, constructive criticism, but compliments. Lots. These can be tricky, because they're like a quick fix. A sugar rush. They're not really good for you. I mean, it's fantastic and uplifting to hear how talented you are, a genius, how this book is going to be your biggest achievement ever, but from a purely professional point of view, you don't need the compliments, you need the criticism. You need the: Well, this is really powerful stuff BUT . . . and I just don't want to hear any buts while I'm writing.

A. M. HOMES: It's changed a lot over time—when I was younger I had more trusted readers, now several have died and others have kind of evaporated. There are people I show things to—the qualities I look for are an editorial eye, and someone who will tell me it's okay, or just not good enough.

JONATHAN LETHEM: I show selected chapters as I go to a few friends—usually different ones on different projects. But I never reveal everything I've got, so if they seem disappointed or dismayed I'll always be able to fall back on my own certainties, the sense that I know more about the project than they do. I don't show the whole book to my editor or agent or anyone else until I've finished it and feel quite confident that everything's up on its feet and working well—my novels usually have enough trickiness in their structure, or unexpected departures of form late in the narrative, that it would be useless to show anyone anything short of a complete manuscript.

MICHAEL CHABON: At the end of a first draft I would reach out to my wife, my editor, and my agent. At the end of the next draft I would hit them all again, and maybe ask another one or two or three. Maybe add another one or two after the next draft. If that's the last draft, let's say, I usually try to find some readers with expert knowledge about whatever subject the novel might be dealing with (comics, Yiddish, New York in the '40s). Always at the end of drafts. The only person I would ever ask to have a look at something half-written would be my wife, Ayelet. It's just too painful, too messy and incomplete, too glaringly flawed. She already knows all my flaws, so that's okay. But no one else.

CURTIS SITTENFELD: I show self-contained sections of my novels (perhaps "self-contained sections" is a pretentious way of saying "chapters"?) to a few people when the writing is clean enough that the people can read it straight through; there are no placeholders or notes where I say "[I'm planning to insert such-and-such here]." As I write, I accumulate lots of questions that require research—I'm trying to figure out what kind of tree would grow in a particular location, or whether a certain expression was used in the 1970s. I make sure to answer all these questions before showing the manuscript to anyone. I also proofread because I hate when other people ask me to read manuscripts with lots of typos. And I send manuscripts in the mail rather than over e-mail because that's how I prefer to receive them.

CLAIRE MESSUD: My husband is my trusted reader. I give it to him when I am done.

ANN CUMMINS: I try to work through most of the problems myself first. I usually come to a point when I think I'm finished with something, a chapter or story, and then send it off to my readers, but the minute I hit the Send button, I'll have new insight. I'm always sending follow-up e-mails saying, "Don't read that draft. New one soon."

GARY SHTEYNGART: I grew up in the post-post-post-Hemingway generation of writers, reared upon the MFA model, for better or for worse. There's a wide range of people who see my work at the first-draft level. I start with a pair of trustworthy U.S. and UK editors, a well-read agent, and a fellow novelist I call "the enforcer," who won't let me get away with being cheap or lazy with whatever talent I may have. Then

I season to taste with people who know something about the subject matter and maybe throw in someone who doesn't really care for what I'm writing, just to feel the first lash of dissent.

ANNE ENRIGHT: When it is pretty much finished.

WHAT QUALITIES DO YOU LOOK FOR IN THESE PEOPLE?

SAŠA STANIŠIĆ: Furiosity.

FRANCISCO GOLDMAN: Absolute trust in their judgment, earned over time.

SUSAN MINOT: Literary discernment.

NELL FREUDENBERGER: The willingness to read a lot of not-very-finished pages. Usually they have to be related to me, or otherwise indebted.

AKHIL SHARMA: It is hard to get readers to read all the different versions of a chapter that I do.

COLM TÓIBÍN: They all love me.

DANIEL HANDLER: They should be writers, I think, because writers are able to give the most useful advice to writers.

JENNIFER EGAN: They need to be on my side—i.e., wanting me to write a good book, rather than a bad book. They also need to be interesting thinkers, and extremely frank. It's hard to find people who meet all these criteria, especially since I didn't get an MFA, where ideally one meets a group of like-minded writing peers. When I find someone who is a helpful and willing reader, I really try to hold on to them. It's also important, when consulting readers, that you give them *permission* to be honest. They are going to follow your cue, and if you give them the manuscript and essentially say, "Tell me you love this," that's what they'll do. Which might be nice, but it's not going to improve the work.

RODDY DOYLE: Don't know the answer to this one.

ADAM MANSBACH: Generally, my readers are professional writers. My editor is the only one of my readers who isn't, but he might as well be. I value readers who are able to see with clarity what is wrong with a manuscript; most people, even if they know something isn't working, can't necessarily sift through all the elements in play in a novel and figure out the real problem or problems, the core ones. So the ability to do that is crucial: to see it, and make me see it. Most of what I look for is simple to say, but incredibly difficult to do: understand plot and character, be able to conceive of alternate versions of both, be able to suggest emotional and psychological directions a character could take, alternate plausible reactions and realities. My editorial process involves long conversations, sometimes agonizing, in which major constructs are torn down, considered, rebuilt, dismissed, etc. Sometimes my readers are prescriptive, sometimes simply diagnostic, and there's a time for both.

EDWIDGE DANTICAT: A good eye. Objectivity.

RODRIGO FRESÁN: That they're gently cruel.

ALEKSANDAR HEMON: Friendship, a sense of humor, so they can see the sadness.

ADANIA SHIBLI: They are usually the five closest people to me, including my sister and my current lover. They often love reading more than writing, or if they write, they do not write prose. They are sincere and honest, and can easily pinpoint when I'm not. But each expresses that differently. One would for instance go into great detail to tell me what he thinks works and what does not in terms of language. Another would refer to the general structure of the novel. The other three would refer to both, in varying degrees of sensitivity to either structure or language. The one who died recently usually presented a view that balanced a criticism of the work structure and its language. Knowing it would be impossible to find a replacement for him, I think his departure will mark any works I'd write in the future. And I will probably be a worse writer, as this was the ideal reader, who could be sensitive to both language and structure equally.

ANNE ENRIGHT: My husband has fifty different kinds of silence; no one's silence is more eloquent. My editor's silence is pretty powerful too—not so close but more focused. My agent's silence is judicious. My friends' silences can be pretty shocked, actually—like, "Who knew?" I am always happy with practical remarks that help me to clarify, amend, correct mistakes. The larger remarks, like "This is wonderful," are not so interesting—but the silences are salutary.

SANTIAGO RONCAGLIOLO: I have a couple of friends with good taste for literature. I tend to agree with their opinions and I give them all my texts. And then, depending on the subject, the genre, or the scene, I'll have specific readers. For *Red April* I used someone who worked with corpses so that I could make the physical descriptions of the bodies convincing.

YIYUN LI: That they read it carefully and tell me what is not working or what is missing from the novel.

CHRIS ABANI: Honesty.

MICHAEL CHABON: Intelligence. Wide-ranging taste. Maybe some kind of connection to the material.

ALAA AL ASWANY: My reader is my former literature professor, a man much older than me. He is one of the most important critics in the Arab world and has supported me from the beginning. I always cross my fingers waiting for his opinion.

CRISTINA GARCIA: I look for people who will tell me the truth as they see it. And usually it's mutual; I don't give work to people whose work I don't read. In other words, it's a bit of a death pact. I mean, if we're not honest with each other, what's the point?

RABIH ALAMEDDINE: My friends have been my readers for so long. I have a friend I call the Language Nazi. He'll correct my use of language. He'll tell me if a metaphor doesn't make sense. He tends to go for voice. Almost anything else he says I disregard. I have another friend who basically always looks for story. If she says that something isn't working, it's because the plot is off. Sometimes I might be going for plot, sometimes I'm not. I have another friend who goes for character. And her best line is, "Can you tell me what this character is wearing?" What she's saying is that the character is not well defined. She doesn't see her.

STEPHEN KING: Kindness and intelligence in equal measure.

TAYARI JONES: I like my readers to be people who are good at understanding narrative. They may not be great writers. Many people read much better than they write and vice versa.

MEHMET MURAT SOMER: Being on the same wavelength with me on where they stand in their lives. Having a shared taste of joy for most things, like jokes, favorite films, music, people, games, politics, even food.

JOSÉ MANUEL PRIETO: They have to be good readers. They have to get carried away while reading a book, but at the same time be conscious of the underlying structure and also what changes can occur in it. Of course, it is always difficult to find such readers.

RICK MOODY: The trusted readers need to avoid bullshit. Often the best reader for me is *not* a close friend because I find I can be rather hard on the near and dear. But I need someone who will not sugarcoat the news and who will be willing to defend their point of view vigorously. I know a lot about what I do, but I am also my own enemy. I have to tease through these paradoxical impulses for the truth.

CLAIRE MESSUD: Strong critical faculties, and a sense of their own rightness.

ANN CUMMINS: Honesty. Openness. Readers who take the work on its terms and don't want to rewrite it on theirs.

JONATHAN LETHEM: I pick people who are likely to be in sympathy with the general drift of the work to begin with. There's no point trying to win over a reader whose resistance to the kind of thing you're trying to do is built in. Literature isn't a campaign of political persuasion, and people mostly only ever try to read books they think they'll like, so that's who you're writing for (and that's what's so dangerous about professional book reviewers: they're doomed to constantly read books they wouldn't ordinarily pick up).

HARUKI MURAKAMI: Being my wife. Honesty. Both, possibly.

TO WHAT EXTENT DO YOU FOLLOW
THEIR ADVICE?

ADAM MANSBACH: I parse it, agonize over it, argue with them about it, force them to clarify it. I divine it, interpret it, and ultimately take a good deal of it to heart. That's truer as time goes on and I learn to trust more completely both my readers and my own ability to differentiate good advice from bad. Coming out of an MFA program, you're conditioned to reject 85 percent of what anybody tells you because it's stupid, it's coming from a place of insufficient investment in your work, it's misdiagnostic. But if you're lucky, what you learn during that period is how to know what to trust. You learn that the criticism that feels like a punch in the stomach is usually right on the money.

EDWIDGE DANTICAT: Probably 80 percent. By the time they're looking at the work, I've been over it so many times and am so sick of it that I assume they're right.

SUSAN MINOT: When my editor suggests a cut I usually comply, 75 percent of the time.

CHRIS ABANI: I always follow their advice. Why ask for what you won't use?

RODRIGO FRESÁN: At its proper measure.

RODDY DOYLE: A good reader's or editor's advice should always be taken very seriously.

NELL FREUDENBERGER: I think most advice is good advice, in the sense that honest reactions are always helpful. Other writers will sometimes make suggestions about how they would have done something differently; you can't always use someone else's "fix," but I think readers know instinctively what needs to be fixed. For that reason I don't think it matters whether the people who read your work are writers. Ideally I think they would just be passionate readers.

STEPHEN KING: Depends on how good I think it is.

CURTIS SITTENFELD: I follow feedback from my early readers when it feels true—it echoes something I already suspected, or I didn't see it as I wrote it but when the reader points it out, I immediately know the person is right. If I'm not sure whether to follow a particular suggestion, I try to sit with it, let time pass, and see if I come down on one side or the other. I think an important part of being a writer is knowing what to ignore, but at the same time, if a number of people are making a very similar point, even if I disagree with it, I need to listen extra carefully.

JENNIFER EGAN: I'll listen to anything because I don't think that listening can hurt me. I try to make sure that in the end I've at least answered for myself all the questions my readers are asking, and that I know why I've made the choices I've made. But ultimately I need to feel inspired to make changes, and excited by the sense that the book will be improved. I don't simply make a checklist based on criticism and tick my way down it; the changes wouldn't work if I did it that way. So the advice that piques and excites me often ends up being the most useful.

DANIEL HANDLER: I consider myself a doctor and my early readers are patients. I don't pay attention to what they think the problem is, but I listen to the description of their symptoms, and where they point when they say it hurts.

SUSAN CHOI: There are only three people I consistently trust with everything I write, and I follow their advice extensively; if I disagree with them, it means I'm enormously confident about the material in question.

SANTIAGO RONCAGLIOLO: Sometimes they sway me, other times they don't. But my readers don't know one another, so if two of them agree on a criticism, even if it doesn't convince me, I consider it very seriously.

YIYUN LI: When I revise I try to keep their questions in mind, but that does not mean I have to address them directly, as sometimes by re-writing a chapter or a scene some of the questions could be answered.

AKHIL SHARMA: They rarely have advice. Mostly they have responses.

ANN CUMMINS: As a new writer, I always thought the reader had a better idea than I did for my work. I rewrote unnecessarily and to the work's detriment. Thankfully, experience has helped me out of that pitfall. One advantage to showing work that's close to finished: there are fewer opportunities for the reader to suggest wily but enticing new directions. That said, my readers frequently have amazingly great ideas that have helped me see potential in characters and stories I couldn't have found on my own.

COLM TÓIBÍN: I don't show them work to look for advice; I show them work as a child shows off a drawing, to look for approval.

MEHMET MURAT SOMER: I trust in them fully, especially my manager and agent, so I follow almost whatever they advise faithfully.

T COOPER: When somebody (trusted reader, agent, editor) suggests something that really pisses me off and sends me down the road of, "They have no idea what they're talking about," usually it's because what they've suggested is *really* spot-on. Sometimes they're wrong, but if I'm having a strong reaction, there's generally a good reason for it, and that reason is that I was probably on the fence or worried about that same thing in the first place—and it's hard to hear confirmation sometimes, but ultimately it's incredibly helpful and for my own good.

Also—somewhat less frequently—there are times I completely, consciously ignore advice. I just know when those times are, and what's great about trusted readers is that sometimes their advice or suggestions serve to remind me to stick with a particular decision or scene or whatever it is. As long as I've considered and reconsidered, I'm fine with ignoring advice here and there.

FRANCISCO GOLDMAN: As there are only two or three readers I feel this way about, I take their advice very seriously.

TAYARI JONES: I have found that most readers can tell you when something is not working. Some people are very intuitive—they know something is off but they don't know why. I sometimes will have, say, a scene, and my reader doesn't like it, but her reason makes no sense. I will then look at that scene and try to figure what it is about it that is hemming people up. Then I figure out how to fix it. So, while I am not taking the advice exactly, I am addressing the issue. Sometimes there is criticism that I just decide to discard, but I think about everything.

JOSÉ MANUEL PRIETO: As I said before, scarcely so. Most times, certain observations are due to superficial readings of the book, or perhaps people don't necessarily understand the logic from which a certain book is written. One has to be careful with this, zealous, of not allowing the intrusion of other people's advice.

ADANIA SHIBLI: Often I do, unless there is something I deeply think is important and I cannot change. But when I haven't, I felt sorry later on, after publishing the work, for ignoring that advice.

JOSH EMMONS: If I agree with the advice or recognize its merit, I follow it, which sounds obvious and self-evident because it is. Since most advice is either good or bad, and the surest way to discern which is which is your own gut response—the alternative, creation by committee, practiced by pop-song producers and the hired guns of Hollywood, would ruin more work than it would help—only take advice seriously that resonates with you. If someone says that one section of your novel is boring and irrelevant and should be cut but you know that it develops an important idea or introduces an intriguing image, keep it. Conversely, if someone points out that the language is weak and clichéd in another section, and upon rereading it you discover ready-made phrases and stock characterization, revise it until the originality and power you're striving for comes through. The more you write, the better your self-editing skills will become, and you may at some point eschew early draft readers altogether. From the beginning, though, trust yourself to separate the useful advice from the misguided.

RICK MOODY: To the best of my ability.

A. M. HOMES: To the extent that makes sense. Grace Paley taught me a lot about creating stories that were true to the characters, so that's what I'm always checking against.

MICHAEL CHABON: To the extent that it brings out into the open all the flaws, weaknesses, and failings that I already knew, deep in my heart, were there, but was trying to ignore.

CLAIRE MESSUD: As much as seems appropriate.

WHEN REVISING, WHAT DO YOU LOOK TO CUT? WHAT IS THE HARDEST MATERIAL TO CUT?

RODDY DOYLE: Clutter. Signposts. Bad writing. The hardest thing to cut is a good piece of writing that actually serves no real purpose in the novel or story. It always seems a shame, but I always feel somehow virtuous when I do it.

AKHIL SHARMA: If it doesn't work, it is out of there. It is easy to generate new material and so I am not loyal to even good lines.

SUSAN MINOT: Whatever I can. The hardest material to cut is writing that I thought was good but doesn't, as they say, serve the story.

HARUKI MURAKAMI: Something tells me.

DANIEL HANDLER: I try to cut anything tedious. (What book is too short?) What is hardest to cut are the parts I've worked hardest on, but I try to be merciless, because let's face it: no reader cares how hard you've worked.

DINAW MENGESTU: The hardest material is always the material that I fought and struggled to arrive at. There were chapters that I had spent months writing, that I had revised and edited until I thought they were nearly perfect. The problem, however, was that they no longer fit into the novel. They had no purpose, or in one case took the novel in a direction it could no longer sustain, so they had to be cut, or saved under a different name so I could always find them again, just in case.

SUSAN CHOI: Absolutely everything that doesn't feel crucial to the book. I cut and cut right up to the end. I've come to find it very gratifying.

COLM TÓIBÍN: With *The Master*, my editor in New York, Nan Graham, pointed out that I was saying everything one and a half times. She suggested, very tactfully, that I should cut the half and just say everything once. I had not noticed this and was mortified. She was joined in her suggestions for tiny little cuts by Ellen Seligman in Canada and Andrew Kidd in London. I will try never to say things one and a half times again. Or try not to get caught doing so.

NELL FREUDENBERGER: I try to cut anything I'm not sure about. As a general rule: if the writer is hesitating, it should probably go. I always want what I write to be shorter, so I don't find cutting very hard.

RODRIGO FRESÁN: I'm a very bad cutter. Generally I add. All the new editions of my books are longer than the first edition. Of course, my editor is already resigned to this.

EDWIDGE DANTICAT: I would rather cut than add so I overwrite to cut. I am sometimes tempted to cut everything. I cut all the appendages, things that don't seem to belong, things that lead nowhere, extra words. I have a weakness for the word *that* from the French "que" so I search for that and cut it as well as adverbs, and also from the French, instances where I have characters *begin* to do something rather than just do it. The hardest material to cut is the stuff you spent the most time on.

SANTIAGO RONCAGLIOLO: I try to cut out everything that isn't narration, especially excessive explanations or rhetoric. The easiest to cut are the sentences that you love but that get in the way of the story. It's like removing a mole near your lip: it looks pretty but it has to go.

AMY TAN: I let go of things pretty easily. I excise things that need to go. I find it technically very apparent where I need to cut—once I know, it's an *Aha!* and it makes perfect sense. I have to remind myself when I do the cuts that I never really lose it. I have it with me, I have the experience within me. And that's never lost—I never lose the experience of that process. I also know that whatever research I've done is often quite extensive and I will probably be able to use it later. I do feel a sense of frustration that I've spent so much time, months and months and months, on a piece that I lose—like any writer, I imagine.

T COOPER: I cut when the prose feels flabby and like it's circling around something but not landing on anything. I cut material that I might really like but that doesn't serve the book as a whole. I've found that if I'm really "in love" with a scene or passage, that's usually a sign it needs to be taken out. I've done that before, and just used some of the material elsewhere in another project in a completely different way.

JENNIFER EGAN: Sometimes the hardest material to cut is the stuff that you've labored over the most, and often the reason you've labored so hard is that it was never quite right in the first place. Those are the most brutal cuts to make, but also the biggest relief once you've made them, because in some way you always knew the stuff had to go.

ANDREW SEAN GREER: I look most carefully at pacing. I think they never talk about that in classes, but for me pacing is the most important part of structuring a novel. I often tell young writers that the important thing to keep in mind is the story—you must be willing to sacrifice anything for the sake of the story. Your best research, characters, scenes, lines, plots, everything. Nothing counts except the story. That seems perfectly simple, but it's hard to keep in mind when you are deep in it. You can fall in love with research particularly and not realize that keeping a few lines seems more knowledgeable than laying out everything you know.

FRANCISCO GOLDMAN: I have tried to apply the rule that the moment I begin to wonder if something should be cut or not, the moment doubt has entered into this relationship, no matter how dazzling I once may have imagined the passage to be, it has to go. This doesn't mean I probably couldn't have cut more.

YIYUN LI: I mostly cut for pacing. Sometimes you really love this character in this scene, but it is slowing down the whole novel, and you have to cut it no matter how unwillingly.

CHRIS ABANI: I cut the parts I love the most. They are usually the most purple or sentimental, you know?

CLAIRE MESSUD: I remember my beloved British editor Ursula Doyle saying to me about a section of my first novel, "I don't know how else to put this, Claire, but this chapter's just a bit . . . boring. It's just boring." When revising, you look to cut what's boring. Because it's probably unnecessary. It's hardest to cut your pretty darlings; but we all know they have to go.

STEPHEN KING: Every useless word. I fall in love with language sometimes. I'm a pedestrian prose-ist, and when I write something good, I hate to cut it.

ALAA AL ASWANY: Usually I go forward for one chapter, and then go back to revise the previous one. Then I write one chapter ahead, and then revise the previous two chapters. And I do this constantly, so in the end the novel you are reading might have been revised thirty or sixty times. Using this method, I keep the feeling of the novel as I move forward.

CRISTINA GARCIA: Backstory. It's the hardest to cut because sometimes it's hard to trust that the readers don't need to know every single thing about your characters' childhoods. You have to figure out just the right and judicious amount of backstory to keep the present afloat without sinking it.

JOSÉ MANUEL PRIETO: Whatever is redundant. Whatever one repeats without noticing because the material is too close. Revision is a time to clearly see those moments. The worst is cutting parts you're happy with for the way they are written, that you think are well written but nonetheless bring nothing to the general argument or better yet hinder the reading, delay plot development.

TAYARI JONES: I cut things that are too digressive. It's hard to cut dialogue that I think is really smart. So I think the key to cutting is to remember that your job is to tell the story, not show the world how smart you are.

YAEL HEDAYA: For me, there are two kinds of cuts. The ones I knew all along that I should make but was avoiding, weak or bad pages or paragraphs or lines that I tried to sneak into the text anyway, knowing all along they shouldn't be there but somehow not wanting to let go; and then there are cuts that my editor suggests, scenes that are too long or repetitive, side plots or secondary characters whom I've let hog the text. But usually the first things to go, my editor's prime suspects, are those lines that I hated anyway but had kept. The stowaways, finally caught by the authorities.

JOSH EMMONS: There aren't any hard and fast rules for what should be cut. When I read a sentence or paragraph or chapter and think, "This is terrible and cannot be salvaged," I strike it out.

RABIH ALAMEDDINE: I've been kicked out of a writing group because I don't listen to what they have to say. I don't know how to correct it. Once I write something, it's difficult for me to cut it. I'm very very lucky in that I have people in my life who can cut. I can do it, for example, if I look at my second book, which is a book of short stories—if I go through it now, I would be able to cut almost three-quarters of it. Usually when I'm writing I don't have the discipline at all to pull back and see it clearly. It takes about two or three years to have the distance to be able to look back at something. For example, I wrote this novella that should have been a short story. There are so many things that are repeated. I make the point once and then I go over it and over it—just immaturity, basically. And neurosis.

RICK MOODY: I love to revise. Writing workshops are all about major surgery—*I think this story starts on page six!*—ignoring in the process the more tricky approach to revision, the part that takes place at the level of the sentence or the paragraph. I feel lucky to have had a period of my education in which I worked at Farrar, Straus & Giroux, whose copy chief, Carmen Gomezplata, was one of the great philosophers in the religion of *omitting needless words*. I improved dramatically as a writer simply because she belittled my catalogue copy. Carmen said to me once, "You will be a better person if you start thinking about your writing this way." And she was correct. I feel better in *omitting needless words*. When I think about how *I talk*, e.g., I am horrified at the abjectness of my spoken English. Writing gives me the chance, my only chance, to improve myself. (By the way, last sentences of paragraphs can often be cut, even though they seem so *profound*.)

A. M. HOMES: I'm always revising, I love to be edited, and I love it when someone shows me how to trim something back for greater clarity. Hardest to cut—the good stuff.

JONATHAN LETHEM: I mostly cut language from sentences, and sentences from paragraphs—almost never do I remove scenes or chapters. If I've put a situation into the book it's usually passed some test of necessity already. If I've written unnecessary scenes something is drastically wrong to begin with in my sense of the work. I cut the language mercilessly—and nothing is difficult to lose, once I get in the cutting mood. The stuff that remains breathes easier, and persuades better, for being freed of anything you can spare.

MICHAEL CHABON: As much as possible. I love cutting. It hurts for a second but it immediately feels great afterward. You feel lighter, relieved of bad dreams and heavy burdens. I can watch two or three hundred pages go down the tubes with the equanimity of a lab assistant gassing a rat.

ANNE ENRIGHT: Some evening, toward the end of the process, I drink a lot of whiskey and go through the damn thing with a red pen. The question, in the morning, is not what I have cut but what I have left in.

DID YOU RUN INTO ANY FALSE STARTS?
HOW DID YOU OVERCOME THEM?

FRANCISCO GOLDMAN: Sometimes I worry that I didn't.

TAYARI JONES: False starts are the story of my writing life. This is how I deal with them. My mentor, Ron Carlson, said that you have to write in a road-trip mentality. One hundred miles down the road, you realize that you have forgotten to bring your wallet. A) Do you get excited and think, "Thank goodness I realized it before I got any farther!," then happily go back home for the wallet and head out again? B) Are you annoyed as you make the U-turn, but once you get home, have the wallet, you happily head back out? Or, C) Are you pissed off as you drive back home and still funky until you get one hundred miles out again? He says you have to work toward the A mentality. I am more of a B, but I am working on it.

JENNIFER EGAN: I cut back to the point when the material seemed to be working organically, and I try to move ahead anew and afresh.

T COOPER: I don't believe in false starts; every piece of work, even if it ends up in the garbage, gets you closer to where you need to be with a project.

HARUKI MURAKAMI: I have not experienced any false start. I prepare very carefully as to when to start.

ANDREW SEAN GREER: The first half a year is false starts. I sometimes think the hardest part of beginning a novel is finding the way to tell it. I don't mean "finding a voice," which is rather magical and unhelpful, but rather the technical way to tell it—first person, third-person close, and even more detailed than that: an intrusive narrator, a wistful tone, a framing plot, alternating viewpoints, etc. That takes a long time to find, and I cannot continue with a book until I have it. It is a very dispiriting process. Then, once I finally get it, I can write pages and pages and pages.

A. M. HOMES: Yes and I find false starts—or as I think of them—good ideas that are not working out, horrible. They feel like a waste of energy, and mostly they happen when you try and rush something, and force a story out when it hasn't had a chance to evolve. It's a flattening effect that doesn't please me. I overcome them by banging against the story until it cracks open again and then I dig deeper into it and, fingers crossed, it's fixed!

STEPHEN KING: Rarely. I almost always know where it starts, and where it ends takes care of itself, but those middles can really suck the big one.

RODDY DOYLE: Not yet. Or if I did, I don't remember.

NELL FREUDENBERGER: Endless false starts! The only way to do it is to start again.

RODRIGO FRESÁN: When I run into any false start, the solution lies in finding out where it belongs in the book. Generally, it fits in the middle.

COLM TÓIBÍN: I did this only once as a way of avoiding writing *The Blackwater Lightship*. Luckily I stopped. It was the opening of a novel about an Irish family, and it was full of material close to what was then happening in Irish life. I just got as bored with it as any normal reader would have. It was like reading a newspaper. But I did not know that because I reread it, but because the rhythms I was using did not enter my own spirit and thrive there. They were tired, sad things.

SANTIAGO RONCAGLIOLO: Starting all over again. The problem with false starts is that you only discover them once you're halfway done, when you realize that the story is poorly presented, or, worse still, that there is no story.

CHRIS ABANI: False starts are a necessary part of writing. It's how you gauge the material, the scale, the terrain, and so forth. You just soldier on. What else is there?

YAEL HEDAYA: Most of my starts are false. It's part of the process. Since I usually never know what I'm going to write about, I start with a sentence or paragraph that flashes in my mind like a neon sign, usually while I'm in the car—which is where I spend a large chunk of my waking hours, being the mother of three small children and living in the suburbs. Not all these opening lines were destined for greatness, to say the least, so I find myself igniting again and again, letting nature take its course. I sometimes feel that the beginning of a text is like the very early stages of a pregnancy. Tentative, iffy, dangerous. There are spontaneous miscarriages. I believe that a text is like a fetus: when the chromosomes match properly, it will survive.

SUSAN MINOT: Always! Begin again and again and again. And if it's still not right, again.

JOSH EMMONS: I run into false starts regularly. It's good to remember that first drafts are provisional, practice, nonbinding, and that your initial entryway to a story may have to change once or twice or ten times before the final draft is done.

AKHIL SHARMA: All the time. I start again.

MICHAEL CHABON: Definitely, and you overcome them, obviously, by starting over. Part of the second-draft process for me is usually taking a look at the opening of the novel and asking myself if that is really the best place to start what has become the story that I might not have quite known, at the time, that I was going to tell.

YIYUN LI: There always seem to be a hundred ways to start a novel. So what I do is I choose a favorite book and arbitrarily force myself to use the opening line of that book to start my novel. (I think for this novel I just finished I started with a sentence that had a similar structure to the first sentence of *The Story of Lucy Gault* by William Trevor.)

MEHMET MURAT SOMER: By dropping the material completely. Forgetting all about it. Making corrections is more difficult for me than starting something from scratch. I don't like rewrites.

TASH AW: False starts are an integral part of novel writing. You have an idea: it's brilliant, absolutely watertight, well planned, original. You start to write: the voice works, right from the start, pitch-perfect, snappy. You write some more: great word count, you'll be done in no time. Then the problems start—little ones at first, characters who aren't all that convincing, awkward plotting, lack of rhythm. And then these little glitches start adding up, and before long, you see that the very basis of your novel is shaky, and you don't know why you're writing it at all. This is what happened to me. I can't remember how I overcame these crash landings. All I know is that there was some tiny kernel in the wreckage that made me think I could salvage the thing and get it going again. The problem is that writing is a balancing act: we are constantly occupying that territory between self-belief and self-delusion. Some writers have an instinctive understanding of what will work and what won't. But most (like me) don't. I need a couple of false starts just to point me in the right direction.

DANIEL HANDLER: All my novels have had lots and lots of false starts. I just write them, glare at them, and throw them out.

JOSÉ MANUEL PRIETO: In order for this not to happen, it's always better never to "begin" at all. In other words, "begin" at any point in the book, so then there are no false starts.

PAUL AUSTER: This has happened only once or twice. What you have to do is throw away what you've done and start all over again.

SAŠA STANIŠIĆ: Many, many times. I don't think there is a secure way to overcome them. Just be honest with yourself and admit: okay, this sucks, I can do much better and redo the thing or start all over again.

CLAIRE MESSUD: Doesn't everybody? Fail again. Fail better.

CHAPTER 7

THE END

WHEN, IN THE COURSE OF WRITING, DO YOU KNOW THAT A MANUSCRIPT IS A NOVEL? HOW?

DINAW MENGESTU: I knew the manuscript was a novel, or wanted to be a novel, from the very first sentence. Of course I didn't know if I could actually make it into that, but there was something to the voice and the first few characters that emerged that led me to believe that it was going to take some time for me to really develop and understand them.

NELL FREUDENBERGER: When I'm interested enough in a person I've created to imagine spending many years with him or her, then I know it's a novel. It's only happened to me twice so far.

EDWIDGE DANTICAT: When I'm almost done, when it's proven that it's lasted the course.

RODDY DOYLE: I know before I start. But when I reach page fifty, I allow myself to think, and say, that I'm writing a new novel. I've met many people who've told me they're working on a novel, but were stuck—on page fifty.

SAŠA STANIŠIĆ: Right now I only have the experience of one novel. I never actually thought of it as a "manuscript." It was pretty much clear from almost the beginning that once I had decided not to write a memoir, I was writing a novel, using techniques and protagonist development, etc., the way I like to find it in a good book.

ALEKSANDAR HEMON: If it looks like a novel, if it reads like a novel, it's probably a novel.

SANTIAGO RONCAGLIOLO: If I finish it, it's a novel. Otherwise, I should have thrown it out a lot earlier.

STEPHEN KING: When the manuscript is two hundred pages long it's a novel. How do you know? Well . . . you number the pages . . .

HARUKI MURAKAMI: Before I start to write it. Just know it.

JONATHAN LETHEM: Well, that's an odd question from my view, since the novels are novels even before I begin setting them down—I feel their entirety and fulfillment implicit in my plans. The whole work is to make that fact evident to another reader, but I know it from the start or I wouldn't begin. It's that fact that drives me crazy with impatience during the long years it takes me to write one—and superstitious about flying in airplanes.

ALEJANDRO ZAMBRA: I don't believe the novel is like a jail cell. For me it constitutes a space without clear limits, without rules, or with rules that only make sense once transgressed. Also, I believe, writing a novel is more akin to erasing than to filling in. The Peruvian writer Julio Ramón Ribeyro expresses it beautifully: "A novel is not like a growing flower but like a cypress that must be trimmed. It must not take form based on a nucleus, from a seed, by addition or bloom, but through its volume, through trimming and removal." I'm never sure of finishing a manuscript. I recognize, all of the sudden, a phrase, a paragraph, a book; this is something written by me, I think, eerily and happily. Then I decide to publish, I decide I'm done. But it is always a decision. A desire to look no more. Perhaps to write another book. For a change in topic, or life.

A. M. HOMES: Because it's VERY long? But seriously, before I begin I know what's a novel and what's a short story, it's the difference between taking a train cross country and getting on when you're three-quarters there. The language and the roll-out of the story is very different from short story to novel.

YIYUN LI: When you read the end and there is no more to write about.

CHRIS ABANI: I set out to write a novel and I stop when it is finished. When all the parts are in alignment, when the story is compelling, the scenes necessary and riveting, and the characters complex and flawed, when there has been a transformational arc, when the work acquires resonance. These are some of the ways to know. The main thing is to be honest with yourself and work hard.

RABIH ALAMEDDINE: I usually know three-quarters of the way and I begin to realize that I can finish this. And the reason I know I can finish this is because I begin to see it as a novel. And I begin to see the art. I know what I'm doing, whether I'm fooling myself or not, I begin to believe that I know what I'm doing three-quarters of the way into the novel. I know how I'm going to finish it, I can see it.

TAYARI JONES: I know a manuscript is a novel if it has a lot of subplots. You can only talk about so many people and their problems in a short story.

MEHMET MURAT SOMER: I take many notes, although most of them become obsolete or useless in time. Then I plan the plot in detail, sometimes even on an Excel sheet. When all the flow, the backbone is done in my mind, it is very likely that it becomes a novel.

RODRIGO FRESÁN: When I can't stand it for a second more.

ANDREW SEAN GREER: I'm not the kind of writer who simply begins to write and discovers what he is writing along the way; I think that's a wonderful process, but it would drive me completely bonkers. Instead, I look at the story I want to tell and decide whether it's a novel or a short story, and sometimes I do write a short story and decide it's really the plot of a novel—too involved, complex, longwinded—and it really comes down to realizing I'm trying to cram too much into a short form.

JOSÉ MANUEL PRIETO: I know it from the first moment, from the length and intensity of what I want to relate. Now then, what is a novel? In a lot of my novels I put that definition to the test. Or I organize the text as a long commentary (*Rex*), or as a detailed dictionary (*Encyclopedia*), etc. So I name them "novels" though they may not be that at all. They're texts. But it is something inherent to the genre, to be always experimenting, looking to widen its form, whatever it may be.

YAEL HEDAYA: Ever since I started writing on a computer, which has been for as long as I can remember, I haven't felt as though I actually have a "manuscript" because there's no actual paper involved, at least not until I get the first set of proofs, and by then the so-called manuscript has not only become a "novel" but already has a publication date, there are arguments over the cover, and publicity. A manuscript, be it a paragraph or page or hopeful, desperate, clingy file, always starts off as one of many "insignificant others" floating around in the My Documents Dating Scene—a literary one-night stand. I know it has become a novel once it receives the

big status upgrade: a shortcut on my desktop, usually and not very origi-
nally named NEW NOVEL—which means the thing has managed to
inch its way into my life, leaving its virtual toothbrush in my medicine
cabinet and genetic material all over my subconscious, showing off the key
to my apartment, which I gave it at some mushy point or another, to all
the other documents. In other words, once there is Commitment.

JOSH EMMONS: When the work's major question or conflict or situation has been answered or resolved or revealed—bearing in mind that
good novels open up more channels of thought and feeling than they
contain, and that a pat, tidy ending can be as unsatisfying as one that
denies closure—and when you *could* go on but believe that doing so
would be a mistake, and when a kind of symmetry has taken shape
around and within the work, you have written a novel.

RICK MOODY: A novel is just *longer.* Once you recognize that something is going to be longer, it's true, you can avail yourself of the more
liberal pacing that characterizes the novel form. For me, only very tiny
ideas are associated with short stories. Anything else is a novel.

MICHAEL CHABON: All my novels have started out wanting to be
novels. Sometimes I begin with the thought, "I need to start another
novel. Which of the various ideas I've had kicking around in my brain
lately seems like it would be the most fun or compelling or sustainable
over the long haul?" And sometimes I begin by thinking, "This feels
like a great idea for a novel. I am going to sit down and start writing it
immediately." But I've never had the experience of being in the midst of
writing, say, a short story, or an epic poem, or whatever, and then suddenly decided that it was a novel.

CLAIRE MESSUD: I'm not sure I can answer that one. Again, the
music. You just know.

HOW DO YOU APPROACH THE END OF A BOOK?

PAUL AUSTER: With mounting anxiety. Of course you want to finish, but then, the moment you finish, you feel bereft.

AKHIL SHARMA: Relief.

CRISTINA GARCIA: With very intense exhilaration, exhaustion, and relief. Yeah, all three. And then a little bit of OCD [obsessive-compulsive disorder] kicks in, and I know when I'm fixated on punctuation and commas that it's time to stop.

COLM TÓIBÍN: Oh, with relief. I always know the end. But sometimes I am wrong and I need to add two more little scenes to bring the novel down, nothing dramatic, just with calmer images.

DINAW MENGESTU: I don't approach it. I see it coming from a distance and then pray that when I get there I haven't gone wrong.

EDWIDGE DANTICAT: With great trepidation. So much seems to depend on the ending. It's the characters' farewell and what most folks will remember. By then I'm also dealing with my own sadness about leaving these characters behind and I have to try very hard not to begin a new series of dramas for them.

RODRIGO FRESÁN: That's the first thing I write: the light at the end of the tunnel, the place to reach.

ALEKSANDAR HEMON: I avoid false closures and cookie-cutter resolutions.

AMY TAN: I know that I'm getting to the end of the book when it suddenly has a kind of momentum, when I can see that all the pieces I have are congealing. When the excess is apparent, when what needs to be removed is apparent. When the meaning of the book is something I feel. And I can't describe that, when the meaning of the book becomes apparent—but it includes all the false starts and all the excesses. I have this sense of being a racehorse, needing to get to the end now that I see it and know what I'm working toward. And that's the period when I work for twenty hours and I can think of nothing but the book and I'm socially inept. If I have a dinner I tend to cancel or at least not talk. And I certainly can't read anyone else's work. This time is the most exhilarating part of the writing.

SANTIAGO RONCAGLIOLO: It's not difficult because I like finales that leave a crater, when there's a collision that gives meaning to everything. Secrets are discovered, things' reasons for being change and the characters complete a transformation. It's a very classic, cathartic structure that dates back to Aristotle.

FRANCISCO GOLDMAN: Dumbfounded awe and moments of panic.

STEPHEN KING: With gratitude.

DANIEL HANDLER: With caution. The endings of novels are often too grand and too vague, because the temptation is to put everything one knows about life into the last few pages.

JENNIFER EGAN: As with the beginning of my books, I usually have a sense of *when* and *where* the end will happen, rather than *what* exactly will happen. I approach the end with fear and excitement, hoping that it will evolve organically from what has come before it, and resolve in a good way. I usually know pretty quickly whether I've nailed it, and if I haven't, it's often because the when and where were wrong—that I was trying to force something unnatural onto the material. It's customary for me to discard my first endings and then reapproach the endings when I move through the material a second or third time.

MICHAEL CHABON: In great haste, with my breath held, making a mad dash for the finish. Just hoping to bust my way through to it and finally be DONE.

T COOPER: Usually with white knuckles clamped onto my desk and with a significant level of terror. It's the final, "Can I pull this off?," and the hardest part of asking that question is that there's never really a correct answer. You do the best you can and try not to control every little thing.

RIVKA GALCHEN: I'm not sure what makes a good ending, but it does seem that weddings and death just don't swing it the way they used to four hundred years ago. I've noticed that lots of great books don't have great endings, not this century anyway. Even *In Search of Lost Time* seems not to have found its period, and of course Kafka claimed none of his books were finished. So maybe it's an epidemic of the now: that endings are maybe harder than they used to be, and, who knows, maybe beginnings are somehow easier? But probably one of the best endings out there—something worth trying to steal from if possible—is in the New Testament, the end of the Gospel of Mark. Jesus has been crucified, then he rises from the dead, and his followers, seeing their resurrected Lord, run away in terror. And in the gospels of Mark and Matthew both, when Jesus is on the cross, he himself seems to lose faith, calling out: My God, why have you forsaken me? That's a pretty fierce way to close. It's like the end of *Don Quixote*, when Quixote forsakes his life of deluded chivalry; in both cases, the hero (or antihero, however you like it) loses his faith, but they lose it too late, when the reader is already firmly converted. I think that's a beautiful way for something to end, in a paradox like that.

RODDY DOYLE: In almost all cases the ending has been a surprise. One day I'm working on the book I've been working on for years and I suddenly realize that I'll be finished in three or four days—and it usually ends up being two.

CLAIRE MESSUD: You don't approach it. It approaches you.

YIYUN LI: Endings, unlike all the possible openings, seem to come very naturally, with fewer variations.

JONATHAN LETHEM: If things are going as they should, with great excitement, which in turn means I begin to hurry, I have to be constantly vigilant in the last hundred pages or so not to become too breathless and telegraphic. I like books to speed up unexpectedly toward the end—but not too much.

MEHMET MURAT SOMER: Slowly and with caution. Trying not to fall into the orgasm trap of finishing it as soon as the plot is solved in my mind. While writing crime novels, the end is usually planned and calculated. So, not many surprises on the way.

CHRIS ABANI: With fear and trepidation. Many a good book is ruined by the ending. Chekhov was a master at endings, as is Stan Lee. I learn from them.

YAEL HEDAYA: With great relief. I'm usually so exhausted by then, so fed up and full of doubt, that I just want to be over and done with it, send it in to my editor and not think about it, as cruel as this may sound.

TAYARI JONES: Gratefully.

RABIH ALAMEDDINE: I wanted so badly to finish my last novel that I forced myself to stay on—not heavy drugs—but things like Vicodin, cigarettes, and wine. I finished it at five in the morning, went to bed, and when I woke up I could barely walk my heart rate was so fast. I was so frightened I didn't know what to do. Luckily I live a block and a half away from a hospital, so I put my clothes on and walked to the emergency room. There was nothing wrong and I was too embarrassed to tell them, so I just had them take my blood pressure and walked back home. I don't think you should print that.

ANDREW SEAN GREER: With great joy and relish—usually, if work has gone well, it feels like a downhill ride. Not so the last time—the ending was the very hardest part. Either way, I approach it with a bottle of wine because I want to be a little emotional (i.e., tipsy) because I really think the ending is the emotional payoff for the reader. And for me!

JOSÉ MANUEL PRIETO: As a moment when what's open closes. Or better yet, stays open, but in a way that the closing falls outside the book's territory, like a ballistic projection of all its elements. Once this is attained, I feel like I'm at the end of the book. And the reader feels it as well, which is more important.

JOSH EMMONS: With fear and trembling. And elation. Approaching the end you become a kind of double helix: along one helix is caution and concern about whether the elements you've had in play for hundreds of pages will come together (or split apart) pleasingly, and along the other is relief and joy that you are about to complete a novel.

A. M. HOMES: I do it backward—i.e., from the beginning.

WHAT MAKES FOR A SUCCESSFUL CONCLUSION TO A NOVEL?

RODRIGO FRESÁN: A phrase with certain resonance. One of those conclusions with an epiphany. Like in a few John Cheever stories, in *In Search of Lost Time* by Proust, in *Moby-Dick*, in *The Great Gatsby*, in *Slaughterhouse-Five*. A conclusion that, unequivocally, closes a door that will be opened many more times in order to spy that ending. Really, in ideal terms, a great conclusion has to be like a great opening. Something that forces you to keep reading and that, upon seeing nothing else ahead, makes you think about everything that happened before.

RODDY DOYLE: It should end before the end. Let the reader end it.

SAŠA STANIŠIĆ: This is a question I could only answer if asked precisely about a particular book or at least a topic. An open ending doesn't fit to every tale, a happy ending could make another one pale and sometimes it's necessary to kill every single person from the book on the last page.

HARUKI MURAKAMI: I don't know. It just comes.

TAYARI JONES: I think that the plot of a novel is really a question. When you have answered that question, or even made a compelling case that there is no answer, then you're done.

COLM TÓIBÍN: No rules. But with me, I am often wrong and once followed advice from an editor and once from a friend who noticed how bad and abrupt the ending was and suggested that I might keep going just to see what happened. I was lucky I listened to them. And with *The Master* I just knew my original plan was wrong, and I needed to add one or two more scenes and much slower, calmer stuff.

ALEKSANDAR HEMON: I don't know. But a bad ending is when everything is neatly tidied up, all the plot strands tied up, nothing left hanging.

DANIEL HANDLER: I think an ending has to be satisfying but also be disguised as an unsatisfying ending—I want my readers to know there's missing information but not to feel its absence.

YIYUN LI: I don't know. I know what I like about different endings of my favorite books. They always make me want to reread the book right away.

RICK MOODY: I do think it's important to avoid tidiness. Tidiness makes me want to vomit. Anything in the happy-ending family of endings should result in the eternal banishment of the writer under consideration. If Jane Austen were alive today, I would banish her to St. Helena, along with her entire retinue. An ending, more properly, is an opening outward. A conclusion of certain thematic ideas, and a proposal of certain others. An efflorescence, rather than a closing down. Is it *Bend Sinister* that ends with the sentence "It was a good night for mothing?" Apparently many printers changed that *m* to an *n* because they thought it made for a more satisfying conclusion. But I figure Nabokov's ending was just right. Because it doesn't close anything down; it indicates possibilities beyond the border of the story just told.

DINAW MENGESTU: I rarely like conclusions that feel like conclusions or that bring all the events to a neat, tidy solution. I tend to prefer ambiguity in my endings.

AKHIL SHARMA: Is it satisfying? Is the end credible? Do we have the answer to the questions that could be answered?

JENNIFER EGAN: If you figure that one out, please let me know. Which is another way of saying, I don't think there are any rules about this; a good ending is, ideally, the surprising yet deeply inevitable unspooling of everything that has come before it.

MICHAEL CHABON: Given the previously described behavior pattern, I have a tendency at first to end the thing too quickly. To stop at *X* or even *W* instead of at *Z*. Good endings are the ones that fall right at *Z*, or just to the left of it.

NELL FREUDENBERGER: I'm not sure that there's an answer for novels in general. I think a reader knows it when she sees it.

SANTIAGO RONCAGLIOLO: It should be unforeseeable and it should give meaning to everything that came before it. It should make you feel that the characters are completing a voyage, and you along with them.

YAEL HEDAYA: Tying up the loose ends, closing circles, watching all the bombs I've planted throughout the book go off. On one hand I feel like a child watching the fireworks on the Fourth of July saying, WOW! And on the other, I'm the responsible adult saying: Yeah, nice, but isn't it just a bit too much? Do we really need all this extravagance, all this noise? All this WOW? So I'd say that a successful conclusion to a novel is a mixture of overstatement and understatement. I'm in constant search of the perfect formula for a subdued, subtle sort of WOW!

STEPHEN KING: You just know.

AMY TAN: When it allows me to feel what the novel has been about. There's a rhythm to a book, and at the very end there's a turn that happens, something unpredictable and yet inevitable. The last paragraph is especially important. And oftentimes I have to cut off those last paragraphs and not let the energy dissipate. Once I've left it with what I would call an ending, something with a sense of direction, of movement, that's when I feel it's successful. Not a pat answer, not a pat conclusion, but a kind of opening.

SUSAN CHOI: I really think that endings should be emotionally cathartic in some way, and that they should almost seem to lift the reader far above the terrain of the novel—so that everything that has come before is "visible" in a single glimpse, from a heightened perspective. It's a feeling that, if achieved, doesn't require anyone to ask, "Was that the end?"

EDWIDGE DANTICAT: The sense that it could not have ended any other way. Full satisfaction for both the reader and the writer. Closure, as we might say in pop psych talk.

CLAIRE MESSUD: Is there such a thing?

T COOPER: Taking up where the last question left off, I think you have to let go a little and think about trusting that you've done your job, and that the reader—if she's still with you after all that time—will absorb and appreciate what you intended.

CHRIS ABANI: It is always different, but I think it is when you leave the door open at the end for the readers to slip through to a place of their own making. Yes, this is essential.

MEHMET MURAT SOMER: For everyone to be happy! That is, the author (me), my manager, my editor, and my beloved readers.

RABIH ALAMEDDINE: If this is a book about how to write a novel, don't take me as an example.

JONATHAN LETHEM: A really satisfying ending is something difficult to quantify or generalize, and may be the rarest thing in all of literature. Just because you've lucked into one once or twice doesn't mean you know how to do it systematically (and the other books, where you had to rely on the usual sleight of hand, are evidence enough of that).

ANDREW SEAN GREER: The feeling, when you put it down, of *Damn!* Perhaps that it feels you have finished something far larger than the few pages in your hands. The sensation, for about an hour, that the world has a certain pattern to it, if a sad one, and if no one calls or disturbs you, that you can sit in that feeling for a while after the book is closed. That makes it all worth it, for me. Also tears.

HOW DID YOU KNOW YOU WERE DONE?

YAEL HEDAYA: How do you know when you've had an orgasm?

YIYUN LI: Tired and relieved. Like finishing a marathon.

AKHIL SHARMA: I just knew.

COLM TÓIBÍN: When I listened to it as though it was music and it seemed right; when it was not just an idea I had but contained images that were soft and organic to the book and oddly natural without being obviously conclusive. I did this by concentrating very hard on certain objects, objects with no obvious symbolic value, which I allowed to carry a mysterious and suggestive weight in the last pages of the book.

RODRIGO FRESÁN: I know it when I myself am done for. But happy.

NELL FREUDENBERGER: I wrote an ending while I was still somewhere in the middle. It wasn't the conclusion of the plot, which I couldn't have written at that point, but the narrator's thoughts about what had happened to him during the course of the story. Then I had to take the action of the story to the point where it would lead naturally into those thoughts; once I'd done that, I knew I was finished.

HARUKI MURAKAMI: Just like making love. Somehow, you know it.

SUSAN CHOI: I'm always wrong about this. I feel I'm finished, and then at the eleventh hour I want to rewrite the ending. Recently I started building in a very long cool-off period to compensate for my tendency to declare a book finished too soon. My last book sat four months between revisions and then another four months before I showed it to anyone, and then I had over a year after it was sold to tinker with it some more—and I was still making substantial changes at the very last minute.

PAUL AUSTER: When I couldn't think of a single thing to change.

EDWIDGE DANTICAT: When I kept putting the same things back in that I was taking out.

T COOPER: A tingling sensation on the back of my neck. I don't know; you just know. You're completely honest with yourself, and you know a movement has ended.

LAILA LALAMI: I turned in my manuscript when I found that I was not making it any better—just different.

GLEN DAVID GOLD: All this is predicated on me knowing what I'm doing, so I'm uncomfortable delivering any sort of definitive message here. What I know is that books I've read and liked have really memorable endings. And I know that at a certain point, I end up writing the ending out of order, and the rest of the writing is about resisting the ending, and failing. Like: it's a vortex I'm being pulled toward and I do all I can to keep my character from getting there. Does that make sense?

ANNE ENRIGHT: I cry.

SAŠA STANIŠIĆ: I scrolled up to the first page and started rewriting. And after that? Before I wrote the last sentence, which was in my head for months, I played my favorite song from a band called the Decemberists, in order to nostalgically overload the moment.

RODDY DOYLE: The band broke up; the baby was born; the father left the house; the rebel got out of Ireland before he was shot. The plot brought me to the end, and then there was a bit of tinkering, storytelling—the craft—to make it a good ending. I hope.

SANTIAGO RONCAGLIOLO: The story tells you. Every story sets its own rules, and thereby its own solutions, and it won't be satisfied until it reaches them.

DANIEL HANDLER: You're never really done. You just reach a point where you can't do anymore. When I don't see any large, gaping flaws, and neither do my few readers, then I feel ready to turn it over to professionals.

DINAW MENGESTU: I knew the end was coming for several days, and by the time I began the last paragraph of the novel I knew it was imminent. As soon as I finished the last sentence I knew that I had taken my character as far as I wanted him to go, and that he arrived at the exact place I wanted him to be.

CLAIRE MESSUD: You're never actually done, I don't think, until years after you're done. You just come to the point where you *can't* anymore. You come to that point over and over again; but at some point, you can get someone else to agree with you; and then, maybe, you're done. It doesn't mean you wouldn't keep at it if you could; but as I say, you can't anymore.

STEPHEN KING: You've said as much of what you wanted to as you can.

A. M. HOMES: You know you're done when if you were to keep rewriting you would in fact write another book. There's a point at which there's no more you can do to a particular book and then it's time to get on to the next thing.

JENNIFER EGAN: I usually decide I'm "done" when I'm making tiny word changes, reversing them, and then making them again. It happens when the distance between what I've got and what I want, while still infinitely subdividable, has become inconsequential.

TASH AW: I didn't. I always feel there's a huge amount I could have done to improve the novel. Maybe that's a good thing, I don't know. With both novels I've written, I've had to force myself to stop tinkering, to stop believing (falsely) that if I had *just two more months*, I'd be able to make the thing perfect. The problem is that two months become four, four become nine, nine become forty-eight, etc. The test I now use is: IF I could afford (emotionally more so than financially) to take another year, or another three years, or ten, to finish this novel, could I actually make it substantially better? I think that at every stage of a writer's career, he or she can only write a novel that suits that stage of their career. I had ambitions with each of my novels, risks and experiments and other things that I would have liked to have accomplished as a writer, but at the time I wrote each one I could only write what I ended up writing. Maybe with the next one I'll be able to do all the things I wanted to before but couldn't. I think it's important to have something to look forward to as a writer, even if it's just an illusion.

Finishing a novel is always linked with shame—or, rather, the lack of it. There's a moment when I realize I'm no longer ashamed of the jumble of words I've produced, that the embarrassment of having written a mishmash of ideas subsides and I'm no longer terrified of the thought of The Public reading it. That is when I begin to think of my manuscript as a novel. I never know when this is going to happen; during the writing of the manuscript, it sometimes feels as if that moment of clarity is never going to arrive, that the novel will never arise from the manuscript's fuzziness of thought and expression. I have friends who read the manuscript in its final stages, and this helps lessen the acute awkwardness of having to go public with my work: their comments give my work a kind of validity, a right to exist.

ALEKSANDAR HEMON: When I can't wait to show it to other people.

ADANIA SHIBLI: When I can no longer enjoy reading it.

CHRIS ABANI: You know. Usually when you run out of words. Short is always better, I think. No one needs seven hundred pages. Okay, almost no one.

TAYARI JONES: I know it's over when I no longer think about the characters.

ANDREW SEAN GREER: I always know the ending before I begin—I write toward that ending. It's the path along the way that always trips me up, and the motivations of the characters to end up where I imagine them. I trust my instinct for where they should go, but sometimes it takes a long time to figure out why.

JOSÉ MANUEL PRIETO: It's not very scientific, but it's something one knows, feels. What's interesting is sharing the same emotion with the reader, or better yet anticipating it. If when I read a book of mine I feel it, feel that emotion and that rise, I know, without a doubt, that the reader, a certain type of reader, will feel it as well.

MICHAEL CHABON: Usually I just hope that I am. I try to convince myself that I am. Then I hope to convince others—my wife, my editor, my agent, other early readers. But I usually fail. Then I have to go back and try to push it a little nearer to point Z.

ALAA AL ASWANY: The end comes when it comes. At a certain point I no longer have control of my novel. My characters are doing the job. After finishing *The Yacoubian Building*, I had very strange feelings about giving it to the publisher. I was proud and happy because I had finished my novel, but there were some sad feelings as well. It was like going to your beloved daughter's wedding, this mix of feelings. You are very happy for your daughter, but you are also sad because your daughter is going to another man.

RICK MOODY: I know I'm done when I have changed "that" to "which" back and forth three times.

ARE YOU ALWAYS A NOVELIST?
ARE YOU EVER ABLE TO TURN IT OFF?

ANDREW SEAN GREER: Yes, absolutely, I can turn it off. Most of my friends could care less, and over a few beers I don't think about it for a moment. But there is a time, when I'm beginning a novel, when I am extremely sensitive and almost every conversation, work of art, piece of music, book I read has its impact on the novel. That is not a time to tell me your deepest secrets in a bar.

HARUKI MURAKAMI: Leaving the desk, I am not a novelist anymore.

ALEKSANDAR HEMON: I am always a writer, the way a basketball player is always a basketball player—the muscles and the brain are developed and toned by the constant engagement and need to play.

GARY SHTEYNGART: Being a good novelist is a tremendous drain on one's emotional and intellectual resources and a serious impediment to the things—the possibility of love, the care of one's family—that can round out a life. Nowadays many novelists believe that they can have it all, that they can keep their eyes glued to the tragedy of our declining world and emerge gay and virtuous people nonetheless. It may happen once in a while. But a novelist, like a doctor, is always on call. It is impossible to look away, to turn off the impulse to catalogue, evaluate, transcribe, embellish, take apart, set right, to drink to excess and collapse in a storm of hot tears. Like a priesthood in a suffering country, this job is all-consuming. But unlike a priesthood, one gets to worship a panoply of *real* gods, from Cervantes to Grace Paley. And that almost makes the whole enterprise worthwhile.

RODRIGO FRESÁN: It's a twenty-four-hour-a-day job. I wish a button existed to deactivate me for a few hours, days, weeks, a year. But it's impossible. And, also, there's the fear that once turned "off" I'd forget how to turn me on.

DANIEL HANDLER: I try to fully incorporate being a novelist into my life, so that it's not a matter of on or off.

FRANCISCO GOLDMAN: I don't ask myself this question.

NELL FREUDENBERGER: I guess I'm always a potential novelist. A lot of times, when you're relaxed and doing something else, you have an idea for a new story, or an idea about how to solve a problem you're struggling with at the computer. I also think there's a tendency that writers have (which comes from reading) to practice writing by narrating their own experience as a kind of interior monologue. Sandra Cisneros describes it at the end of *The House on Mango Street* and George Orwell talks about it in *Why I Write*. It can be a very dull experience, and I think it's often told in the third person. ("The girl went into her parents' bedroom. She took a book from the shelf and sat down on the carpet," etc.)

ANNE ENRIGHT: No, I am not able to switch it off.

PAUL AUSTER: Never.

EDWIDGE DANTICAT: I think it's like being a parent or a child, you can't really turn it off.

GLEN DAVID GOLD: Not entirely sure what that means, but post-therapy, I'm a human being first, novelist second. Much happier that way. But I'm always making stuff up, more or less every waking hour, and some of that is used in fiction and the rest of it just amuses me.

AKHIL SHARMA: I am always myself. As a novelist I am just a more focused aspect of one part of myself.

RODDY DOYLE: Always a novelist. I'd hate to turn it off. Turn off the light—will it go back on? But I'm able to function as a regular human being too. If someone I love dies, I'll grieve. Years later, I might be rooting around for the words and spaces to describe grief, trying to recall the feelings. But I won't be taking notes at the funeral.

SANTIAGO RONCAGLIOLO: I'm a storyteller. I never manage to abandon that role. My work allows me to make use of everything, because life is my primary material: my frustrations, emotions, fears—it all winds up incorporated in my writing. At the same time, this condemns you to a certain existential marginality. You're always an observer. I don't have clear opinions on a lot of things because I'm always more interested in hearing foreign ones.

STEPHEN KING: On some level, I guess. It's an embedded part of my personality. Are you ever able to turn it off? Sure.

T COOPER: HAHAHAHAHA.

YIYUN LI: I don't know. I like writing stories and novels for different reasons, and I don't think I turn it on or off consciously.

CHRIS ABANI: Always writing; never turn it off.

CRISTINA GARCIA: Oh yeah. I have a daughter who's going to be sixteen. I've pretty much been writing about as long as she's been alive, so I've always had to negotiate what I consider fairly mutually exclusive roles. Having a child and raising a child is very, very present tense and demanding and can be all-consuming when you're doing it and it's very piled-up like a novel. Anyone who says that raising children and writing are compatible is nuts!

CLAIRE MESSUD: I don't know. You are who you are. If you were somebody else, well, you'd know, then.

RABIH ALAMEDDINE: No. I'm one of the lucky ones: the first thing I ever wrote was published, though I was, in some ways, a novelist or a storyteller before that. Unfortunately, that's sort of become how I identify myself, and I'm not sure that's healthy.

TAYARI JONES: All the time. I guess I'll turn it off when I'm dead.

AMY TAN: Good question. I think of myself as a fiction writer when I'm writing a nonfiction piece. And I'm always still a writer. Novels are the work that's under contract. The best way people describe me is as a novelist. I will say as a writer I'm always thinking of life in terms of being a writer and probably in terms of the novel that I happen to be writing. When I hear a certain sentence from someone, it clicks to me that it has to be part of my novel. Or I make an observation and it seems serendipitous because it has to be part of my novel. Turn it off? Why would I want to turn it off? Writing to me is very much about discovering the meaning of my life.

MEHMET MURAT SOMER: I think I am more like a surveillance camera. The novelist within me acts more like an engineer, filtering these recordings, sorting out, plotting and planning.

YAEL HEDAYA: I don't know if I'm always a novelist but I'm always a writer. Words are like calories. I ingest them and burn them off all the time. Sometimes I binge. When I was younger, there were days when things got written in me automatically, like there was a demonic keyboard in my brain typing words all the time. It was exhausting and exhilarating. Today, I'm usually too preoccupied with other things (like life, etc.). I can shut off this device whenever it gets too noisy in there, though I must admit that sometimes being in control makes me miss not being in control.

JOSÉ MANUEL PRIETO: I don't think I can disconnect. I see it as a "professional deformity." I notice it because in whatever information, book, or story told, I find the genesis of a story, the key for a character, etc. It's something that never stops.

ALAA AL ASWANY: Any novelist is two people: you have the person who is living in the world, who is doing what other people are doing; and you have another person, the novelist, who is holding a very sensitive camera, taking pictures, trying to adjust this camera, trying to record every single scene the person is living. I know that deep inside me there is another, very curious person carefully observing the very tiny details and expressions of the senses.

JOSH EMMONS: Other than writing novels, the activities that unite novelists include observing their surroundings closely, listening to stories, reading books and people, safeguarding their solitary time, and daydreaming. These are hard to stop, so out of necessity I'm always a novelist.

MICHAEL CHABON: I'm not sure I could, if I wanted to—and why would I want to?

RICK MOODY: I could also be a librarian, or an arbitrage specialist, or a Jungian psychoanalyst. These are things I wouldn't mind being.

A. M. HOMES: In the sense that I'm always working, always living, thinking, I am never able to turn it off; that said, it takes me five years to write a novel and I can't just go from novel to novel, there's a recharge period during which I write some short stories and other things.

JONATHAN LETHEM: Sigh. Yes, always a novelist.

ANN CUMMINS: I am able to turn the notion of being a novelist—a writer—off. For some of my social circles, it has little relevance, and though I do make mental notes of the odd, interesting story ideas that pop up throughout the day, I think that's different than identifying as "the novelist." Identifying as anything—the teacher, the friend, the wife, the writer—all feels claustrophobic to me. Sometimes I'm not able to turn the work off. When I was in the final six months of writing *Yellowcake*, I was deeply caught up in the novel, which frustrated Steve, my husband. One day he said, "Will you show up!" I didn't realize how much I was living in that other world.

SAŠA STANIŠIĆ: Definitely. I don't even believe that there is such a thing as being permanently inside of your own head and those of other people thinking what good story is here or there. It's one of the legends that authors need in order to not come off as too boring.

COLM TÓIBÍN: Try me.

APPENDIX

MARIO BELLATIN'S ANSWER

I sent Mario Bellatin the same questionnaire I sent everyone else. He responded with a long prose poem, excerpted below. —Daniel Alarcón

THE CONDITION OF FLOWERS

Text written as an attempt to answer a series of questions posed to Mario Bellatin during the month of April 2008.

ORCHID SEASON

It seems that what I look for in a text, as with any other artistic manifestation, is the possibility to travel through a space under its own principles. I don't think that it is only within books or the arts that you can find these characteristics. I feel they can be found in religious spaces, in dark rooms, in houses of horror at fairs . . . and in intimate conditions, especially in exalted states.

ROSE SEASON

This exercise of availing myself of alternate states makes me unsure of whether or not I actually read books. I more likely contemplate them, admire them, and pry inside them. To carry out such a program, one requires the presence of numerous volumes simultaneously. Each with different characteristics as well. I recall times when I was trapped in fifteen books or more. This is most likely for personal rather than artistic reasons. Among other things, I don't suppose, while I am trapped, that reading in such a way will later serve me in composing my own work. It may even seem strange to make a similar association: to think that the act of admiring books before reading them is somehow a way to build my own creation. Although if I take into account the method I utilize in approaching books and the structure I later shape them in, it seems the mere act of appreciating a book is a way of creating it.

CLOVER SEASON

As is well known, such a quantity of books exists that it is impossible to count them. To impose order upon this endless game that I am a part of—that of appreciating books before reading them—I make the conscious effort to return only to sacred texts. The Torah, the Old Testament, and the sacred Koran—the missing clover—are my works of reference, principally because from them I can easily formulate the idea that all books are infinite, even the most elementary ones, infinite as the space separating one letter from the other.

CHRYSANTHEMUM SEASON

Each one of the books is a part of the book I've been transcribing since I was a child, based on the shape of those hardcover white catechisms that traditionally carry a chrysanthemum trapped within its pages. The first one took shape at ten years of age. It was about dogs I knew. About my vision of them. I think I continue to seek something similar. To establish a certain view of things. I practice it now with a camera that, when it came on the market forty years ago, was thought of as simply a toy.

BIRD OF PARADISE SEASON

I understand the need of some writers to hurry. This tends to happen with writers who are just beginning. Nonetheless, in literature, those moments just prior to concluding a work have no beginning or end, nor can they be measured according to any traditional criteria. Possibly the task to be accomplished might be to give the impression that, in a first instance, the work before you was composed in the manner it is being read.

CAMELIA SEASON

When the process of writing occurs under these conditions—during moments when the figure of the author is diluted—many times the result itself no longer matters, whether it's a short story, novel, or any of the labels used to standardize the literary. What becomes fundamental is only the exercise of writing. It is placed above other considerations. The act of looking at one letter then another appearing, and finally the completed word. An almost physical exercise whose joy is found from the possibility of seeing how one page ceases being an empty space. A pleasure that derives from who knows where and whose destiny is unknown as well, but that along the way leaves a series of disparate works that, curiously, due to their apparent disjointedness, form a sort of everything.

SPRING RAIN SEASON

These manifestations, both the ones produced by my mind and by my body, I face as a part of life. I try to not do anything against them. I don't recall ever having to turn down anything in order to dedicate myself to writing. If this is understood on a superficial level, one can ascertain that any event is of more importance. Including mental breakdowns. It's untrue, I know, but a sunny day will always be more important than making a book.

SEASON FOR THOUGHT

Although I more or less believe that one never stops writing. Not while sleeping or during wakefulness. I remember the times I have gotten out of bed at midnight to type texts that I could not even recognize the next day. Structures that attempted to reflect my previous dreams. And that's without counting the mystic dreams I experience occasionally, especially when I faithfully complete the duties imposed on me by the Sufi mosque—Tekka—to which I have belonged for fifteen years.

WALLFLOWER SEASON

On many occasions forgetting what I have written causes me serious problems with some readers who want to know more about something they read in my books. When they realize that I have no idea of what they are asking me about, and that I don't even remember writing or publishing such a thing, they feel cheated. Many times they think I'm playing a joke on them, the wallflower trick, among others. It seems impossible to them that an author could be unaware of what he has written.

CRESS SEASON

I perceive as reality an indissoluble whole. Only by reading—and the more distance, the better—what is written, can I arrive at certain conclusions. I can find answers to definite questions I pose myself while writing. But I don't think they're the questions that certain critics might believe an author asks himself. I don't ask myself, for example, whether to take characters from real life or not, if those characters are believable or if they're strong, and I don't ask myself whether a scene is difficult or not. Rather, I'm concerned with even more abstract questions, with precisely those doubts that have not been resolved after my readings of reality, of artistic manifestations, including those which have no form or time or place. Questions like, what would happen in a story where beauty and death confront each other? Is it possible to translate a book that does not exist? Can an author write a book in a nonexistent language? Questions of this sort, it seems to me, the more absurd the better.

BROOM SEASON

In regard to questions about the things I narrate, I find scenes that I don't believe myself capable of creating in any other way. Planning them, for example. I'm convinced that as creators we are better than ourselves.

STATE OF DETACHMENT

I've been conscious that the exercise of creation is based on a constant becoming. At a certain moment I had the need to free up the central writing space precisely so that this empty space might generate new writing. The presence of that unpublished book made the flow of words difficult. It would erect itself like a static block that ran the risk of ruining its very own content at any moment. So then I went to a novice editor, with whom I agreed to release the book under the system of prepublication vouchers, consisting of a set of cards that I had to sell and that could later be exchanged for the book once it was finished.

STATE WITHOUT MEASURE

Thinking of nothing else but selling the vouchers, I dedicated myself to the task in the most committed manner possible. I knew that to stop and think about what I was doing would ruin everything. To the printer's surprise, in one week I was able to sell eight hundred vouchers, which allowed for the printing of the book and a book-release event. At the time I thought the most important thing had occurred. To free myself from the manuscript. To be free of its presence and to have the printed word as protection. Only later did I understand the most important thing about that operation. My act created a writer. The fundamental thing was not the finished book but the fact of having introduced eight hundred books into the world. That action generated an interest that, I'm sure, a traditional publication would not have received. From then on the effect continued, until now, when I have to turn in books that I have not made and whose editorial deadlines have generally passed.

STATE OF DEATH

I think they will get rid of me when they discover I am an impostor who does not care whatsoever for the existence of books once they have been published. Who does not read the reviews regarding his own work.

Someone whose life has not been changed by publishing his books, who has learned nothing by writing and publishing miniature novels, and who, at the same time, is a fraud who can never stop being a writer. The out-of-focus photographs taken with a child's camera and expired film may prove it.

AURA ESTRADA'S
DIAGRAM OF *THE LOSER*

"Even Glenn Gould, our friend and the most important piano virtuoso of the century, only made it to the age of fifty-one, I thought to myself as I entered the inn. Now of course he didn't kill himself like Wertheimer, but died, as they say, a *natural death*."

So begins Thomas Bernhard's unyielding torrent of a novel. *The Loser* is a meditation on genius and the unraveling of genius filtered through the relentless logic of a compulsive mind. The narrator of the story, a virtuosic piano player himself, steps into an inn brooding over the suicide of his friend Wertheimer. Wertheimer had days earlier traveled many miles to the residence of his estranged sister. He hung himself from a tree outside her house.

These three men—Gould, Wertheimer, and the narrator—were friends and rivals and, briefly, piano students together years ago at the Vienna Academy. For Wertheimer and the narrator, however, studying alongside the great Glenn Gould proves to be their undoing. Gould's prowess so disheartens them that they both give up the piano despite their respective substantial talents. Gould, for instance, offhandedly pigeonholes Wertheimer as a weakling, and it's this that triggers the man's eventual decline: "Wertheimer's disaster had already started the moment Glenn called Wertheimer *the loser*, what Wertheimer had always known Glenn said out loud." Wertheimer slips into middle age and

Eeyore-minded madness. The narrator too caves before his friend, the mighty Gould: He sells his prized piano and wastes decades trying to write a book titled *About Glenn Gould*. Now, after Wertheimer's just done himself in (Gould is long dead of heart failure), the narrator travels to Wertheimer's funeral, and later to his country mansion. The whole of the book constitutes the narrator's thoughts as he recreates the downfall of his and Wertheimer's piano careers in the face of Gould's utter dominance at the ivories.

The book is classic Bernhard. Its form—a barrage of thought set forth in a way not unlike Joyce's *Ulysses*—and its approach to the subject matter—using a famous figure as a fictionalized foil for Bernhard's own self-exploration and storytelling—is typified in other works by this Austrian-born novelist. Bernhard's philosophically inclined, monologue-based novels rank with the stories of Beckett and Kafka. His intelligent belligerence rivals the irritated affects of Mark Twain or Dostoyevsky. But the voice Bernhard conjures—a lacerating, idiomatic, piercing, and for brief moments frail and sad stew—is his own.

It is indeed his ruinous but rewarding energies, his wild-eyed cackle, and the roar of the onslaught of his prose that makes reading Bernhard's work akin to plunging forward into a strong headwind. It is an even braver task to attempt to break down his texts into their related parts. But this is precisely what we have here for *The Loser*. Here, Aura Estrada teaches us as much about her methods of thinking as she teaches us about Bernhard. Here, Aura Estrada sheds light on the structure of a novel she returned to again and again in her own novel-building. Here, we have a lantern, a shrewd and crudely rendered map, a small but elemental machete by which we might make our way through the marvelous forest of Bernhard.

—*Jesse Nathan*

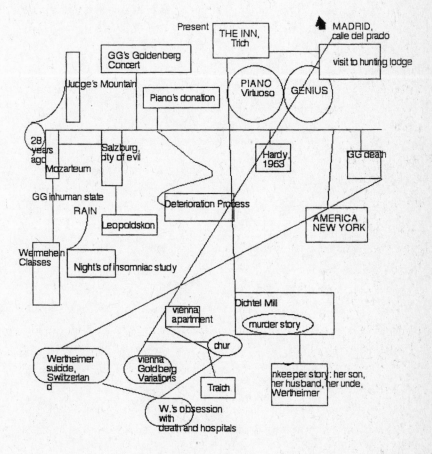

Present

THE INN,
Trich

MADRID,
calle del prado

visit to hunting lodge

GG's Goldenberg
Concert

Judge's Mountain

Piano's donation

PIANO
Virtuoso

GENIUS

28
years
ago

Mozarteum

Salzburg,
city of evil

Hardy,
1963

GG death

GG inhuman state

RAIN

Deterioration Process

Leopoldskon

AMERICA
NEW YORK

Wermehein
Classes

Night's of insomniac study

vienna
apartment

Dichtel Mill

murder story

Wertheimer
suicide,
Switzerland

vienna
Goldberg
Variations

chur

Traich

nkeeper story: her son,
her husband, her uncle,
Wertheimer

W.'s obsession
with
death and hospitals

INDEX OF WRITERS, ARTISTS, MUSICIANS, AND DIRECTORS MENTIONED

ACKNOWLEDGMENTS

Thank You, Thank You

826 Valencia runs on the big-hearted benevolence of thousands of volunteers, contributors, and supporters. Here are just a few who were especially helpful with this project: Ines Austern; Elissa Bassist; Bennet Bergman; David Aloi; Kyle O'Laughlin; M. Rebekah Otto; Royanne Curtin; The Deborah Harris Agency; Ellen from the office of Amy Tan; Etgar Keret; Andrew Leland; Steph Long; Brian McMullen; Abner Morales; Francis Nisly; Théo Sersiron; Chris Ying; Molly Bolten; Ted Weinstein; and the generous and talented authors who shared their great ideas with us here. Special thank-you to Adam Mansbach and Vinnie Wilhelm for helping write the questionnaire.

ABOUT THE EDITOR

Daniel Alarcón

Daniel Alarcón is associate editor of *Etiqueta Negra*, an award-winning magazine published in his native Lima, Peru. His fiction and nonfiction have been featured in magazines such as the *New Yorker*, *Harper's*, and *Granta*, and his second book, *Lost City Radio*, won the 2008 PEN USA Novel Prize. His most recent story collection, *El rey siempre está por encima del pueblo* (*The King Is Always Above the People*), was published in Mexico in 2009.

ABOUT 826 NATIONAL

Proceeds from this book benefit youth literacy

826 National is a network of seven youth tutoring, writing, and publishing centers located in seven cities across the country. Since opening 826 Valencia, our San Francisco center, in 2002, our goal has been to assist students ages six to eighteen with their writing skills while helping teachers get their classes excited about writing. Our mission is based on the understanding that great leaps in learning can happen with one-on-one attention, and that strong writing skills are fundamental to future success. Due to overwhelming interest from others around the country, 826 Valencia now also serves as the headquarters of 826 National, a tutoring and mentorship model that has been duplicated in six other cities: New York, Los Angeles, Ann Arbor, Chicago, Seattle, and Boston.

Through volunteer support, each of the seven 826 chapters provides drop-in tutoring, class field trips, writing workshops, and in-school programs, all free of charge, for students, classes, and schools. 826 centers are especially committed to supporting teachers, offering services and resources for English Language Learners and publishing student work. 826 programming reaches students at every opportunity, in school, after school, in the evenings, and on weekends. Each of the 826 National chapters works to produce professional-quality publications written entirely by young people, to forge relationships with teachers to create innovative workshops and lesson plans, to inspire students to write and appreciate the written word, and to rally thousands of enthusiastic volunteers to make it all happen. By offering all of our programming for free, we aim to serve families who cannot afford to pay for the level of personalized instruction their children receive through 826 chapters.

The demand for 826 National's services is tremendous. Last year we worked with more than 4,000 volunteers and over 18,000 students nationally, hosted 368 field trips, completed 170 major in-school projects, offered 266 evening and weekend workshops, welcomed over 130 students per day for after-school tutoring, and produced over 600 student publications. At many of our centers, our field trips are fully booked almost a year in advance, teacher requests for in-school tutor support continue to rise, and the majority of our evening and weekend workshops have waiting lists.

826 National volunteers are local community residents, professional writers, teachers, artists, college students, parents, bankers, lawyers, and retirees from a wide range of professions. These passionate individuals can be found at all of our centers after school, sitting side by side with our students, providing one-on-one attention. They can be found running our field trips, helping an entire classroom of local students learn how to write a story, or assisting student writers during one of our Young Authors' Book Programs.

All day and in a variety of ways, our volunteers are actively connecting with youth from the communities we serve.

To learn more or get involved, please visit:
826 National: www.826national.org
826 in San Francisco: www.826valencia.org
826 in New York: www.826nyc.org

826 in Los Angeles: www.826la.org

826 in Chicago: www.826chi.org

826 in Ann Arbor: www.826michigan.org

826 in Seattle: www.826seattle.org

826 in Boston: www.826boston.org